Praise for *Dispatches from the Sweet Life*

"Bill Powers is a wonder, a brilliant and bighearted writer able to transform the most ordinary moments of daily life into exquisite epiphanies, rich with discovery. *Dispatches from the Sweet Life* charts the luminous frustrations and giddy pleasures awaiting all those who choose to opt out of the high-speed addiction to progress, allying themselves instead with a real community immersed in the life of the animate earth. Powers is a one-of-a-kind reporter bringing necessary news from that mysterious edge where our gorgeous ideals meet the parched and rock-strewn soil of reality."

— **DAVID ABRAM,** author of *The Spell of the Sensuous*

"An enchanting personal story of a long journey in search of simplicity, home, and the 'Sweet Life.'"

— **DAVID KORTEN,** author of *When Corporations Rule the World* and *Change the Story, Change the Future*

"A compelling tale of leaving Manhattan to embed in a small, rural Bolivian town with all its wonders, differences, and commonalities. *Dispatches from the Sweet Life* is the vivid personal chronicle of a bold adventure in search of sustainable development — and pondering what really matters."

— **THOMAS E. LOVEJOY,** professor of environmental science and policy at George Mason University and former chief biodiversity advisor at the World Bank

"William Powers actually does what many of us in the Global North dream about and talk about but ultimately may not have the chutzpah to pull off: become an expat-on-a-budget in a place where life appears to be simpler, happier, and ultimately better. In this age in which the tyranny of time, scale, and efficiency robs us of moments to envision an alternative, Powers's description of homesteading in Bolivia is self-effacing, funny, and strikes at the core of what is missing today: a chance to get off the combine before we get pulverized by the system. Do we need to travel far to learn what's deep inside us all? The short answer is: probably yes."

— **RICHARD McCARTHY,** executive director of Slow Food USA

"While *Dispatches from the Sweet Life* is full of useful information wrapped in compelling, colorful stories, it carries something unusual for those of us steeped in the American Dream of progress and prosperity: a feeling for a life woven into a specific place on earth. How many of us actually make a place our own by letting its creatures and vegetation and characters root in us as we settle in them? This book is part memoir, part Transition Town case study, part permaculture how-to, but in largest part an invitation to absorb through all the senses — physical and spiritual — how you might feel outside the angular edifices or your work and your daily life."

— VICKI ROBIN, author of *Your Money or Your Life* and
Blessing the Hands That Feed Us

"In essence, the Transition movement is a network of storytelling, as people around the globe share their tales of trying to build more resilient, diverse, and connected communities in wildly varying settings. The story told in *Dispatches from the Sweet Life* is a powerful, fascinating look at trying to do Transition in one particular place. Its pages drip with illumination, insight, and wisdom."

— ROB HOPKINS, founder of the Transition movement

"William Powers's writing is hopeful, warm, and kind. He makes us question the old American Dream, and at the same time, he offers up a new dream. *Dispatches from the Sweet Life* points us toward days made richer by spareness, days made meaningful through focus and care."

— MICHAEL HARRIS, author of *The End of Absence*

"The multigenerational project of cultural renaissance is the Great Work of our time. In *Dispatches from the Sweet Life*, Bill Powers gifts us with an engaging and intimate look at the personal challenges, risks, and joys of reinventing human community and of imaginatively loving our interdependent and sacred more-than-human world."

— BILL PLOTKIN, author of *Soulcraft*

"The foundation of the 'Sweet Life,' this book makes clear, is a deep connection to community and the natural world. William Powers's description of the search for that life in a small Bolivian town is often inspiring, sometimes tear-jerking, and always thought-provoking."

— HELENA NORBERG-HODGE, founder and director of Local Futures

Dispatches from the Sweet Life

Also by William Powers

Blue Clay People: Seasons on Africa's Fragile Edge

Whispering in the Giant's Ear:
A Frontline Chronicle from Bolivia's War on Globalization

Twelve by Twelve:
A One-Room Cabin Off the Grid
and Beyond the American Dream

New Slow City: Living Simply in the World's Fastest City

Dispatches from the Sweet Life

One Family, Five Acres, and a Community's Quest to Reinvent the World

William Powers

New World Library
Novato, California

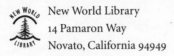

New World Library
14 Pamaron Way
Novato, California 94949

Text design by Tona Pearce Myers

Library of Congress Cataloging-in-Publication Data
Names: Powers, William, [date]– author.
Title: Dispatches from the sweet life: one family, five acres, and a community's quest to reinvent the world / William Powers.
Description: Novato, California : New World Library, [2018].
Identifiers: LCCN 2018020042 (print) | LCCN 2018027595 (ebook) | ISBN 9781608685653 (ebook) | ISBN 9781608685646 (alk. paper)
Subjects: LCSH: Powers, William, [date]– | Urban-rural migration—Bolivia. | Sustainable living—Bolivia. | Alternative lifestyles—Bolivia.
Classification: LCC HT381 (ebook) | LCC HT381 .P69 2018 (print) | DDC 304.8/840747—dc23
LC record available at https://lccn.loc.gov/2018020042

First printing, September 2018
ISBN 978-1-60868-564-6
Ebook ISBN 978-1-60868-565-3
Printed in Canada on 100% postconsumer-waste recycled paper

New World Library is proud to be a Gold Certified Environmentally Responsible Publisher. Publisher certification awarded by Green Press Initiative. www.greenpressinitiative.org

10   9   8   7   6   5   4   3   2   1

A tree holds up the seven skies. We venerate all trees because we do not know which one holds up the world. — Chief Gaspar of the Bolivian Chiquitano, as told to William Powers

Contents

Preface

I wrote *Dispatches from the Sweet Life* for anyone who questions, even slightly, the dominant American lifestyle today. I hope that in the wake of the inner and outer struggles in these pages, the reader will emerge with some knowledge and a good deal of curiosity about how we might live more integrated lives.

This is the third book in the Beyond the American Dream trilogy, which began with *Twelve by Twelve* (2010), about a guy in an off-grid tiny house in rural North Carolina seeking a minimalist, sustainable existence. It was followed by *New Slow City* (2014), about a newlywed couple in a Manhattan micro-apartment trying to re-create that same Slow life in the midst of urbanity. It culminates with *Dispatches from the Sweet Life*, about a young family self-exiled to South America, searching for balance, humanity, and happiness in a Bolivian town. Though thematically and chronologically connected, each book in the trio stands on its own.

There's no single definition of the South American idea of *vivir bien* or "living well." The Quechuas call it *sumak kawsay*; the Aymaras, *suma qamaña*. It also draws from the Guaraní idea of harmonious living (*ñandereko*) and the path to the noble existence (*qhapaj ñan*). Some, like Bolivian philosopher Javier Medina, call this alternative culture *la vida dulce* or "the sweet life": happiness achieved through deep human community in balance with nature.

From the moment I first arrived in Bolivia in 2001, I was fascinated by this new-and-ancient Bolivian dream. Fleshed into the larger society, the Sweet Life worldview seemed the opposite of my own culture's "American Dream," which positions the individual — via competition — atop a set of natural resources for exploitation.

Then, in 2005, while I was writing *Whispering in the Giant's Ear: A Frontline Chronicle from Bolivia's War on Globalization*, the indigenous union leader Evo Morales won the presidency on a pro–*vivir bien* platform. A cultural meme, at once alluring and sustainable, was now primed to shape a modern nation. This released a powerful question: Could the Sweet Life provide an alternative to the more-is-better hegemony of the American Dream?

Though *memoir* names this book's genre, I've layered in a four-part structure corresponding to the four components of the Sweet Life: the search for balance, the complementarity of diversity, a unified vision, and initiation. I've culled these from Bolivian academic writings (by Javier Medina and Pablo Solón, among others) and from conversations with friends like Chiquitano Chief Gaspar and horse tamer Kusi. I imagine each of the four components, metaphorically, as part of the Chiquitano tribe's "tree of life that holds up the world." Each of the four parts corresponds to a section of that venerable tree — roots, trunk, branches, and sky (yes, in Bolivia that's part of the tree, too). Thus, we climb the tree that both supports and *is* the enigmatic Sweet Life.

There's no instruction manual for "living well" because it is a state of growth, a journey rather than an end point. What works for someone else may not work for you, and the multiplicity of "sweet" paths is its very fragrance.

I share this very personal story aware that I am a man with a US passport, relative economic security, and education. This is part of what made it possible for me to choose to move to Bolivia. For many Global North foreigners, moving abroad is a privilege, in the sense that risk-taking is. The discriminatory immigration policies in today's United States and Europe make the advantages of my citizenship feel especially poignant. The ability to physically move, so easily, between the United States and Latin America is extraordinary. Our family's and community's honest efforts to live ancient values in their new "transition" expression today are also an attempt to subvert the very status quo that supports our privilege.

Because this is a true story, I chose to protect identities and specific locations, including the name of the actual Bolivian town it describes. I have occasionally collapsed multiple conversations into one or telescoped the chronology of certain events to tighten the book's narrative.

I also include at the back of the book a glossary of terms and translations of some of the Spanish, Quechua, and Aymara terms sprinkled throughout the text. If you are interested in learning more about some of the ideas in this book — like Transition initiatives, permaculture, international development, and so on — please visit my website (williampowersbooks.com) for a list of resources.

Finally, memoir is not diary, but rather literary art seeking a migration from fact to truth. I hope this book might catalyze reflections, emotions, and inspiration in you...toward harmony within that broad, inclusive tribe called *us*.

The Town
Chorrillos
Amboró National Park
Bergwald
La Posada del Sol
Paredones
Santa Cruz
Latina Cafe
The Church
Republika
The Plaza
Flor de Montaña
Tierra Libre
The Market
N
W
E
S
La Vispera
Tierra Guapurú

Tierra Guapurú

← Town

Cacti

Hillock

Gate

N
W · E
S

Eucalyptus Border

Creek

Frog Pond

Wild Blackberries

Carnaval Grove

Orchard

Tula Trees

Pacay Trees

Creek

Casa Guapurú

Guapurú Forest

One Acre

Grey Water

Black Water

Prologue

My howl for help echoes into the silence. Incensed, I kick a rock, which sails over the edge of the bluff upon which I'm marooned and tumbles toward the river below.

I hear a rustling as the rock flushes out a *duck* like none I've ever seen. The thing flaps wildly up out of the gulch, its neck elongated like that of an egret, its feathers chartreuse, orange, charcoal. It nearly wings into my face, but then it banks upward, leaving behind a feral pungency.

I wish I could fly out of here, too. There's no going forward, since the rock face is too steep and brittle. Nor backward, since the path I edged in on has crumbled away.

That leaves right here. Alone in Bolivia, where the Andes meet the Amazon, far from the familiar. I feel a feverish rush, the mosquito-borne *chikungunya* disease working its way through my muscles. My wife, Melissa, is five thousand miles gone. She departed during the visceral aftermath of a horrifying crime that just went down in our adopted town — a two-hour drive from this ledge, along an isolated dirt road — resulting in a xenophobic surge of anger against us and other foreigners.

Steady. Grab the torso of a *tula* tree for support. Sweat. Soak up the last warmth of the sun about to sink. Shiver. A cold night is coming. Thirst. Focus on the aquamarine ribbon of river below. Breathe. Remember that all paths are the same: They lead nowhere.

Inhaling silence, I'm on the threshold of understanding something that has long baffled me: My mind has internalized and been calcified by the Dream, a worldview that goes beyond

1

the "American Dream" of capitalism and social mobility and encapsulates the broader Western Dream of progress and left-brain reductionism. The Dream computes humans as muscle and synapse in an agnostic cosmos. It says, trapped here, I'm severed from my wife, from my Bolivian neighbors, from nature.

Then fear falls away, as the Dream becomes brittle as the rock face behind me. I connect to a deeper, untethered wisdom. I remember Don Carlos Peralta ("The giant hummingbird told me you were coming"), the be-a-bee Bolivian Amazon Chief Gaspar, the "Transition Town" visionaries in Suraqueta, even that dazzling duck — they populate a different dream, another story. From the precipice of almost certain death, and in a flash that mirrors the last rays of today's sun, I finally grasp something: an incredible stratum of joy within the Sweet Life enigma.

I. ROOTS
The Search for Balance

One

In January 2013, my newlywed wife, Melissa, and I visit the Bolivian town of Suraqueta, where we discover a beautiful piece of land that's for sale. Five acres of rolling hillside, a tadpole-filled creek, and a grove of wild *guapurú* fruit trees, whose tangy-sweet purple fruits grow out of their velvety trunks. We spend hours walking the land. "It feels like we're in the country," Melissa says from the property's main hillock. "And yet that's town-center, a stroll away."

I gaze out over Suraqueta's clay roofs and white colonial façades, the green hills cupping it, framing a scene that could be Tuscany if not for the sparks of green-and-red parrots flaring over our heads. Strong notes from mariachi trumpets drift upward from a wedding somewhere below, and I catch the invigorating scent of eucalyptus. Higher mountains loom to the north, and there lie cloud forests of rare giant fern trees in the biodiversity-rich Amboró National Park bordering the town. Over my shoulder is a massive jaguar-shaped Inca ruin. A breeze releases soft static from the yellow-flowering *carnaval* tree overhead as my half-Bolivian daughter, Amaya, swings from its branches, yellow petals snowing down.

Amaya lives with her mom and maternal grandmother in the nearby city of Santa Cruz, two and a half hours away. Melissa and I have come here on vacation from our home in New York City to visit her and to scout out properties. Eight-year-old Amaya, whose name means "beloved first daughter" in Quechua and "spirit" in Aymara, announces where "our house" would be, and I notice the joy she exudes by inserting herself in that *our*.

5

She climbs down from the *carnaval* and begins plucking purple *guapurú* fruit, popping the grape-size morsels into her mouth.

We follow Amaya's lead. The juice warm on my cheek, I imagine ditching my American life for a simpler one abroad. We could build a custom adobe house on this very hillock and grow much of our own food on these acres — mandarins, pomegranates, bananas, vegetables of all sorts. We'd reforest the agriculturally degraded flatter portions of it to create more habitat for the native guinea pigs and iguanas I hear rustling in the *quiñe* shrubs, and re-channel the creek through the land to create fishponds. I imagine rising with the sun, working part time via laptop and Wi-Fi, opening abundant time to raise my family in community.

Melissa and I try to conceal some of our enthusiasm for the land as we begin negotiations with the property's owner. He inhabits a concept of time different than our own. He's in no rush to sell, and no, he won't divide the acreage. We make an offer. He counters. It's still too high. By US standards, his price for five perfect acres would be reasonable, but for us, it would mean going deep into debt, which we're determined to avoid. We stay up late huddled over the table in our rental cabin, offering the calculator multiple scenarios, trying to figure out how we might afford the property.

One afternoon we visit the Suraqueta (pronounced: Soo-rah-QUE-tah) Refuge, a halfway house for wild animals that started life as pets. Surrendered to the refuge as adults, the creatures wait for release into Amboró National Park. Habituated to humans, several animals roam free. Nuño, a thirty-pound, ginger-haired howler monkey rests on my shoulders, his leathery tail wrapped around my neck. Cheetah, another howler, arranges herself on Melissa's shoulders. Amaya and some of her friends feed papaya to giant tortoises, while Melissa stroke's Cheetah's head.

"It's gorgeous here," my wife says, her hand dropping from Cheetah to her belly's bulge. Melissa is six months pregnant. I feel calm in Suraqueta, and I imagine our baby would, too, but I'm conflicted. Giant fern trees rise into blue skies, but so do the support struts of the George Washington Bridge in Manhattan. The gleam of the river feeding nearby Cuevas waterfall is the Hudson River's gleam. "Yes, it's gorgeous," I counter, "but so is New York."

"Sandy wasn't so gorgeous," Melissa says.

A few months ago, in October 2012, Hurricane Sandy smashed our Manhattan neighborhood. It left behind boarded-up restaurants and drowned subways and closed offices for weeks. We waited twelve days for electricity. Sandy, dubbed by the media as a "Frankenstorm," caused $65 billion in damage and left a hundred people dead.

Like many New Yorkers, we roamed the debris-filled sidewalks, none of us very happy. We felt helpless and unproductive without the electricity that supports every aspect of modern life. I hit an emotional low as I envisioned an umbilical cord connecting me to OPEC wells. Petroleum as amniotic fluid. I felt ashamed to be an oil-dependent, overconsuming human and ambivalent about bringing another of my kind into the world.

On a gray afternoon atop Tar Beach, our name for our downtown apartment building's rooftop, I improvised for Melissa a bit of a grim stand-up routine from Doug Stanhope. The comedian cites an Oregon State University study, which found that the greenhouse gas legacy of one child dwarfs — by twenty times — the impact of employing environmentally sensitive practices, like recycling or using energy-efficient appliances for one's entire life. Stanhope then jabs cynically about the decision to have kids. Melissa laughed, a laugh tinted with sadness that unfortunately has become habitual to us. A laugh, at root, of antipathy toward ourselves.

Contemplating a new life in Bolivia, we are well aware of our privilege. Melissa has a permanent post as an expert on women's political participation at the United Nations' headquarters. I teach sustainable development to grad students at New York University, write, and give speeches around the country. So why do we feel discontent in the global hub where you live when you've made it? We talk about how we're umbilically attached to a kind of Franken*Dream*: Work-and-spend. Drill, baby, drill. Buy, baby, buy. Our attempts to go minimalist and Slow in New York have begun to feel not enough for us, and we know we face a major choice. We can remain in our society's Dream of more-is-better — find a bigger apartment, deploy our social capital toward career advancement, synch our offspring to the addictive viscous fluid of competition. Or we can wager it all for something richer …and cut the cord.

THE DAY AFTER BONDING with howler monkeys at the Suraqueta Refuge, we meet up with a longtime Bolivian friend, a thirty-three-year-old backcountry scout and wild-horse tamer named Kusi. She's beautiful, with a thin frame and deep large eyes. She likes to "go *macha*" — tough girl, with loose-fitting military khakis and short hair. A decade ago, on a conservation project I managed in Amboró National Park, Kusi worked as an Andean bear and jaguar tracker on a wildlife census. Now, at Posada del Sol — a Suraqueta café owned by Trent, originally from Texas — Melissa, Kusi, and I pass around a wooden cup of yerba máte and discuss our stay-or-go conundrum.

Adjusting her red bandana, Kusi says, "*Aca existe la vida dulce*" — It's the Sweet Life here. She adds that *la vida dulce* is not about hedonism, as the phrase might initially conjure; it doesn't mean pleasure all the time with an aversion to struggle. The Sweet Life is another way of expressing *vivir bien* (living well), an idea with ancient roots that is being freshly reinvented in modern Bolivia. She boasts that the country's new constitution and also its "Law of Mother Earth," the highest decree of the land, endow Pachamama — Mother Earth, sometimes called Gaia in the West, a feminine omnipresence or the planet as a living body — with "Earth rights" similar to human rights, like the right to not have her vital systems interrupted by big development projects.

Kusi's enthusiastic talk reminds me of Bolivian philosopher Javier Medina's important contrast between the Western "Better Life" — steeped in individualism and progress, what I call the Dream — and the Amerindian "Sweet Life," which emphasizes "the sufficiency of the good" and respect for diversity. Medina writes, "The Western worldview puts natural resources at humanity's disposal, whereas in the Amerindian worldview humankind is understood as '(s)he who helps Mother Earth give birth.'"

Kusi explains, in her lispy colloquial Spanish, that, in keeping with the Sweet Life vision, Suraqueta — her hometown and "the place to which of course you should move" — has been designated as one of Bolivia's twenty-four "eco-municipalities." This designation anchors the lofty concept of Earth rights to specific places through government support of organic agriculture, clean energy, and community-based ecotourism.

This discussion inspires me, relieving the murky mood I experienced in New York. In contrast to America's dark and divided political climate, Kusi describes how Earth-care is now enshrined in Bolivia's constitution, how a broad-based citizens' movement brought the current indigenous-socialist government to power, creating a welcoming context for foreigners like ourselves. Suraqueta, it's dawning on me, is *glocal*, a contraction of "global" and "local." Should we move here, Melissa and I would join a small but vibrant group of expatriates (3 percent of the town's population of five thousand): Dream-skeptical, revillaging foreigners from thirty countries, along with Bolivian urban refugees from less-than-Slow Cochabamba, Santa Cruz, and La Paz. We've already met some of these people. A detethered Parisian runs the French bistro Latina Café with his Suraqueteña wife; erstwhile Istanbulites have just inaugurated the Turkish La Cocina; an Australian couple tends bar at Republika. There's a doctor from Cochabamba and a sculptor from La Paz. In the plaza, we've overheard conversations about fledgling meditation retreats,

Brazilian massage therapy, and at least ten organic farm start-ups. And there's not a chain store within a two-hour drive.

Suraqueta features communal work parties and *pasanaqus* (or community savings mechanisms), and 90 percent of perishable food is locally produced. Many of the expats, predominantly Europeans and other South Americans, blend into the dominant Bolivian milieu by joining these cooperative social structures with an enthusiasm I've not seen in other expat havens — like San Miguel de Allende, Mexico, or Vilcabamba, Ecuador, which tend toward bubble colonies of gated wealth.

Further, Kusi says, people are talking about making Suraqueta Bolivia's first "Transition Town." Worldwide, about sixteen hundred Transition initiatives currently exist, part of a global Transition Network, in which local communities foster "glocal" low-carbon economies through alternative energy, local consumption, organic agriculture, and more. Size doesn't matter; "Transition Streets" encompass a single city block. All Suraqueta needs to do to join the Transition movement is to get a core group of community members to declare their intention to form a local chapter working toward the movement's goals, then take practical steps to achieve them.

Trent swaggers over, sits down, and inserts his perspective into Kusi's sales pitch. An émigré from hospital middle management, Trent is one of only two Americans living here. On Christmas Day, 2004 — fifty-two years old, divorced, and fed up in West Texas — he met a woman from Cochabamba, Bolivia, online, flew to a country he'd never seen, and got hitched. The couple moved to Suraqueta, and with very little initial capital, founded what is now a flourishing backpacker hostel and café. "Bolivia was the best thing that ever happened to me," Trent says, a faint echo of Texas in his drawl. "I haven't been back to the US once in ten years. My advice? Cut the umbilical cord."

AFTER ONE MONTH IN COUNTRY, our real estate negotiations stall. The landowner asserts his *oferta final*. Our vacation ends in a few days. My new semester starts next week. Melissa's boss expects her back at the UN in three days. She's so pregnant that this is the last week she can safely fly. Decision time.

During one of our last Suraqueta nights, Melissa and I swing in hammocks outside our rental cabin, gazing out at the silhouettes of banana trees and vines heavy with passionfruit. Salsa music from a nearby party reverberates softly from hard surfaces; frogs peep from the stream trickling below the nearby bamboo grove. We sway to and fro in our indecision but lean toward taking out a loan.

"Let's gamble the known," Melissa affirms.

I mutter inwardly: Gamble steady jobs? Gamble abandoning our families and friends? Expose our newborn to inferior rural health care in one of the poorest countries in the hemisphere? And Kusi's enthusiasm aside, how welcome will we really be — privileged gringos buying land, driving up prices, and helping to "gentrify" Suraqueta to foreign tastes? Is it really wise to go into debt to buy this land and build a house within a political context that has recently been threatening for foreigners?

Yes, threatening. The country's popular indigenous president, Evo Morales — simply called "Evo" by most Bolivians — used to end his speeches with the crowd-rousing cry, "Death to the Yankees!" The United States has a sketchy sixty-year résumé in Bolivia, with a history of unwelcome intervention that overshadows, in the eyes of many Bolivian citizens, any counterbalancing do-good efforts.

I weigh this history against our personal desires. When Evo came to power as the victorious MAS (Movement Toward Socialism) candidate in 2006, Bolivia made a choice to cut its own umbilical cord to the United States, in the form of dollars, in the wake of a tumultuous half century. In 1953, Bolivia enacted significant land reform that broke up the enormous haciendas owned by descendants of Europeans in the western part of the country, and the government distributed ample terrain to indigenous farmers. However, this failed to address the deep-seated racism of lighter-skinned, Spanish and other European elites toward the country's indigenous people, who until the 1950s were not even allowed to walk into Plaza Murillo, the main square in La Paz. Then, in the 1980s and 1990s, a series of Dream-friendly, neoliberal presidents privatized many of Bolivia's national resources, angering many ordinary Bolivians who wished to keep those resources in local hands.

Evo, the country's first indigenous-descendant president, proceeded to enact strong antidiscrimination laws, and he nationalized the hydrocarbon, telecom, and aviation industries. He also went after the United States. The US Agency for International Development? Morales kicked it out of Bolivia. The US Drug Enforcement Agency? Ditto. Peace Corps? The United States pulled them out after its volunteers were accused of spying. Even the US ambassador was booted. By settling here, Melissa and I would leave behind the known certainties of our relatively privileged status up north for the unknown and, yes, potentially hazardous status of foreigners in Bolivia.

That night, barely able to articulate what this change to our lives might mean, I stuff these uneasy thoughts somewhere deep. I assure myself that Melissa and I are both experienced citizens of the world. We will gamble the known.

In the light of day, buoyed by our love of Amaya, of Suraqueta, and of the exciting post-Dream paradigm emerging in this eco-municipality, we accept the *oferta final*.

Melissa flies back to work, and I stay on to navigate the bureaucracy of Bolivian land tenure, teaching my first classes at NYU remotely via Skype. I consult with a land rights lawyer, track down papers, and queue up with Bolivians in administrative offices. We take out the loan, do the bank transfer, and finally receive an embossed document: the deed to our five acres in Bolivia.

SEVERAL WEEKS FROM HER DUE DATE, Melissa's pregnant belly seems particularly huge on her thin frame as we shuffle together arm-in-arm down Manhattan's Sixth Avenue. The baby has been pushing up against Melissa's sciatic nerve, so each step causes pain to shoot up her left side and through her lower back. Sweating in my wool coat, I act as a crutch.

We're both nervous about the natural birth we've planned — with midwives, without comforting doctors or equipment — and the flared sciatic makes us more apprehensive about safely bringing our baby into the world.

Now that we're close to leaving New York, I'm nostalgic. All the familiar background scenery is fresh again, like the first kelly-green daffodil shoots pushing up through Washington Square Park's thawing soil. As Melissa leans into me, saying her back feels a lot better, I imagine us as an elderly Greenwich Village couple, shuffling through these same streets. Melissa holds a Slow City calm; she gazes upward, out of the buy-o-sphere and into the biosphere, and points out a third-story gargoyle. I notice the waning moon. An indignant heat rises in me. I do not want to leave New York. Manhattan is our life. Now that an expiration date threatens that life, I cling tight, white-knuckled.

Greenwich Village is our neighborhood; the Hudson is our river. These subways and buses belong to us, and I am not ready to go. I love Small Liberia's palm butter and Murray's bagels; I love the Met's Chinese decorative arts and fire-lit Jones Street jazz. I love teaching at NYU, riding a yellow ten-speed bike along the Hudson. I'm happy on Tar Beach, I've adapted to our tiny flat, and maybe our baby could, too.

Inertia grips me, that blurry psychological state that keeps people doing what they're already doing. Maybe the Sweet Life will sour. Maybe the socialist government will take our land away. Maybe we'll just shift from being privileged Manhattanites to privileged expatriates. Maybe we'll deprofessionalize. Maybe we'll be lonely.

We can still change our minds and stay in the winner's circle instead of migrating to the tenuous. New York is our habitat. Will we really cut the umbilical cord to *this*?

"PUSH!" I shout.

It's a month later, in the birthing center. And it's time.

Melissa pushes, howling.

To bond with my offspring from the get-go, I, the "natural-birth father," assist the nurse and midwife at each step. I massage her hands, her lower back. I help move her from the bed into a tub of warm water.

After sunset, the midwife flips off the light and asks me to light candles. The nurse floats a flashlight sealed in a plastic bag on the water. Melissa's beautiful face glows in the flicker of candles and from the bobbing flashlight.

I'm anxious. Melissa pushes. And pushes.

Nothing. It's taking too long.

I get up from where I kneel by the tub to play the mantras. Sat Nam. *My path is truth.* I realize Melissa is mirroring the mantra in slow drawn-out guttural sounds. The primal sounds of a mother on the perilous edge of bringing life. I kneel again beside her. She grips my arm. I notice something wrong in the illuminated water. Our baby's been crowning for a half hour, but now, in the dim light, I'm certain I see a tiny eye. A tiny nose.

She's too small.

My heart ticks faster. I'm imagining a tiny preemie.

But all at once, after a final loud grand push, our baby — Clea Luz — arrives on a wave.

The midwife guides her to Melissa's chest, where she splays in all her purple splendor, not yet oxygenated to pink. Clea is large and healthy. Eight pounds of moist, weeping love on her mom's chest. She's got a hint of my red hair. Melissa's green-blue eyes. My heart pounds joy. And what I'm feeling most acutely, inexorable from the love, is my own heightened *wildness*.

Melissa's happy, primordial tears, the salt of ancient oceans, fall onto our screaming mammal. Life, uncaged, whispers to my heart.

It says *move*.

There must be life beyond the Dream. We can smother inertia. Gamble the known. Venture into the Global South to join a community's resurging Sweet Life, with both Clea *and* Amaya at our side.

My hands shake as I receive the surgical scissors. I know what this father must do. Steadying myself, I cut the umbilical cord.

Two

"Could that really be an ostrich out there?" Melissa asks. It's September 2013, and we're in a taxi driving through the Grand Chiquitano plateau, a scorching Amazon basin rich with the honeyed scent of palm nuts.

"They're rheas," I answer distractedly, watching the fowl roam the grassy expanse around us. We've just deplaned at Viru Viru airport and are heading for Santa Cruz, Bolivia's biggest city, with a population of two million, which is a half hour away.

But the splendor of the grasslands is soon gulped up as our driver whizzes past soy granaries, industrial tractor clearinghouses, the gilt of an amusement park called Playland. Clea Luz — now six months old — ogles at all of this from my *lap*. It's making me edgy, since it's her first time riding without a car seat. Before we got in, the taxi driver puzzled over said foreign object, which we'd scavenged from a Brooklyn curb. I explained what it was and how it's installed, but I found no seat belts in his 1992 Ford station wagon with which to secure it.

So the car seat jostles in the back along with all of our belongings: seven bags. Schooled in Manhattan minimalism, we rejected a container shipment, whittling down the already sparse contents of our tiny apartment to such an unmoored paucity. We are unmoored, too. We've arrived without a sponsoring institution. Pre-coupledom, Melissa and I have a combined sixteen-year history in Bolivia, writing and doing environmental and human rights work, but always connected to contracts or fellowships, and always with the security of having our "real" home waiting to the north.

On top of all this, my heart thrums at the thought of hugging my firstborn daughter. Amaya, now nine, is elated to meet her baby sister for the first time. "Daddy, I'm shaking with joy," she told me on the phone the other day. I ache for her embrace but wonder how the two sisters will get along.

We finally arrive at Hotel Milan, a two-star hotel a half block from the city's historic plaza. The owner, a diminutive, seventy-year-old *señora* with black-dyed hair, screeches with joy at the sight of Clea, taking charge of *"mi nietita"* — my little grand-daughter — as Melissa and I, in well-honed nomad mode, shuttle our bags. We've spent the six months since Clea's birth on a kind of gypsy-parenting US tour to ensure long stretches of time with loved ones before migrating: two months with newborn Clea in the co-housing community Arcadia near my parents in Carrboro, North Carolina. There, with her four grandparents present, we blessed Clea in a "welcoming ceremony" in a loblolly pine grove, each of us sharing a thought or poem chosen for Clea. Six weeks at Melissa's parents' adobe-style home in Santa Fe, New Mexico, where Clea was blessed by the minister on the altar of her grand-parents' Episcopalian church. A month in my sister's solar dome in Vermont, swimming in creeks, picking blueberries, and pre-paring communal meals. A month in a clapboard summerhouse with more of Melissa's family on Cape Cod, carrying the growing Clea in her sling through Barnstable Harbor's salt marshes.

During this period, challenges abounded: packing and un-packing, adjusting to others' rhythms, the baby wailing at night. I struggled to fit an abbreviated workweek of writing and remote World Policy Institute project management into the shifting back-drops. On the whole, however, gypsy parenting invigorated. We didn't buy anything new for Clea, relying on hand-me-downs and thrift shops. We didn't rush into full-time work. We took back our time, gave it to Clea, and watched her smiles bring delight to innumerable folks on the road.

Now, in Santa Cruz, the nomad tour's last stop before Suraqueta, we take a *micro*, a small urban bus, to the gates of the city's fifty-thousand-student public university, Universidad Autónomo Gabriel René Moreno. We're here to pick up Amaya, since her grandma works here, and a bus drops Amaya off each day after school. Amaya's mom, a Bolivian of part Tacana Indian ancestry, is a biologist who works for a network of indigenous tribes that defends the Amazonian protected areas in which they live, and she is traveling for work. We scan crowds of students for a redhead. Nothing. As we anxiously wait, Melissa explains to Clea for the umpteenth time that she's about to meet her sister.

Suddenly, a flash of auburn. Amaya spots us and runs over, the ensuing moments every bit as primal as Clea's water birth.

"*Clea!*" Amaya cries out, looking into her sister's eyes. Our infant, who has been calmly strapped onto Melissa in her carrier, starts to kick her pudgy legs against Melissa harder than she ever has, her face unbridled wonder, her guttural utterances elated.

Melissa unsnaps Clea and she tumbles into Amaya's arms with a shriek of bliss, a sound she's never made, inextricable, it would seem, from the genetic link to this other person. Amaya's grandma sidles up, beaming at the encounter, hugging Melissa and me. Then the three of us gawk as the two sisters explore each other's eyes.

For the next two days, the two are never apart. Feeding the plaza pigeons, splashing in a city pool, Amaya changing her sister's diapers in our hotel room. When the joyous weekend is over, Amaya back to school the next morning, we know, having decided to move here, it's not good-bye for long. "See you soon" are the three lovely words Amaya speaks; she'll be with us in Suraqueta on her vacation.

The next morning, we schlep our seven bags and small daughter to the hole-in-the-wall office of the Suraqueta bush-taxi union off Avenida Grigota, whose sixty independent owner-drivers run seat belt–free, natural gas–converted Toyota Noahs and Nissan Sunnys along the half-dirt Santa Cruz–Suraqueta stretch. Clea in Melissa's lap — the car seat getting accustomed to its new home amid luggage — our driver, a shy acquaintance named Jerónimo, streaks west past Santa Cruz's high-rises to the throb of merengue music. Melissa asks him to slow down, which Jerónimo does, a touch, but all we can really do is swallow distress and watch the palm trees and small, clay-roof-and-cinder-block tropical towns like Puerto Rico and Limoncito and Santa Martha blur by.

After an hour of flatlands, we bump and rattle out of the tropics and up into the cooler Andean foothills, detouring mammoth boulders, the semi-bulldozed remnants of the mudslides that intermittently seal off Suraqueta for days. The Piray River bubbling below, Melissa and Clea pin noses to the taxi window, taking in the Jurassic Park–reminiscent Cuevas pinnacles. When we reach the peak of a long incline, Jerónimo, heretofore mute, cries out: "Suraqueta!"

We edge to the front of our seats. Below us, down in the valley, is a striking colonial town of hundreds of *teja*-roofed adobe houses, the green mountains rising up around it into Amboró National Park's cloud forests.

Rolling into our new community, a surreal scene unspools. It's familiar, of course, but feels entirely fresh now that we've come here with everything we own to *live*. I watch it all fly by: cupolas, black derby-hatted farmers and layer-cake-skirted Quechuas, papaya trees, a geodesic dome — no, a yurt — a black Brahmin cow wandering down the side of the road, flicking its tail, and productive little orchards wrapping around and through everything.

We wind up a narrow track to our destination: LA VISPERA announces a colorful, hand-painted sign, above the words, in Spanish, "Organic Farm, B&B, Herb Shop, and Garden Café." We step out of Jerónimo's ride into brisk mountain air and a terraced acre of two-hundred varieties of food plants. Oil palms stretch their long arms overhead; horses graze in an open field; and down the path from the spices and oils workshop bounds our longtime friend and Finca La Vispera co-owner Pieter de Raad.

The seventy-year-old proprietor is so tall he has to duck

under a bluebell arbor to reach us. A wool jockey's cap over his bouncy gray curls, he gives me a crushing hug. Behind him, gliding with a more serene, Buddhist-monk gait, comes his wife, Marga. Both Dutch, and having worked as psychologists in their homeland, they abandoned their European careers four decades ago and went AWOL in Latin America. While traveling through the area in 1983, they fell in love with Suraqueta and purchased these thirteen acres, cheap. A degraded cattle pasture in the early days, their parched hillside bloomed over the ensuing decades. Each part of La Vispera emerged instinctively, without an overall design, and today it's less of a business than an ecologically centered community of employees, neighbors, and short- and long-term volunteers and guests.

Marga and Pieter lead Melissa, Clea, and me to their newest creation, a three-bedroom circular, thatched, hobbit-like adobe house. We step into the hush of rounded earth walls, a wood-burning stove, an arched ceiling held by a vaulting single *tajibo* post, and a stunning mural, a rendition of a phoenix coming out of the ashes, an image to which I relate right now. Clea gazes up at a high ceiling inlaid with fine bamboo. There's a handmade wooden crib for her, beds with crisp linen, and a view over cultivated fields of every type of vegetable and fruit to mountains beyond. As natural as Amaya and Clea's connection, so do I click into this place. Marga hands us cups of passionfruit juice from the farm and asks: "*Listos para 'vivir bien'?*" — Ready to 'live well'?

WE'VE SLEPT, breakfasted, and are relaxing in hammocks in front of our hobbit's house when Kusi pulls up on a dented purple Yamaha dirt bike. She wears her trademark military khakis and, for protective headwear, a red bandana. I hug our friend. "You chose the Sweet Life!" she says.

Then, incongruously, she reaches down to pull her pant leg a few inches to show us something she's duct-taped to her calf. A hunk of uncooked beef.

"To seduce my worm," Kusi explains, ultra-casually.

Clea's eyes abulge, Kusi explains how the *Dermatobia hominis* fly lays eggs under your skin and its larvae are near-impossible to extract. But the meat covers the breathing hole and begins to suffocate it. "When my worm comes up for air," she says, "she'll burrow into the beef and I'll wrest her out!"

Meanwhile, a wasp approaches, hovering a few feet from my face. It's three times the size of a typical American wasp. Kusi says: "*Es un poquito malo*" — It's a tad bad.

I press Kusi to define "a tad," and she finally admits: "Its sting slays, instantly."

"*Pero no pasa nada*," she adds — But no problem — "because it fortunately doesn't attack humans. It only kills poisonous snakes."

Melissa's eyes widen. "Poisonous snakes?"

"The green vipers aren't lethal," Kusi assures us, her voice as nonchalant as it was when discussing the "*poquito malo*" executioner wasp.

"And the nongreen...vipers?" Melissa asks.

Kusi coolly lists off coral snakes and café-colored *chutos*, the larger *corredores*, and rattlesnakes. All of them poisonous. All inhabiting the land we bought.

Kusi didn't mention any of this during her Law of Mother Earth sales job at Texas Trent's café before we moved. When I point this out, she smiles and tells us, metaphorically, not to worry: "*El equipaje se arregla en el camino*" — The luggage arranges itself en route.

After Kusi leaves, I ponder this. It seems to capture a core Bolivian ethos. Don't worry about prudently packing the car, the saying has it. Just throw it all in the trunk and the road's bumps will bring everything into place. Risk tolerance is *otra cosa acá*. Families of four cruise through Suraqueta on a single motorbike, all unhelmeted. Car seats...well, we know about that one. And when, at Melissa's insistence, I walk down to Suraqueta's very basic La Florida Hospital and ask whether they stock snake venom antidotes, the on-duty nurse shakes her head. She says they stabilize "bitten ones" for evacuation to Santa Cruz. "But what about when mudslides block the road?" I ask. She answers with a luggage-shall-arrange-itself shrug.

Beyond such worrisome news about our new creepy-crawly neighbors is the problem of shelter. Pieter and Marga told us upfront that they have long-standing reservations for the hobbit's abode and our tenure is limited. Long-term rentals, however, are scant in Suraqueta. We need to build our house. And quickly.

Eager to start, Melissa and I walk across town to our land and traverse — all the while alert for serpents — the cattle-denuded middle of our property, settling down on a picnic blanket on the hillock. There we open our bible: Johan van Lengen's *The Barefoot Architect: A Handbook for Green Building*.

This four-hundred-page, diagram-rich, and rather seditious book has become dog-eared since I purchased it at SoHo's McNally Jackson bookshop a year back while we were still Manhattanites. Seditious, because the book breaks two belly-of-the-beast rules. First: Shoes required. In New York, amid fields of pavement, how delicious it was to dream of dewy grass between the toes! Second: Let the experts do it for you. With this DIY guide to building, we will sidestep specialization and design our own home!

We've since considered the tome's every approach to house framing and gray-water systems, water catchment and plumbing, site selection and room layout. Now we riff on a design for our home, a minimalist sculpture of art and ecology. It will be small: one bedroom, plus a mezzanine over the open-plan living/kitchen/dining room, holding an additional queen-size bed. We think of it as a "trial house" to learn bio-construction, to see how the landscape accepts us, before committing to a future three-bedroom, at which point this would become a guesthouse or a rental or a workspace. (We'll see.) With colored markers, we enthusiastically sketch niches for books and kitchenware impressed into adobe walls; we draw a sofa, desk, and table into some of the home's many curves, exploiting the ease of sculpting adobe walls; and we add a hammock-strewn, covered outdoor patio to broaden our living space into the landscape.

Later, surrounded by the cleverly built walls of the hobbit house at La Vispera, we scan our drawings with an impartial eye and realize our colorful diagrams are great for dreaming but unworkable for building. Bare feet, alas, come easier than draftsmanship. We seek out Pieter for advice and find him harvesting persimmons near the "Feng shui eco-home," as Marga calls their jazzy *casa*. He tells us he's about to take a break, welcomes us into his adobe, and with no additional verbiage, begins to play a prelude of Johann Sebastian Bach on his 1892 antique grand piano.

As horses graze outside in a field beside a mandarin grove, I soothe into a sonata in pleasant consort with the aroma of lavender from an open round window. As Pieter leans his large form into the piano, the afternoon sunlight gilds his gray curls. Every detail in their home, I notice, seems exact. Thin *caña hueca* bamboo is beautifully inlaid between the living room's *tajibo* ceiling beams, and the couple's books and CDs snuggle into their niches in the curving adobe walls. Pieter segues from Bach into a tune he wrote, inspired by the valley thrush; as he plays, a thrush swoops over to the lavender bush window and warbles along, kindling sparks in Pieter's crystal-clear blue eyes.

Thirty-five years, I think. That's how long he and Marga have lived in Suraqueta.

The feeling crescendoing in me while listening to aviary-in-the-ivories is a desire to emulate, nay, to imprint on such an elder. At last, the music ends, and Melissa and I clap, Clea coos, and I eventually share our dilemma: the difficulty of designing a house.

Pieter listens, a breeze from Amboró blowing across his acres. "*Caminar preguntando*" — Walk questioning — he finally says. "That's what Marga and I learned from the Bolivian friends with whom we dwell."

The pragmatic American in me is actually hoping for a referral. But Pieter has lived in Bolivia long enough to have adopted Kusi's enigmatic style of offering advice.

"Can I ask one while seated?"

Pieter smiles. "You just did, Billy boy. Have another?"

"Who was your architect?"

WE WALK OUR QUESTIONS and sketches over to Salome, the *arquitecta* who designed Pieter and Marga's home. She's already an acquaintance of ours, and she meets us at the front door of her pink-and-fuchsia-streaked adobe eco-citadel, six blocks from the plaza. A striking Bolivian woman of mixed local and German parentage, the midforties architect revillaged to Suraqueta a decade ago to escape a harried life in Bolivia's third-largest city, Cochabamba, along with her husband, Salvador, and a revolving selection of their combined eight children — "*los míos, los suyos, y los nuestros*" — yours, mine, and ours — as she puts it to us with a soft but reserved smile.

The chic ruralite sweeps us through her self-designed home's layout: five bedrooms organized into two wings joined by a high-ceilinged living room. The lofty kitchen's not round, she explains; she used, rather, a shell-like spiral. We trail Salome out a sliding glass door and across a tree-shaded patio to two other homes she designed, those of her close neighbors, a Viennese masseuse named Sukkah and a jack-of-all-trades from Madrid named Juan Pablo, both of whom live in loose community with Salome, Salvador, *y familia*.

Salome's as-built portfolio wins us over. Between her Vispera work and these creations, Melissa and I feel confident that we share a vision of permaculture and bio-construction, the use of local materials like adobe, and a spirited deference to the *teja*-tiled pueblo's atmosphere.

Over the next fortnight we walk questioning with Salome, spinning out draft after draft in her home, at Café 1900 on the plaza, and up on our hillock. We finally settle on a two-story central dome that curves, wavelike, across the foyer and bedroom. Her fee for the complete set of executable designs? "Four hundred US dollars," she says, with a wink toward Suraqueta's reasonable cost of living. Her low fee also recognizes an unstated "gift economy" in which skills are often passed around at below-market rates with the assumption that, in community, the favors will circle back. Plus, as Salome says, she simply likes doing it. Hypertransactional Manhattan could hardly seem further away.

Meanwhile, we've been *caminando preguntando* — walking questioning — at La Vispera, too.

At first, much of the finca's produce seems another lexicon of fruiting foliage, but we ask incessantly about preparations for native fruits like *guapurú* and *guayabilla*, leeks and *acelga* (chard), and soon our hobbit-house kitchen begins to sizzle with veggie stir-fries, our blender churning with new fruits. Each day we ingest salads of myriad greens and edible flowers.

On Wednesdays, Pieter and Marga rise early, joining their dozen well-paid, mostly long-tenured staff for the weekly harvest. The finca's energy intensifies, with everyone focused on fulfilling the week's orders of organics for the Santa Cruz market. But not in a speedy New York minute; the vibe is unhurried efficiency. "We left overscheduled Europe behind," Pieter says to me at one point while packing a container with nasturtium-topped baby lettuces. They're not workaholics, it dawns on me, but rather *osiologos* — leisureologists — existing in an equal balance of practicality and aesthetics. Marga, who is tall, with a Buddhist's cropped hair, regularly meditates in a little cottage capped with a "green roof," and she seems to bring that meditative quality into her silent hours tending the fields, sometimes accompanied by her husband's distant piano melodies.

One afternoon, I step outside of our hobbit house...and gasp. An unknown man is climbing one of our portico posts.

"*Hola!*" he cries, sliding back down the post and extending a confident hand. Dark of eyes and hair, with a thin, compact build, the twenty-something man wears flared jeans and a T-shirt revealing sharp-cut biceps. It's only when I notice the five-color air-brushed van parked outside — flamboyant with information on his business making straw-bale, rammed-earth, and adobe constructions — that I realize who he is.

"Rulas Maradona?" I ask.

Of course, he says, seemingly stunned by the question mark. He was climbing up the pole to straighten out a *teja*, he explains, as he sidles into our house — *his* house, he says, since he built it for Pieter and Marga — and nods admiringly at his work. "My walls breathe," Maradona says, his muscles flexing as he pounds a wall. "No paint on either side. I'm the best in Bolivia at mud coverings because I possess the secret mix of cactus juice for water resistance."

Spotting Clea on her baby blanket on the floor, Maradona strides over and — strongly, tenderly — strokes her cheek, while telling Melissa what a beautiful child she's given the world. Melissa, no doubt taken by this Suraqueta Don Juan, croons: "I love your work," then adds, exploring the music of his name, "*Rulas Maradona*."

He takes a minibow and asks to see the final design we developed with Salome, now in 3-D printouts. Maradona scrutinizes it, while Melissa raves further about his work. "It's the burrow-like comfort of sleeping in a bedroom sunk two meters into the earth for additional thermal mass."

Maradona slowly places Salome's design on the kitchen table, then turns his full thermal mass to us and pronounces: "I insist on my own improvements, but I'll do it."

We more or less agree right there to work together. The spontaneity of the decision, I'd see later, is more than just our being seduced by his poise. It is a first step into the Bolivian flow. *Caminar preguntando* isn't intellectual. The path you walk on is revealed as you walk and question and learn; each step is a single swoop of Ask-Act. The "decision fatigue" from which we and our stateside friends suffer, that exhausting pro/con parsing of micro-decisions, is rare here. After a few days of settling on details with Rulas Maradona, we sign a contract. He and his team of five other strapping bio-construction dudes will start in two weeks.

Yes, two weeks. The deepest gripe among folks wanting to undertake ecological construction in the United States is the endless permitting. Our house is to have gray-water reuse in the gardens, an evapo-transpiration-"banana tree circle" system of recycling human waste, and an experimental dome over the round portion. Browse the eco-building blogs, and you'll see that such a house might take two years, two dozen inspections, and thousands of dollars for approval. But here it's zero years, zero inspections, zero dollars. Suraqueta has no building codes.

Unleashed from codes and decision fatigue, I wake up one morning and acknowledge that we no longer inhabit a cage beneath Tar Beach in crowded Manhattan. We live in Rulas Maradona's "breathing" house on an organic farm embedded in a gift economy. The worries we had upon arrival — killer wasps under eaves, vipers underfoot, worms under skin — have not materialized. The luggage, indeed, *is* arranging itself en route.

So we flow. Flow up to our land with Salome and Rulas to stake out the exact site for our future home and to arrange for a *ch'alla* — an offering to Pachamama — in advance of laying the foundation. Flow into town, a five-minute walk from our land.

There Melissa and I bump into Suraqueta-born Cesar "Koki" Herrera, a longtime friend and author. He invites us to a book signing that evening in the town's cultural center. We attend. Instead of an airless reading, Koki's directing a group of local actors who perform scenes from his new book. Next there's local wine and a signing. While we're sipping, another Suraqueta-based writer, Uruguayan Emilio Martínez, author of the Bolivian bestseller *Ciudadano X*, about Evo Morales, tells me Koki finished the book six weeks ago and his Cochabamba publisher pulled the manuscript together and published within a month. I mentally compare that with Western publishers, who take well over a year between acceptance and publication. "That's Bolivia," Martínez says. "A little anarchy of creating and doing."

The next day, walking through town, I'm woozy with this new flow we're in, this "little anarchy" of Small. There's Theresa greeting us with a basket of hot empanadas. There's my longtime friend Doña Serafina at the market, who becomes our *casera* (our go-to market-stall green grocer), throwing in a little *llapita* (gifted bonus) of bananas on top of the avocados and cacao we purchase. There's an old artist acquaintance Pedro carrying scrap timber up to his workshop. There's *happiness*. Everywhere I look, smiles and a stress-free pace. On the plaza, a group of teenagers chats and laughs, smaller kids biking circles around them. An octogenarian couple strolls through this scene, the husband with a hoe over his shoulder. A sparse sprinkling of expatriates blends colorfully into this tableau. There's Frank, a German, from Road Runners tour company dropping off Amboró National Park hikers at Tierra Libre Café. There's Japanese-Bolivian Don Asano selling the *cuy* — guinea pigs — he raises on his organic farm. This isn't another-world-is-possible theory — it's another world that exists today.

I'm excited about the upcoming screening of the 2012 documentary *In Transition 2.0*, an event intended to galvanize community support for forming a new "Transition Suraqueta" group. As Kusi originally promised, some locals want Suraqueta to join the sixteen hundred Transition initiatives already underway in fifty-five countries.

These initiatives seek to transition to a new, postcarbon lifestyle. They are grassroots community projects that aim to increase self-sufficiency and reduce the potential effects of climate change and economic instability. Refusing to wait any longer for governments to act on our behalf, these groups of engaged citizens take things into their own hands at the community level. The Transition movement is characterized more than anything else by its defiant positivity, showing by example that this process can be liberating and fulfilling, involving practical approaches to energy, waste and recycling, food production, and transportation. Further, joining the movement takes little more than the will to take action.

I wonder if the supposedly inevitable trend toward near-total global urbanization is really inevitable. Could an insurgency against the FrankenDream be as possible as fifty thousand revillaged communities like Suraqueta?

WE GATHER AT OUR BUILDING SITE on a crisp morning.

Rulas Maradona and his wife are here, along with Salome and Salvador, Kusi, and other friends for the customary *ch'alla*. In Bolivia, it would be unthinkable to build without conducting such a ritual offering, and Melissa and I have attended many *ch'allas* over the years, for house construction and rental-apartment christenings, weddings and first-haircut initiation ceremonies. Today, we are conducting a specific type of *ch'alla* called a *k'oa*, laying out a colorful circular offering, a mandala of coca leaves, flowers, aromatic herbs, and "object representation" trinkets on a large piece of paper. As each person lays another bit of the mandala, he or she shares intentions toward our home's future Sweetness. We also honor the other humans who have dwelled here — from the Spanish back through the Inca and Guaraní and Chané. We offer to the animals living on our land now: the iguana pair living in a hillock rock pile, the wild guinea pigs, ferrets, parrots, even the snakes. Then, when the mandala is flawless — with every seed and trinket organized just so, a piece of art to treasure — we scorch it.

Melissa and I, embodying the Aymaran concept of *chachawarmi*, a unified male-female energy, place the meticulous mandala over a bonfire Rulas has lit. Silently, we all watch the smoke convey our *k'oa's* intentions skyward. More than just a nuclear family's intentions, it's a community's intentions for itself and nature.

That evening at La Vispera, Melissa spots a creamy yellow cactus flower and points it out to Marga. Her eyes light up. "It blooms for just a single day each year," Marga says. "And you discovered it."

As the sun sets over the valley, I feel like this flower. Something uncommon has opened. It's astonishing to contrast with New York this free sense of walking questioning, of designing and building a natural house. The cynical humor, the asphalt, the cramped nature of my former life departs day by day. Sitting in La Vispera, now, with Melissa and Clea, focused on that yellow cactus flower, my mind returns to Tar Beach and our Manhattan jobs, to familiarity's gravity and how we nearly abided inertia.

Melissa captures something of what I'm sensing. "This is our place," she says, contemplating the rare yellow bloom. "But to see that, we really did have to gamble the known."

Three

Too euphoric for sleep, I rise before dawn, boil coffee, and carry it, along with empanadas from La Vispera, across an awakening Suraqueta to our land. Rulas Maradona and his team will break ground this morning.

As the sun cracks our east ridge, I extend my palms to receive its first rays, as has been done here by indigenous Bolivians for at least two thousand years. It's now November, but this practice traditionally marks June 21, the winter solstice in the Southern Hemisphere and the Aymara New Year. Sunlight sets ablaze the pines and *sotos* on our hillock, spilling down into the dale at our land's center. I sip coffee next to what remains of our charred communal *k'oa*, abuzz with excitement. A home. Melissa and I will build our home on this blessed ground.

My jubilation wanes as the agreed-upon hour arrives and passes. No Rulas. No strapping bio-constructors.

At last someone appears. A silhouette is moseying up our northern dirt path.

It's Rulas's dad, short, sixty-five-year-old Papa Maradona. Though his skin has wrinkled and his posture slumped, he still possesses the same dark good looks he passed along to his son. He plops down with his knapsack under the *noki* tree and draws out a bag of coca leaves. One by one, he places several of the dried green leaves into his cheek.

I watch him, forcing patience as he loads up. Coca chewing is a ubiquitous ritual in Bolivia, like tea in England. And like tea and coffee, coca leaves are a mild stimulant that yields a caffeine-type buzz — though the drug cocaine can indeed be *extracted* from

33

coca through a complex process of boiling, adding chemicals, and so on. Coca is central to many aspects of Bolivian culture. On a daily basis, it's used by millions of folks, like Papa Maradona, to get the juices flowing for work, but it's also consumed in abundance during *ch'allas* of all kinds, during patron saint festivals in August, and for Day of the Dead in November, at which time many Bolivians honor the deceased by staying up all night until dawn chewing the leaf.

Finally, I can't contain the obvious question: "Where is everyone?"

Papa Maradona nods and continues to wordlessly accumulate leaves. He doesn't speak until his cheek swells like a guinea pig's. "They're not coming."

In the middle of another job, he adds, rising to his feet.

Papa Maradona starts working, alone. Not on our house, unfortunately, but rather on a temporary corrugated-iron storage shed for sheltering building materials and tools. He digs a foundation, fells one of the giant eucalyptus trees on our land, and frames it. That takes a week. Then two. Still no Rulas and no team.

I track down the junior Maradona, but despite our contract, there's no getting on with *our* show. The flip side of the lovely spontaneity of our snap agreement is that a parallel spontaneity might alter the pact. Finishing a roof elsewhere has taken priority. "But you do have your materials lined up?" I ask.

Rulas frowns. "*Como?*"

It turns out that he doesn't buy materials. He'll build the house, period. Rulas is not, as we'd thought, a general contractor who will oversee the entire project. So Melissa sits down with him that evening to create a materials list; she purchases cement, stones, gravel, and iron rods in the pueblo, and I travel to Santa Cruz for plumbing fixtures in that city's agreeably chaotic Ramada and Alto San Pedro bazaars. Then I ship our wares back to a "work" site still graced by nobody but the coca-wired shed-builder Papa

Maradona. Melissa and I become reluctant barefoot contractors. We enlist a plumber and an electrician, a water-meter installer and an *adobero* (adobe brickmaker), a foundation digger and a blinds maker. There's even a "glass guy" to recruit, available only in Santa Cruz, who is to cut and install windowpanes, as well as a "wood guy," the soft-spoken local thirty-year-old nicknamed Eterno — Eternity — because that's how long he's said to take to deliver posts and beams. As luck would have it, we also need a carpenter for the finer, detailed work. Melissa and I, Americans after all, sit down one by one with each of these tradespeople and hammer out agreements for completing each respective piece of the construction puzzle following a SMART work plan: *s*pecific, *m*easurable, *a*chievable, *r*ealistic, and *t*ime-bound. This renders awkwardly from Manhattanese into Spanish. Do the delighted nods we receive indicate agreement or bafflement?

Meanwhile, we're about to be exiled from La Vispera. Though I petition Pieter to hobbit-house us a little longer, he reminds me of his paid reservation, which was made more than a year ago. Unfortunately, long-term rentals in Suraqueta prove to be even scarcer than imagined. With less than a week until homelessness, Melissa and I pursue every lead. We find nothing.

At last, Rulas Maradona and his six bio-guys do appear. They don't just begin work; they attack the site. Working with Rulas, it would seem, is akin to trench warfare, with extended phases of silence interspersed with deafeningly brutal engagement. Insisting on eleven-hour days, with corresponding overtime, Rulas and crew dig and lay the foundation and raise the adobe in a feverish cloud of dust.

But then they stop, bottlenecked by missing tradespeople. Our SMART plan proves otherwise. No window or door frames from the carpenter, no wiring from the electrician, no beams from Eternity. Alas, planning is a Western import presupposing linear time (time as an arrow). Bolivians — and this may be the actual "smart" part — live within recurrent time (time as a cycle). Like seasons or tides, "time" comes and goes. It will come back again, *hombre*, so what's the worry?

Our worry is a timepiece tyrant, ticking toward dislodgement from La Vispera. I console myself, however, in the much-awaited Transition launch. On the designated evening, thirty people gather in a backroom of La Taboada, a chocolate shop on Calle Bolívar, to view the documentary film *In Transition 2.0*. In it, folks in England demonstrate the alternative currency they created to encourage local consumption. An African American woman in inner-city Baltimore talks about how their Transition street helped unify the local social fabric. The film celebrates this flourishing movement, with thousands of initiatives worldwide becoming increasingly and powerfully linked, and it lays out the tools for Suraqueta to become Bolivia's very first Transition Town. As the credits run, I'm certain everyone feels as enthused to form a core group as I am!

Thiago, a thin, receding-hairlined, bespectacled Mexican friend who's been living in Suraqueta for three years, clicks off the projector. I hear a yawn. Shuffling. "We're already 'in transition,'" *arquitecta* Salome says.

"Exactly," rejoins organic coffee farmer Juancito, who points out that all of us watching the film tonight, both Bolivians and expatriates, and a hundred others in town, are already on a path of local consumption and already embrace local traditions and ecological awareness. "So why do we need the big 'T'?"

Glances toward the exit. Thiago, who took the lead to organize the film screening, tries to change the energy in the room: "*Esta bien*," he says, "but if we don't organize ourselves, corporate marketing will undercut all of that, turning Suraqueta into another consumer colony."

Thiago's observation falls like a stone tossed in water that creates no ripples. Instead, comments reflect a freethinker vibe: Yes, Transition is cool, but people live in Suraqueta to sidestep organizations and meetings. This sentiment is akin to that of our planning-allergic tradesmen: Locals prefer to let the luggage spontaneously arrange itself en route.

But this is not the same as passivity. Bolivians are extraordinarily rebellious. In 2000, they rose up to toss out the powerful Bechtel Corporation in the so-called Cochabamba Water War (to stop privatization and higher utility rates), and in 2003, they blockaded all national highways for a month to remove the neoliberal president Gonzalo Sánchez de Lozada after he declared he would import petroleum through ports in Chile, Bolivia's historic enemy. This is a nation, however, suspicious of anything that appears to undermine community autonomy. As Bolivian anthropologist Silvia Rivera notes, generations of powerful Aymaran anarchist unions have subverted central power in whatever form it takes.

And the *amigos* assembled tonight in the Taboada chocolate shop backroom seem to reject the film's Transition Town blueprint. The evening ends with neither a core group nor identified next steps. The SMART planner in the room departs, downhearted.

WE HEAR THE RUMOR: My old acquaintance, an Austrian-Bolivian mechanic named Jörg, has just put his house up for rent. I met Jörg in the early 2000s at Mosquito, Suraqueta's former rocker bar, a living-room-like watering hole where anyone could go behind the bar and play DJ, and drinks payment was haphazard. Lanky Jörg opened Mosquito as a sideline to his main job as town mechanic, after returning from a near-mythical stint as a US rock-band roadie, including a rumored gig as Michael Jackson's bodyguard. Born and raised in Suraqueta, Jörg, after siring two kids with an Argentinian woman here, divorced and moved to Hamburg, where he negotiated an eleven-hour-a-day contract that permits him three months' annual leave back in Suraqueta with his children. That leave, it appears, has just ended.

I fast-walk my questioning to Bergwald, an Austrian hotel / café / art shop on Suraqueta's north side. Out of breath, I knock on the front door, hopeful the house is not already rented. The door opens, and there's Jörg's father, Ludwig. Scruffy, gray-bearded, and clad in a black leather biker's cap, it's hard to believe diminutive Dad shares the same genes with his towering son.

Yes, he tells me, Jörg's house — which forms part of the Bergwald hotel complex — is still available. The pad could hardly be more different from what I imagined of *la vida dulce*, but we're out of options. Ludwig accepts the first month's rent in cash, dismissing my offer of a security deposit and signed contract with a laconic "This is Bolivia."

After hugs with Pieter and Marga at La Vispera, Clea, Melissa, and I bush-taxi our seven suitcases to Bergwald.

"Holy moly," Melissa says when we arrive. The view from Jörg's porch is a surreal mini-Austria. The swimming pool winks invitingly amid manicured fruit trees and flowers. Inside, our modern, cinder block–style three-bedroom, two-bathroom, newly applianced home is a shrine to Queen and Dire Straits, Elvis and Hendrix; their framed posters, vestiges of Mosquito and Jörg's roadie romp, canvas the walls.

Clea is to ripen, it would seem, in Hard Rock Café meets Planet Hollywood. Her playroom pays homage to Freddie Mercury, and in our shared bedroom each morning she awakens in her crib to images of James Dean and Marilyn Monroe. To our offspring's primate brain, these representations could only be of revered ancestors, with none more esteemed than the ones at hearth center and deserving of the largest icon in our dwelling. Clea stares up at these godheads from her baby blanket, cooing to Jagger, Richards, Wood, and Watts. We humans venerate (the Rolling) Stones.

It's at Jörg's that we celebrate, three months after moving to Bolivia, our first Christmas, gone. Christmas can be hot in Suraqueta, in the eighties, though mountainously cool at night, the days streaked with thunderstorms mixed with sun. It's the Southern Hemisphere summer, the rainy season. In lieu of pine, we adorn a baby bougainvillea with decorations, its root ball snug in plastic; we imagine the plant will climb a pillar of our someday-adobe. Jörg's mother, Frau Anna, gifts us faultlessly wrapped candleholders she kiln-fired on-site, then painted in Christmas cheer. Melissa bakes Swedish *nisu* bread for Anna and other friends, wrapping the braided golden loaves in a red bow, as her mother has long done for neighbors in her native Santa Fe, New Mexico. Beside the swimming pool out our window, a tree drips with ripe avocados. I hear them thump the earth during my twice-daily swim; lemons, limes, and tangerines gleam above my backstroke.

It's with jubilant hugs that we welcome Amaya to Planet Hollywood. She spends two several-week visits with us during her summer vacation (December and January) between fourth and fifth grade. Amaya watches Clea take her first steps beneath Jagger's leering gaze, and we take enjoyable walks around town: the plaza, Amaya's Suraqueta-friends' homes, and on our land.

"I know I should feel nothing but gratitude," Melissa says, one mid-December afternoon. She's in her bikini by the pool, and we're watching Amaya pick a mandarin off a tree and feed it to her sister. "So why do I miss that piney scent and the chance of snow?"

Gone. Gone feels free — we're unbound, of course, from customs or expectations, and can create our own holiday culture — but we are also clumsily detached. By leaving America and tiptoeing onto the margins of a foreign society, we've removed a veneer, behind which lies a void. I miss my mother and father, my sister and nephews, even details like the sound of Burl Ives crooning carols.

Gone is an emotion. As the days pass, it's the one that surfaces the most. I stare wistfully at our random bougainvillea Christmas bush under Mick Jagger, coveting the holiday culture of my late 1970s and early 1980s childhood at my family's Long Island home, the traditional trees, the modest number of gifts, the stockings to be stuffed. Grandma, Uncle Ed, Aunt Michelle, and cousins Heidi, Alisa, Judy, Matthew, and Andrew, and my little sister, Amy, and me. That sense of arriving in a warm winter coat at a nearby relative's house with Pyrex dishes of stuffing and sweet potatoes in hand, of the threshold between the cold outside and the physical and emotional warmth of hearth and family inside. With all of us planted in or near New York City, there was no air or train travel. I never would have imagined raising a family a hemisphere away.

"HEARD OF THE GRATEFUL DEAD?" I ask Amaya. It's nighttime, and she's reading on Jörg's couch.

"The *what*?"

"Mmm… '*los muertos agradecidos*.'"

Amaya frowns and cocks her head back. I've had the Grateful Dead's "Box of Rain" in my head for the last few days, partly because it's been drizzling intermittently. The tune brings me back to Cheryl Strayed's memoir *Wild* and how she dubbed Oregon a "box of rain" because the Dead is popular there, and also because Oregon is box-shaped and forever drenched. Part of why I like the song is that I don't quite know what a box of rain is. There's a similarly sweet ambiguity with another Dead song, "Ripple," which peaks with Jerry Garcia crooning, *If I knew the way, I would take you home*. The songs capture a state of melancholy and unmooredness to which I relate.

I play "Ripple" for Amaya, and "Box of Rain," and the rest of the 1970 album *American Beauty*.

She listens while she reads. Later, I ask her what she thinks about it. "It's fine," Amaya says.

She looks at me sleepily, blankly. I continue: "I saw the Dead live in Madison Square Garden when I was in high school. In 1988." I realize she's adrift. Her cultural reference points are *cuñapé* pastries and the band Los Kjarkas, the Santa Cruz plaza and reggaeton. Amaya may be a redhead who speaks English, but she's Bolivian.

"You saw the Dead…*live?*" she finally says, forcing a smirk through her sleepy face.

The next morning, while we're all Skyping with my sister's family in Vermont, I say to my sister's husband, "We thought of you last night, Andrew. Amaya listened to the Grateful Dead for the first time."

"Which album?" I tell him it was *American Beauty*. He nods: "Good place to start." Over Andrew's shoulder, I peer into a streamed version of my old, familiar life: my sister's family's living room, the toy shelf, the wood-burning stove, and a huge boulder down by the creek that they've dubbed Big Rock Candy Mountain after the old Harry McClintock folk song about a hobo's idea of paradise, where lakes of gin and cigarette trees abound. In the kids' version they sing in their family, "Your birthday comes around once a week, and it's Christmas every day."

I feel my tear ducts activate. The Christmas stockings hung on the mantle, the decorated tree. A silvery, sparkling New England through the window. Probably the scent of pines.

We elected to put an equator between us. *A box of rain will ease the pain.* I question our isolation, wondering if the cost of Bolivian sweetness is an equivalent portion of American beauty.

ON OUR LAND, two days before Christmas, I cut a trail with my machete while Amaya and her friend, Soami, spend a morning helping adobe brickmaker Estuvio and his brother, Ali. Up to their nine-year-old thighs in mud as they stomp in straw, the girls then help pour the goop into wood frames to bake in the sun. Meanwhile, Rulas and Papa Maradona, having raised the adobe walls but still lacking needed materials from the other tradesmen, are all but stalled and leave shortly after Soami scampers home for lunch. Estuvio and Ali continue to shape adobe, but very gradually.

We pay Estuvio well — two and a half bolivianos a brick. From my still-very-gringo mindset, this is an incentive to generate critical building materials ASAP. Though Estuvio and Ali do indeed come to work, stomping hay into wet earth, then pouring the brown brew into wooden molds, they don't rush, happily passing time lolling under our venomous-to-the-touch *noki* tree. There they smoke the Mairana-grown-and-rolled tobacco *cigarros* that sell for one American penny apiece in the Suraqueta market, and they amass formidable coca wads that dwarf Papa Maradona's. Brother Ali, evidently understimulated by nicotine and coca, adds swigs of cut-rate grain alcohol from the plastic bottles that, over the weeks, mound up under the *noki*.

Later that day, Amaya and I take a chill-out cue from Estuvio and Ali and rest together on our hillock in impeccable 75-degree sunshine, getting lost in conversation interspersed with comfortable silence. The pueblo hidden behind the hillock, we're in father-daughter country. After a while, clouds form and it starts to drizzle. "Maybe we should go back to Bergwald," I say to Amaya, feeling the mist on my face.

"It's hardly anything, Daddy," she says, and recounts a dream she had the previous night. In it, her teacher took the class to Cancun and turned them over to "a lady who was supposed to take care of us, but instead she handcuffed all twenty kids together!" Amaya recounts how she busted out of the handcuffs, triggering a chain reaction that snapped open the cuffs of the rest of the kids. Impressed by her escape, the lady handed Amaya $3,000; the rest of the students got $100 each. "And then," my daughter concludes, "we were free to go by ourselves to the beach to spend the money."

As she relates her dream we move from the side of the hillock, where it is now gently raining, to the shelter of a big *soto* tree. I sit into its base, my spine curving into the rise of its trunk. How good it feels to have this arboreal support. Eventually, the drizzle stops and we return to the hillock, in the sun, leaning back in silence and looking into the sky. I affirm Amaya's heroism and inventiveness, even if it is in dreamland, happy she's sharing her thoughts. But I find myself — in a lull where Amaya evidently rings up her Cancun purchases — uneasy. I'm trapped in my own dogma and fears and unable to be fully with her. Is our vision of Suraqueta as Transition Town, as part of the future of a simpler, postcarbon world…delusional? Did Melissa and I shape this image out of a desire to escape a FrankenDream that we likewise conjured? And worst of all, is our quest yet another example of the colonial impulse, of outsiders imposing their cultural desires on the already established way of things in Suraqueta?

Macy's. That's the unlikely locale that pops out of these questions.

My thoughts slip out of Cancun beach-shopping and into a snowy Christmas Eve day in Manhattan several years ago. I had ducked into Macy's midtown ("the world's largest department store") for a last-minute gift and rode a thronged escalator between the third and fourth floors of the magnificent retail fortress.

I had expected to abhor myself for bending to the "shopping season" consumerism that was expected of me, but instead I found myself totally into the Jennifer Lopez song pulsing through the place. *Don't be fooled by the rocks that I got,* J Lo told us, because she's still the same old Jenny from the block. *Used to have a little, now I have a lot. No matter where I go, I know where I came from.*

Oh, how I wished to resist! J Lo was hocking the "rocks that she's got": the disease called affluenza that trashes the climate and makes us unhappy.

But my body felt customer heat, wool-coated torsos pressed against me on the escalator. Our faces were harried as we rushed to purchase, but our guts and hearts pulsed along to J Lo. We reattached on the next escalator, fluorescence bright, rocks asparkle. *Buy, baby, buy* isn't logical; it's a primal ritual. We the people didn't need anything as romantic as *suma qamaña*, the Bolivian philosophy of a "sweet life" of harmony with community and nature. We were blood-bound by Jenny titillating together up into More.

And we're never bored because when we get to More, there will always be More above. Climate change? Famine in Africa? Amazon rainforest destruction? Temporary glitches. Specialized *Homo sapiens* will crack these complications through More ingenuity!

"Daddy?"

"Huh?"

It's Amaya. I'm not in Macy's. I'm on a hillock in Less.

"Your head's been bobbing, kind of... weird," she says, looking concerned. "You okay?"

I nod, orienting myself under a Southern Hemisphere *soto*.

"Good. Because now I'm going to show you the dog trails."

Taking my hand, she leads me into a day turned foggy. Stalwart clouds interlock over the pueblo below, blotting out the blue sky and the hundreds of orange-clay roofs. Then the clouds drift like a flotilla up our hill and swallow the construction site and *guapurú* groves. Amaya guides me into mist. "Wow," I say through the gauze. Anywhere we look are scraps of cloud, thicker patches within the all-enveloping one. I follow Amaya down a long path I've never noticed, skirting the cow manure heap I've trucked in for future fertilizer, along a thin canine trail through the fog, beat down by the packs of pueblo dogs that have been traversing our property for years. They're practically another species, mostly dog, but slightly wolf-reverted.

Each time she's on our land, Amaya goes explorer like this, climbing *tula* trees, wading in the creek, and now she's discovered this hidden network of dog trails across our land. But where do these trails go?

In the end, to Monte Oscuro.

Some translate Monte Oscuro as "Dark Jungle," but I prefer

a slightly different translation based on my Liberian-infused experience: The "Dark Bush." Monte Oscuro is a tiny, nature-enveloped settlement bordering Amboró National Park, but the term "Dark Bush" has, for me, increasingly become a metaphoric shorthand for "wilderness" in general. It's a state of mind beyond the Dream.

My daughter, this holiday season, is on ancient paths, instead of on the scent of a Manhattan purchase. Degrooved from J Lo, far from the highway called More. This feral dog track leads to a lonely locale invisible to Dreamers, to a place even beyond revillaging.

Along this bush-whacked path are renatured mutineers like Amerigo Vespucci, a forty-year-old American émigré organic farmer who lives outside Suraqueta. Midwestern-born and a founding guitarist in the metal band System of a Down, Vespucci adopted an assumed name when he arrived in Bolivia twenty years ago, never returning to America. He married a Bolivian woman, had kids, and cultivated what is now a productive agro-forestry farm. Amaya met Amerigo Vespucci at Bergwald last week. He arrived at Jörg's with a crate of organic mandarins and hibiscus juice for us from his farm. He also brought as a holiday gift lemongrass roots to transplant, as well as seeds from, he said, "a highly drought- and bug-resistant squash I've developed."

This is also the trail of Suzie, another local American who mutinied from her upper-middle-class Virginia family, married a Honduran fisherman, and now makes jewelry on a farm her family caretakes several miles from town. She's seen barefoot, when she's seen at all, which is rarely, since she prefers absorption within the nearby virgin forests. Suzie has not set bare feet in the United States for fifteen years.

Further still, past Amerigo Vespucci's and Suzie's stakes, Amaya's wild dog trails lead to the hamlet of Monte Oscuro, the very last settlement before Amboró's giant fern cloud forests tumble into the Amazon. The Dark Bush is the farthest point, both real and metaphorical, from spend-it-in-Cancun. It's the point after which humans are scarce.

Melissa and I have Dark Bush acquaintances, like Margarita, a Colombian thirty-year-old mom of two. When I met her outside Tierra Libre the other day, she told me that she and fellow pioneer families are "into a rhythm where we're nine days in Monte Oscuro and two days, to trade, in Suraqueta." That's the very maximum they can be in the Dark Bush and still have enough cash for essentials, she explained. Margarita was dropping off the necklaces and handbags she'd made at the artisan-owned cooperative craft shop beside Tierra Libre near the plaza. "Yesterday," Margarita told me, "a mother capuchin monkey came out of the forest with her baby on her back. And I was walking with *my* baby on *my* back. We gazed at one another for a long, beautiful moment."

Four

"Why do Bolivians throw trash everywhere?" I overhear a Bergwald hotel guest say, *auf Deutsch*, down at the pool. "This town is *schmutzig* (dirty)!"

Amaya is back in Santa Cruz, Melissa is taking a nap inside with Clea, and I'm relaxing under the mango tree after a dip. The woman speaking is Bavarian. As she continues to inveigh on Bolivian littering, I half wish I didn't understand German.

Later that afternoon, while on a walk through the Campeche neighborhood, I'm attuned to garbage as I cross a public soccer field below the biggest hill rising over the town, Cerro de la Patria. The Bavarian traveler is right; from a Western vantage point, Suraqueta is *schmutzig*. As if to illustrate these thoughts, a cluster of chitchatting Suraqueteña preteens pass me, and the tallest of them, in knockoff Levi's and with lipstick bordering a mouth of twinkling braces, tosses a drained red Pilfrut yogurt bag onto the ground, yards from my feet.

The group giggles cheerily across the field, sidestepping cow dung and litter, but I'm frozen, looking down at the bag and remembering my irritation at the Bavarian back at the pool. At least a dozen times I've heard "first world" visitors disparage Bolivian littering. One day, when I found myself doing the same thing, I realized that I was judging Bolivia's trash without acknowledging the more insidious, invisible trash that I've tossed: the 400 ppm of carbon dioxide my lifestyle has littered into each square foot of Earth's atmosphere. The average American carbon footprint is nearly twenty times a Suraqueteño's.

These thoughts make me feel self-conscious about my own privilege. I see Suraqueta as almost a community of islands, with spotless expat and elite-Bolivian atolls speckling a sea of trash-strewn public spaces. From émigré Texas Trent's Posada del Sol's happy-hour *caipirinha* cocktails to the French-Bolivian-owned Latina Café's Parisian jazz *avec steak frite*, and from La Vispera's organic spinneys to Bergwald's poolside *Deutsch*, the isles are un-marred by the rest of the town's debris.

I recall my very first flight to Bolivia, back in 2001. I was en route to serve as a fresh-faced aid worker in La Paz, and the man in the adjacent seat, a missionary, must have pegged me as a newbie. "There's just two things you need to know to survive in Bolivia," he said in an Oklahoma accent. "First: patience. And second..." He lifted his chin. "Eyes up, partner."

Arriving in an unhurried La Paz, I immediately caught his first reference. But the second? It took a while to connect the mess underfoot with the Okie's survival tip.

Eyes very much down now, I consider picking up the red Pil-frut bag but check myself. Oddly, I'm okay with the girl's litter-ing. Not because I like garbage. I blush to realize I'm privileged enough to want Suraqueta to be *edgy*, to want the islands (La Vispera, Bergwald, Latina Café) to be islands, and the sea, with its flamboyant coral of trash, to be the sea.

I bristle, conscious that desiring a certain quantity of trash as a kind of beauty mark highlighting the village's appealing face is as aloof as the missionary's desire for his own hygienic ideal. While he sees Bolivia, perhaps, through the lens of a Tulsa suburb, I view it through that of an Austin bumper sticker: Keep Sura-queta Weird.

What about the girl who tossed it? She litters, perhaps, be-cause her parents do. Plastic garbage is novel here. Until recently, rural Bolivian refuse was mandarin peels, eggshells, and other biodegradables. Plus, Suraqueta, to her, is not an aspirational lo-cale but rather a springboard to the jobs and diversions of Santa Cruz. She and her friends are *Sura-trampada*, a local joke mean-ing "trapped in Suraqueta." For now, she's pleasantly enmeshed in local dances on festival days and the web of her extended family, but all the while she's wishing for the very Dream that I — the odd *extranjero*, or foreigner, still staring stupidly at a Pilfrut baggie — left behind in order to become voluntarily *Sura-trampado*.

Beneath this speculation prowls a dread that the town's immigrant-local rift could be a fuse on a very big bomb. I shove that fear aside, focusing instead on the current conundrum of a red baggie, which, in the end, I leave be.

In Suraqueta, as Melissa and I learn, garbage eventually gets repurposed.

At the market, Melissa buys cookie sheets forged from discarded vegetable oil tins, and I pay two bolivianos apiece for cast-off fifty-kilo bulk sugar bags to collect "vegetable manure" for our garden-to-be. In a street stall outside the market, a man razor-blades expended car tires into foot-long soles, trimming the inner lining into footwear uppers to produce the *albarca* sandals worn by the majority of local *campesino* men. Two-liter plastic bottles get retooled; I see them on every third patio used as soil-filled planters strung up on beams with "monkey tail" cacti drooping over the sides. One day, the municipal electrical cooperative distributes to each of its sixteen hundred members, ourselves included, a reused two-liter bottle with a little opening cut into the side and a clasp fitted on the back. Why? In a town without mailboxes — ahem, without mail service — it keeps the monthly electric bill dry. Many Westerners might find rubber-tire sandals and two-liter mailboxes gauche, but here they're handy, hence worthy.

Our friend Mateo, a striking six-foot-two Spanish transplant, catches the wave. I spot him one Saturday trolling the pueblo for discarded glass bottles. "I turn them into drinking cups and lamps," he says. "It's my new business." Mateo invites me around the block to his workshop in progress, and I'm astonished to see thousands of bottles separated by size and color, along with several apparatuses he's rigged up to cut and buff. In his first month, he'd already sold thousands of bolivianos' worth of product (or several hundred US dollars).

As I explore the workshop, his Brazilian partner of six years, the svelte Ivete, strides into the shop, beams "*Hola*," and smelling like lavender, plants a kiss on my cheek. Six years back, she and Mateo met in her native Salvador de Bahia, fell in love, and decided to travel the world in search of a place to settle down. Their four-year journey started in Suraqueta, passed through Latin America, Europe, and North Africa, and ended on the sixteen acres of river bottom they purchased in La Misca, nine miles outside town ("Suraqueta won out," Mateo says). They ooze verve, happy homesteaders who intend to build an adobe house on their property when the money's saved. For now, they've charmed their way into a long-term housesit in town, where Ivete, a third-generation Brazilian *curandera* (healer), provides acupuncture and massage and makes clay-based soaps, while her beau regigs hip-flasks and rum empties. I order a set of three-bottle hanging lamps for our house-to-be, then hoof back to Jörg's place.

Jörg's parents, Bergwald owners Ludwig and Anna, are Mateo and Ivete three decades fast-forwarded from now. The Wi-Fi password at Bergwald is "1983" — the year the couple arrived, pioneers, with the likes of La Vispera's Pieter and Marga, in Suraqueta's eighties wavelet of European settlers. They bought an acre of pastureland just below a north-facing lip of hill five blocks from the town plaza and began to create. Though Ludwig earned well in his contracting job in Austria, both he and Anna needed to escape what they felt to be a rigidly structured Europe.

In Suraqueta, their inventiveness thrived. Amid raising no fewer than ten children — two biological (rocker mechanic Jörg and his older brother, now a hotelier in Austria), plus eight kids they bigheartedly adopted from an orphanage in the city of Sucre — they built their rustic hotel themselves over the years, room-by-room and cabaña-by-cabaña, into an attractive complex. Along the way they dug the pool and terraced their sheer slope; erected an on-site bakery now run by adopted son Castro, who twice a week brings warm bread to our door; and built a jam-making kitchen for the ten varieties of jam they jar from their harvest and sell in their shop. Ludwig also devised a meat-curing oven, where he crafts cold cuts for their breakfast café, and Anna set up the art studio where she fires up the kiln for ceramics and paints bright canvasses, both offered in their restaurant gallery. Not to mention the metal shop where Ludwig and his sons have produced, largely from recycled scraps, most of Bergwald's furniture, its planters, and the playground equipment. They've even assembled their own working jeep from junkyard remainders.

ONE CLEAR MORNING, Clea is baby-talking with a tangerine sapling when I notice a pair of blue eyes. They're peering over the edge of our porch, watching us.

"Pretty in the bags," says a voice, in German-inflected Spanish, "but...*get them in the ground.*"

A full face floats up. It's Ludwig, now perched on tippy toes to see over the portico. Donning his black leather biker cap, the Bergwald owner's eyes carry their characteristic gleam, at once amused and mischievous.

Ludwig is talking about our tiny fruit trees, still in their black bags: avocado and fig, apple and mandarin, star fruit and guava, chirimoya and *pacay*. I bought them from a Bolivian friend's nursery on Calle Campero. Sixty saplings — twenty-seven species of fruit in all — to populate our someday-orchard.

"They'll be in the ground soon," I tell him, knowing it's unlikely. Melissa and I, when not changing diapers and barefoot contracting, are busy being work-addled gringos: I'm on book deadline to finish — speedily — *New Slow City* and to design and coordinate an NYU travel course on Bolivian sustainable development that I will teach, while Melissa manages a World Policy Institute project under our joint charge.

Ludwig, seeming to intuit that we're neglecting our sprouts, tells me to follow him.

I strap on Clea and trail Ludwig through a tiered Shangri-la of Suraqueta's unique "niche ecologies." Our adopted town, it so happens, lies at a spot where Andes foothills meet Amazon jungles meet Chaco drylands, and micro-environments bud at the nodes. Andes-Amazon-Chaco, moreover, is not just a three-by-three permutation because *dozens* of degrees and types of overlap flourish (as in, strong Andean–weak Chaco; medium Amazon–medium Andean, and so on). Into these ecological niches Ludwig and Anna have cultured hundreds of plants, from tropical palms and rattans through an array of desert succulents and cacti. On our way down the terraces, jasmine and honeysuckle scents escort us past apple, peach, and mandarin to the bottommost tier, out of which upsurges the largest eucalyptus I've ever seen.

"*Mira!*" Ludwig cries, gazing up into its canopy. Clea's head tips back, her mouth parting into an *O* so perfect it burlesques wonder.

I trace their ogles upward. Through strata of branches, the blue sky looks like veined sapphire, reminding me of something my friend the short and wiry Chief Gaspar once told me during my community conservation days in Bolivia in 2002. The sixty-year-old said that his people, the indigenous Chiquitano, believe that "a tree holds up the seven skies," and that each sky is what we today call an ecosystem. An Amazonian sky, an Andean sky, a Chaco sky, and so forth. We venerate all trees, Gaspar explained, because "we do not know which one holds up the world."

After a long silent moment, Ludwig says: "When I planted this thirty-five years ago, it was the same size as those in your little black bags."

Clea remains lost in branches above. "You understand?" Ludwig asks.

A tree holds up the world, I think, but I say: "Get the trees in the ground?"

Pleased, Ludwig nods.

That night, stirred to action by our biker-capped landlord, Melissa and I decide where we'll clear the thorny brush from a thousand-square-meter circle within our five acres and plant our sixty fruit trees. Our guiding philosophy is that of permaculture, a holistic system of agriculture and community which centers on, first, observing a given ecosystem's natural patterns and then designing landscapes and human settlements in harmony with those patterns. The term *permaculture* was coined in 1978 by two Australians, environmentalist David Holmgren and biologist Bill Mollison. The word was originally a conjunction of "permanent" and "agriculture," but was later revised to encompass "permanent culture" as well, thereby integrating social structures into a truly robust system, partly as inspired by Masanobu Fukuoka's natural farming philosophy. Melissa and my go-to volume, Mollison's *Permaculture: A Designers' Manual*, tells us to cluster tropical-niche fruits for easy tarp-covering during frosts, which in Suraqueta are infrequent. Now we're barefoot horticulturalists. We diagram a compass pattern that eschews rows, with lines of trees shooting out like spokes from the center.

The next morning, I wake up enthused, reciting Ludwig's muddy-hands mantra: *Get the trees in the ground.*

I call Kusi, and together we machete the selected patch out of our property's undergrowth. It's grueling because our worn soil sprouts mostly scrubland-loving, thorn-covered *quiñe* trees. As we work, Kusi confides that she's tired of being tough, sovereign…and *alone.* "I'm thirty-four now," she says, "and aching to be more mammalian, like I see with the horses, and in the cloud forests. Give birth! But I want to do it with a mate, in clan, and the men I like are either married or not into *this*" — she hoists her machete over her dirt-covered shoulders, warrior style.

After we've cleared an area, I ceremoniously lift a hoe. Our first hole!

I grin at Kusi, who returns a more skeptical grin. Brandishing my implement, I release it upon the ground. But the hoe hurdles back upon impact, as if striking asphalt. Pain radiates up my arms.

An unsurprised Kusi hands me the tool *she* brought along: an industrial-strength pickax.

I smash the ax into the ground but manage to nick away only a hockey puck of the hard soil.

Granted, I'm aware that Melissa and I did not purchase loamy tillage, but I'd yet to feel the pickax reality. A month ago, following a *Permaculture: A Designers' Manual* suggestion, I researched the history of our property, learning from Kusi and others that our acres ache with the effects of decades of tractor tilling and overplanting of corn and potatoes, with cattle grazing between plantings and no fallow time. Only abundant toxic pesticides and fertilizers kept our progressively feebler soil producing.

These are, of course, not native practices; for centuries, Suraqueta was all organic, from the Incas farming the terraces above us through Kusi's grandparents' agroforestry plots. But Dream agriculture arrived with Harry S. Truman's Point Four Program in 1949, and according to Georgetown University professor Kevin Healy, for sixteen years, Bolivia had the best financed and longest-standing agricultural development program in the hemisphere. Sheep and cattle were airlifted onto the high plains of the altiplano to replace "inferior" llamas and alpacas, even though their camelid hooves were adapted to the local terrain and did not lead to the erosion and desertification caused by the new livestock. Truman's program also attempted to replicate the American Midwestern bread basket in eastern Bolivia, complete with big tractors and agrotoxins, a regionally ill-suited plan that led to major rainforest destruction. In the 1970s, the UN Food and Agriculture Organization joined US efforts in the Suraqueta region in promoting "technological packets" of hybrid seeds and chemical pesticides and fertilizers, with little consideration for Suraqueta's locally adapted organic practices. The result, according to the Bolivian agricultural think tank AGRUCO, was an increase in production, but without consideration for grave effects, "the majority irreversible, to the soil, water, air, and the health of humans and animals."

In the end, that's why our soil is junk.

IN BERGWALD'S METAL SHOP, Ludwig and another of his adopted sons, Carlos, are welding salvaged junk metal into chairs for their café. They could purchase the chairs, but as Carlos tells me: "We like doing it." Castro, meanwhile, drops by to deliver our Wednesday bread. Anna's under the avocado tree painting pots she cast. Ludwig takes a break from blacksmithing to relieve himself into a clutch of agaves. Passing me on the way back to the shop, he declares: "The day I can no longer pee outside is the day I leave Bolivia."

Later that day, I run into Mateo and Ivete a block west of the market. The couple is walking back from an orphanage organic farm in the Los Sauces neighborhood a kilometer from the plaza, with bags full of pick-your-own produce. Mateo says my bottle lamps are ready. We chat — no rush, the cheerful hubbub of pueblo life around us — and at some point Mateo remarks: "Back in Europe, I loathed the overwork and the hyperscheduling. I wasn't *me*." He looks up into the *carnaval* tree beside us, its leaves so radiant in the afternoon light that they could almost be lacquered. "I used to be trash, and here I'm repurposing myself."

Later that evening, I realize Mateo has captured a Suraqueta ethos that says: Freecycle yourself into something dodging classification. Pieter and Marga assembled La Vispera from joy, not to become "organic farmers." Bell-bottomed Rulas Maradona builds beautiful houses because he loves it. Ludwig and Anna create Bergwald without consciousness of being "DIY homesteaders."

Such pigeonholes don't appear to exist here. If a philosophy threads through the Suraqueta spirit, it's Pedro's direct dictum: *We like doing it.*

So it's with a groan that I survey my own inner rubbish:

comparison. Endless striving. Like Staten Island, I'm built on a landfill. All the meditation I've done, the striving (ah, there it is again!) toward an "alternative" lifestyle, even this continental translocation can't biodigest what's Made in the USA. To wit, I recognize something of myself in this passage from upstate New York organic farmer Shannon Hayes's book *Homespun Mom Comes Unraveled:*

> In pursuit of our self-sufficiency, I didn't realize that I had actually become a *type*. Even if we've never met, *you know me....* We are the over-educated over-achievers, sidestepping the conventional rat race in favor of an alternative maelstrom. In school we were taught that our careers could be our lives, and instead, we've opted to make our lives our careers. You can see us every week at your farmers' market.... We knit sweaters, sew quilts, and hand-stitch Halloween costumes; we gather eggs, we milk the family cow, weed the vegetable patch and eviscerate chickens with our babies strapped to our backs; we compost everything from dinner scraps to organic diapers to placentas.

Hayes channeled her overachieving into her noncareer. Are Melissa and I up to something similar? We're still controlled by a kind of Dream software, an American Dream that's become a warped FrankenDream of busyness, constant action, and control. Yet we are trying to inhabit an emerging Sweet Life counter-story, a Bolivian Dream, and it has to do with the Aymara ideas of seeking balance and finding complementarity instead of competition. This other dream is embodied by Mateo and Ivete, Pieter and Marga, and Ludwig and Anna. Right now, though, I need to get to the other side of my deadlines.

OUR HOUSE CONSTRUCTION moves from stalled to evidently lifeless. The wood guy, Eterno, lives up to his name. *"Mañana"* is Eternity's answer to my daily question of when he'll deliver our beams. Melissa and I want to foment the local economy, so we're hesitant to order the wood from Santa Cruz suppliers. Plus, exports soak up Bolivia's entire certified ecologically harvested wood supply, and we know Eterno responsibly harvests the *quina-quina* hardwood we need from his land in Bella Vista, forty kilometers away.

Glass-man Diego (the window and door panes we need are only available in Santa Cruz) could perform at the Comedy Cellar. His assistant came to Suraqueta six weeks ago to take measurements, and Diego was to have SMART-ly delivered the glass a week later, thereby receiving an agreeable heap of bolivianos. But humor apparently interests him more than cash. Each excuse is more inspired than the last.

"I was on my way to Suraqueta with your glass," he says over the phone one day, "when a car in front of me…umm…blew up. *Siii*, it exploded into flames!" I repeatedly ask him why this affected his ability to transport our glass, but he just keeps talking about the "twenty-meter flames."

Three days later Diego says he's "on the road to Suraqueta." I call him an hour later, "I'm in Angostura!" he shouts. I think I hear Diego suppressing a chuckle, but tell myself I'm imagining this. Angostura is an hour away. I'm thrilled; the glass, finally.

An hour passes, then two. Diego doesn't answer his phone.

I have his assistant's number and ring her. "Diego? No, he's here in Santa Cruz."

"*Como?* But what about our glass? *Familia Powers de Suraqueta.*"

I hear paper shuffling. Then: "We hope to get to that… *mañana.*" The glass is not even cut.

The plight of our "eco-house" worsens when Rulas tells me he's out of adobe bricks again.

"But you said we needed four thousand for the project," I say. "And that's what Estuvio eventually made. He delivered."

"I underestimated."

"When do you need them?"

"*Ahorita*" — Right now.

I plead with our *adobero* Estuvio and his brother, Ali, to return and hasten production. They return, but slowly, smoking and chewing coca under the *noki* tree. Time isn't money here. *Time* isn't here. I scramble for adobe bricks to purchase and find a stack, but with the rains, no truck can get the heavy cargo up our muck road.

Then, some very un-Bolivian tension breaks out among the tradesmen. Rulas informs me: "Tell Fito he needs to finish the electrical wiring!"

Fito is the electrician. "He was at the site this morning," I say.

"He was here for ten minutes and then left."

Puzzled, I hang up and call Fito. He's at the plaza, and we meet there. "I don't want to do the work in front of Rulas," the nineteen-year-old Fito says from a chilled-out park bench. Just arrived from his native Portugal, Fito is lanky, with a permanent dreamy expression.

I ask him why.

"He watches how I wire and might copy my mojo."

The only other electrician in town is booked. So all we've got is adolescent Fito, who boasts 168 hours in a technical school in Lisbon and zilch work experience. I extract a promise from Fito to go up at dawn for covert wiring.

Dawn comes and Fito works — for twenty minutes. Then he returns home to snooze. I track him down, and he promises to go the next day. And he does. For twenty more minutes.

I get a peeved phone call from Rulas. His men will soon be idle again "because of that *pelado*" — "the peeled one," "he of smooth cheeks," that is, "green." So the next day I accompany *pelado* Fito up to the site. He and Rulas eye each other, two alphas on a turf. Fito climbs a ladder, stuffs a few meters of yellow wire-casing into the chiseled-out adobe, and then comes back down. "I need six-millimeter cable."

I order the wire from Santa Cruz, and it arrives on top of a bush taxi. But I can't order a work ethic for he of smooth cheeks. Fito continues to appear each day, cut a canal or two into the adobe, insert tubing, and then get bored and leave. "But Fito," I urge, "you have the plan."

"I'm sorry," he says, his brown eyes baleful as ever. "I promise to do it tomorrow."

"No, Fito, *today*."

"Oh, okay, I'll go up now."

He doesn't. Riled, I climb our hillock. Others have built homes here, so why are we failing?

I know impatience is a core fault of mine. But I convince myself that this time my exasperation is justified. *Nothing* is working. "Transition" is off to a false start. We're five thousand miles from our families. We live in an exclusive Austrian enclave, separate from the larger community. In pursuit of an enigmatic Sweet Life vision, we've indebted ourselves to buy a bunch of asphalt soil and a house in limbo. Furthermore, our income may not be able to cover that debt, especially if we can't meet our current project deadlines. Frustrated, my hands constrict into fists. Into this anxious, foul mood flies…a honeybee. It lands on my forearm, and I'm about to shoo away the intruder when I remember something, another lesson I learned from Chief Gaspar.

Gazing at the pollen-laden creature, I feel a bit of the tension ease.

About a decade before, I was managing a community development program in the Bolivian Amazon, hundreds of miles due east of Suraqueta. One afternoon, while driving three village chiefs through the jungle for an important intertribal meeting, I planted our jeep in a cavernous mud hole.

We were fifty miles by dirt road from the nearest settlement. I spotted fresh jaguar tracks five feet away and shuddered. My friends, the three village chiefs, looked at me with pity, but being strong rainforest men, they didn't complain. Ximén was barrel-chested and slightly cocky. Sebastián, though plump around the middle, hunted crocodiles. Gaspar, by far the smallest of the three, had a constant smirk on his face. They grabbed their machetes and got to work, and I joined them.

As we slid felled logs under the tires, I shooed away honey-bees. "The bees have found us," I complained to Gaspar, but the chief said, cryptically, "They will come." When we finally had the logs in place, I noticed a crescendoing buzz. A handful of bees had become hundreds, perhaps thousands. "*Now* the bees have come," Gaspar announced with a smile.

I yelped with the first sting. "I'm not getting into that hive," I said, staring at bees covering the jeep's dashboard, the seat, the wheel. But the chiefs pushed me toward the truck. No one else could drive. There was no choice, they told me, because more bees would come and it would only get worse. The chiefs knew from long experience that the bees were searching for salt.

The loathsome insects slid away as I sat down in the driver's seat. But as I touched one of the jeep's buttons, a bee stung my finger. I sprang up, howling and slapping, and received five more stings. I sprinted fifty yards from the truck, swatting all the while. Ximén, the stocky one, eventually caught up to me, laughing. "You screamed like a little kid," he said. Gaspar ran over and said the alarm lights were on. "The battery will die!" he exclaimed. They both insisted I get back into the jeep, turn off the alarm lights, and most importantly, get the pickup out of the mud.

Then Gaspar changed tack. He put a hand on my shoulder and said: "You are a bee."

I momentarily forgot the pain of my stings and looked down at Gaspar. He told me that, by tensing up, I was going against the "bee energy" and *causing* the insects to sting me. He was advising me to go with the flow.

I walked back toward the dreaded pickup. As the buzzing built, I repeated to myself, "You are a bee. You are a bee." I slid into the front seat, repeating Gaspar's exhortation, and gently shooed a bee away and placed the key into the ignition.

The chiefs took positions around the pickup. I felt the chassis rising as additional logs were shoved under the spinning wheels. Meanwhile, a bee headed up my nostril. There was one in each ear. They perched on my eyelashes and eyebrows. *You are a bee. You are a bee.*

And — to my shock — I became a bee! I didn't receive a single sting. All I sensed was a light tickle from their tiny legs. I felt fully relaxed, the communal buzz a gigantic *om*. Slowly, beautifully, the pickup rose up out of the hole. The chiefs climbed in, and we moved forward through the Amazon, bees finding their way out the windows one by one, like parachutists leaving a plane.

You are a bee, I tell myself the next morning on the way to our construction site with good news for Rulas Maradona and company.

After my honeybee wake-up call, I shift my approach: We'll throw a party for all the tradesmen and their families. This Saturday at the worksite. A barbecue, with beer. Time may not be in the local DNA, but fiesta is. What Gaspar taught me — and it's a lesson I've had to relearn many times — is that going against "bee energy" only ends up hurting oneself. Could it be that SMART plans and an impatient gringo attitude has actually been *causing* our *casa* woes?

When I announce the party, delight warms the faces of Rulas and Papa Maradona, Fito and Eterno. On Saturday, the crew rigs up an ersatz grill to roast the meat, while their wives make salads. Chilled Paceña beer flows to the sounds of *cumbia* music. And amazingly, we laugh.

Amid the disarray of our half-wired, glassless, unroofed house, we tell jokes and stories and enjoy one another. Kids jump into Estuvio's mud pit, helping with impromptu adobe-making; the *adobero* grins bigger than I've ever seen. I get to know Rulas better, and it turns out that five of the strapping guys in his crew are either siblings or in-laws, with the sixth, Hipolito, a close friend. Papa Maradona, as we've been calling him, is actually named Eduardo. Everybody becomes more real to us, and we, it seems, to them. Somebody jokes that this is the first time "the peeled one" has been here for more than twenty minutes. Fito's smooth cheeks flush, and he takes a swill of Paceña beer.

As the party ends, Eterno slaps me on the back and promises to deliver the wood we need. "*Ahori-*ti-*ta,*" he says, leapfrogging *ahora* (now) and *ahorita* (right now), straight to *ahoritita*, the nowest-of-now.

Come Monday, Eternity does deliver the wood. This allows Rulas and crew to raise the bathroom and bedroom roofs. And Fito, with the help of a friend, wires everything up in a few days.

It's not that everything is seamless after my attitude adjustment. The glass guy still invents outlandish excuses, and the massive dome we've designed seems destined, should we raise it, to collapse. But when my inner New Yorker gets vexed, I recall Chief Gaspar's honeybees. Impatience is the trash I must freecycle. US-style efficiency has no place here in Suraqueta.

Five

Carnival in Suraqueta is yellow. Yellow sunflowers, mustard *comparsa* dance costumes, and the wincingly bright gold of the February-blooming *carnaval* trees. As summer ripens with abundant rains, Amaya arrives from Santa Cruz for the March 2014 carnival with the smock, hat, and protective glasses she dons while side-arming water balloons at her friends on the plaza. She seems to have grown an inch since Christmas; this is the first time we let her roam town alone, and she's sozzled by the festivity and her new independence within it. This gets Clea stretching for more freedom, too. One hot carnival day at Bergwald, Clea, donning her bright-red boots *y nada más*, toddles solo past the apple trees, baby-talking all the way down to Ludwig's mammoth eucalyptus.

On Friday evening, a solemn procession of hundreds leaves Suraqueta's centuries-old church hoisting statues of saints and of Jesus. Then carnival floats rising with *comparsa* queens and accompanied by ambulant brass bands stroll down Calle Bolívar, ourselves out among the festive thousands. It's a multigenerational extravaganza, as children, parents, and grandparents dance together in matching smocks and hats. Some of the floats are Pachamama- and harvest-themed. As corn matures on hundreds of small plots, so too do carnival groups flourish with a yellow-corn theme. A friend dancing in one maize ensemble passes me a bottle of the corn-based, home-brewed alcohol called *chicha*, which I swig and pass back into his dancing. The parade's biggest float is decked out in blossoming *carnaval*-tree branches, and on a pedestal, one of the more beautiful queens wears a crown of the buttery yellow flowers.

Pieter, also in the festive spirit, gifts us ten trees from La Vispera: five *toborochis* and five palms. On a warm morning, I machete through an area near our creek, where the soil is less junked than in our in-limbo orchard area, and dig holes. I'd stayed up the previous night reading *Permaculture: A Designers' Manual.* As with *The Barefoot Architect*, this book's pages are frayed, and last night I double-underlined this sentence: "Every element must have multiple functions, and every major function must be served by multiple elements." The sentence feels liberating. Nature will work for us! While laboring, I envision Pieter and Marga's palms as a windbreak, a view-texturer, and an eventual source of palm nuts, this single element serving three functions.

I've been sweating for several hours to nail down the *Manual's* element-to-function triple-billing when Kusi stops by. She watches me.

I wave but keep grunting away in combat with the underbrush. When I glance up again, I notice a slight smirk creeping up one side of my friend's mouth.

I put down the machete, pick up a shovel, and begin digging another palm tree hole, wondering how the heck we'll get our sixty fruit saplings — still in their little bags — in the ground without an army to help. Looking up, I see Kusi's smirk has swelled, and annoyance rises. *Okay*, I think to myself, *why don't you utter one of your Sweet Life nuggets right about now?*

Finally, I blurt out: "What is it, Kusi?"

Unhurried, she ambles down the slope toward me. Saying nothing, she begins to pick up felled baby trees. A tiny *tipa*. A *soto* treelet. A *carnaval* sapling.

I'm appalled to see I've hacked native trees from where they were naturally growing in order to put in the foreign ones Pieter and Marga gave us.

Kusi still hasn't said anything. She continues to assemble a little mass grave of the horticultural newborns I've slaughtered.

I feel silly. Steeped in permaculture theory, I've been clearing out the undergrowth without bothering to look at what's in it.

Kusi picks up the machete and gracefully edits away grasses, spiky *quiñe*, and scrub *tula* trees, leaving behind two tender *carnaval* trees, one of them winking with a single yellow flower.

"Don't sweat," Kusi says, delivering that nugget after all, "uncover."

For the next hour, Kusi and I uncover what is already there: a future forest of diverse native trees, many, like the *tipas*, with medicinal functions. We bring to light more *carnavales* with the most gorgeous flowers and scents. We uncover blank spaces, too, and that's where we transplant Pieter's palms.

THE FOLLOWING AFTERNOON, I'm sitting on a plaza bench next to my friend Thiago, the intellectual-looking Mexican permaculturalist, looking up through a view tunnel in a patch of full-on yellow *carnavales* to our distant hillock: our *sotos* and eucalyptus, and the rising eco-house beyond. Freshly installed windows wink in their glass. *Teja* roof tiles cap the bathroom, foyer, and bedroom. Bee-like, Melissa and I have been triangulating with Ludwig, Kusi, and others, gathering information on everything from the proper angles for retaining walls and roof pitches to plumbing-tube diameters and stairway step heights. We've been feeding our gleanings to Rulas and the tradesmen, helping bring the house to near-completion. Except, that is, for one seemingly impossible task: the physics-defying dome roof.

Thiago follows my gaze and asks if I've ever heard of the *minga* tradition. I tell him I've seen and participated in *mingas* over the years in different parts of Bolivia. *Mingas* are labor-sharing work days; somebody invites friends and neighbors over to plant a field, weed a stubborn acre, frame an outbuilding. Everyone labors together, with the host preparing lunch. A few weeks later, someone else calls a *minga*. Thus, tasks are accomplished and social capital is forged outside the cash economy. Thiago reflects on why Transition floundered after the film-viewing, saying it had the feel of a top-down imported blueprint.

"Like an American 'SMART' plan," I groan.

He nods. There's a pause. I regard the town's sundial across from us; erected in 1808, it has functioned continuously as a working timepiece for over two centuries. It's so much a part of Suraqueta to be hardly perceived. I consult it for the time, occasionally, but this is the first time I've actually noticed it. Similarly invisible were those native tree saplings yesterday, until Kusi helped me see them.

With these thoughts, a piece of the Sweet Life puzzle clicks into place: *Suraqueta's a tree.* That's the strange image that comes to mind.

It's a "glocal" tree. Glocal is a response to cookie-cutter globalization. Instead of the Dreamer's sole highway called Progress, "glocalization" sees ten thousand inimitable eco-cultural organisms into which modernity textures. Ten thousand...trees. Suraqueta has branches of internet and asphalt, of plastic bottles and their corresponding trash, but the trunk is a regional cultural blend of Chan and Inca, Spanish and, yes, recent expatriate, with strong limbs of *carnaval* and of other cultures and local economies, including what Thiago just mentioned: *mingas.*

My mind traces the *minga* branch. These work parties are increasingly infrequent as the economy monetizes. The year before Melissa and I arrived, Thiago and others attempted to reignite the tradition, and several enthusiastic *mingas* took place. Then they sputtered out, perhaps because those *mingas* weren't connected to the glocal tree. Could a "Transition" bough, which grows out of Suraqueta's trunk-strengths of community, a low carbon footprint, and a strong independent economy, be strengthened by reviving *mingas*?

A yellow *carnaval* flower falls onto Thiago's shoulder. "I know the place for the first Transition *minga*," he says.

"Where?"

He nods up toward our acres.

AMID INVITING FRIENDS and neighbors to the upcoming fruit tree–planting *minga* on our land, Melissa uncovers our new roof design.

"Look up," she says, as we walk under a *carnaval* tree on the way to market. "A 'dome' should be like the sky, almost ephemeral. But what about *structure*? That's what we're missing."

I notice how the *carnaval* branches structure the tree's biomass and appear, from below, to "hold up the sky," as per Chief Gaspar's Chiquitano story.

"Could our roof," Melissa asks, "be a tree canopy?"

She heads over to Salome and Salvador's house, and our imaginative architect and her husband sketch out a new design and send it to an engineer friend in Cochabamba, who tweaks it. The result is a roof that's no longer a dome. It remains attractively circular, but trades a cupola that might have crumbled with the first earthquake for Melissa's bio-mimicked matrix of wood beams capped with a round skylight. Rulas studies the design. "We'll do it," he says, but I hear hesitancy in his voice. No one has attempted this type of roof here at this scale.

Meanwhile, I notice fresh aspects of the "glocal" tree called Suraqueta after an encounter with an Israeli tourist.

We're both separately enjoying empanadas and steaming coffee one afternoon at a stall in the market. "What a fantastic town," the thirty-something from Jerusalem says.

When I tell him I live here with my family, his face goes pensive, appearing to ruminate on what such a scenario might look like for him. "Are there jobs here?" he finally asks.

I shake my head. "I'd need a job," he says, shrugging.

He's right, I think, after we've parted. In the "formal" economy, you do need someone else to give you a job. But here the ethos is: *Create one.* It's more than Rulas building eco-houses and

Ludwig blacksmithing furniture. It's more than Kusi freelancing in jaguar and Andean bear tracking or our Doña Serafina opening a successful vegetable stall in the market. It's those examples times a thousand. Part of what author Emilio Martínez meant when he quipped that Suraqueta is "a little anarchy" is that it has no larger employers besides the municipality and state governments, which engage less than 3 percent of the population. Over 90 percent of the ten thousand souls in the municipality of Suraqueta — that is, our town plus the forty smaller villages and hamlets around it — are entrepreneurs.

Northern governments and mainstream economists have a word for this: *failure*. The Dreamer narrative on Bolivia is that, in failing in the 1990s and 2000s to achieve the so-called "Washington Consensus"–approved goals of liberalizing trade and opening up fully to foreign direct investment, Bolivia remains burdened with the worst of evils, a large "informal" economy. But this failure is rich soil for the glocal tree. The informal economy is nothing less than freeholders like Theresa selling her empanadas and Estuvio shaping his adobe bricks. It's the fifty women organic farmers with their farming cooperative sales point on Calle Bolívar and our friend Diego who runs the local radio station and emcees events.

This is not to say, of course, that large employers are in all cases bad. Jobs with benefits are desirable and necessary for workers, particularly in today's corporatized Global North. Nor is valorizing the "informal" small-entrepreneurism in Suraqueta and elsewhere in the Global South an implicit argument for deregulating companies. Extreme outsourcing, for example — the social-fabric-shredding way that companies swell bottom lines at the expense of worker pay and benefits — must be regulated. But it's vital to see that positive substitutes to hegemonic Dream economics — glocal "trees" — already exist. They can be nurtured and cultivated. One such alternative is the *inter*dependent, small-holding culture in Suraqueta that sustains Pachamama and people alike.

One April afternoon, a week after the pueblo has eased its way out of the annual release and *chicha*-hangovers of carnival and gotten back to work, I find myself rounding Calle Campero, my thoughts on our fruit saplings, when I notice a change: the yellow *carnaval* tree usually seen from here is blotted out in red.

Puzzled, I continue walking toward the plaza, also wondering where the normally visible sundial is. It's blocked by what, from this angle down the narrow cobbled street, looks like a barrier of red. Curious, I quicken my pace, noticing that the bloodshot intrusion has also rubbed out the church and family-owned shops on the plaza. Finally reaching the plaza, I see hundreds of Suraqueteños gathered under the trunk...of a giant red tree.

It's not a living tree, providing oxygen. Not a branch of the glocal tree that evolved here over time. And it's certainly not Chief Gaspar's Amazonian tree that holds up the seven skies. Branchless, it's more of a monolithic trunk. My eyes trace the two-story inflated massif, in the shape of a bottle actually, and land on the words *Coca-Cola*.

In the place where Clea usually frolics with friends, where Thiago and I imagined *mingas* under the sundial, and where teenagers cluster to chat and elders to play chess, an external force has shaped a new configuration. To a fierce pulse of reggaeton, the masses push and grab toward the free bottles of Coke handed out by good-looking, red-shirted young Cruceños, or residents of Santa Cruz.

A nine-year-old I know, Pablo, approaches me with caffeine-wired eyes and exclaims, "My sixth!" He swills the rest of a bottle, opens his schoolbag to proudly reveal his stash of Cokes, then runs back up to seize another.

Old-timers, who gather beside me on the margins of this frantic rite, are less impressed than little Pablo. "*La chicha americana*" — American *chicha* — one of them hisses, disparaging the soft drink. I feel anger rise, wondering who consented to Coca-Cola Inc. driving in a convoy of vans and transforming our public space into a commercial one. Who, indeed, allowed the firm to give out thousands of dollars in free product toward transforming locals into Coke consumers? A mere glance at the adobe city hall on the plaza's southwest answers these questions: The same "little anarchy" that allows thousands to informally prosper beyond big companies also means few limits are put on anyone.

THE COKE PILLAR DEFLATES and the vans motor off, leaving behind a record wake of plastic bottles overflowing the town's few garbage pails, peppering the streets with red.

I kick an empty Coke, hard. It's the gray day after our canceled *minga*. Rained out. "*Mingas* are difficult, anyway," Kusi laments to me, when I give her the rescheduled date. "Few want to work cooperatively anymore. They crave cash and *la chicha americana*. That's probably why I can't find an interesting man and will die childless. A Kusi born in the wrong era."

I think about another rumored piece of news: A Santa Cruz company wants to build a ceramic tile factory in Suraqueta. They're already mining the red clay around the town, shipping the raw material to Santa Cruz for processing. Why not build a plant here? Smokestacks will cough into the sky, but the company could create hundreds of jobs, formalize people.

SOME WEEKS LATER, up at our house worksite one morning, Rulas says: "I'll be handing over your keys soon."

If the roof holds, I think, a little sullenly.

The normally self-possessed Rulas shifts his feet. I can tell he's searching for words. I wait, gazing over our hillock, across the town's vineyards and orchards to the spot on an adjacent hillside where Rulas is building his own home. He and his wife, with their three young kids, rent for now, but Rulas has been pouring the money we're paying him into their future. It's amazing to see the walls of his own minimalist, wattle-and-daub eco-house growing. The artisan is innovating, filling the walls with three thousand wine bottles he scavenged over two years, and constructing a whole interior wall out of discarded TV screens from a Santa Cruz e-waste dump.

Finally, Rulas speaks. "My crew and I want to thank you and Melissa. If not for you and others building adobe houses, we wouldn't be here."

I ask him where he'd be.

"In *Sauna* Cruz, probably," he says, using a pun referring to how sweltering that tropical city is. "On a work gang building one of the skyscrapers.... Here, at home, we're free."

As he says this, I feel tears begin to rise up and look for escape hatches. Holding back my emotion, I watch Rulas climb the mishmash scaffolding and continue interlaying *tajibo* beams in what looks like a tenuous "tree" of a roof. Rulas has just articulated one of revillaging's benefits — as urban Bolivians and foreign transplants graft into this thriving glocal tree, folks like him can not only avoid migration to alien urbana but also literally transform city trash into a Suraqueta home like Rulas's. But what if Suraqueta, in the end, gets formalized, the *minga* flops, and our roof doesn't hold? What if the tree is felled, the tree that keeps us together, the tree that holds up the world?

My dreams darken. Or rather redden. A trickle of blood after the incision.

It's a recurring nightmare I used to have in Manhattan. I started having it when an expanding Google paid $2 billion for a square block near our micro-apartment, and around the time of my first spottings of Google Glass.

The trickle of blood becomes a gush. I imagine Amaya's head cut open.

I discover that Google's corporate mission statement says it's at root pursuing artificial intelligence. Google's cofounder, Sergey Brin, says: "If you had all the world's information directly attached to your brain, or an artificial brain that was smarter than your brain, you'd be better off."

Surgeons bend over Amaya. One of them holds something shiny in a pair of tweezers, then inserts it in her head.

Google Glass is a bridge technology. The company already has chip-in-the-head prototypes, your synapses, sponsored, the Dream manifested.

DE COLORES, friends and neighbors stream in. With hoes, shovels, and machetes, dozens ascend our hill in unexpected numbers for the *minga*.

Though it may not be a direct reaction to the beverage giveaway or tile-factory rumor, there's a tinge of counterpoint in this cooperative upswell. A purple-shirted Maximo — our Cochabamba-immigrant neighbor who raises bees and has a hole-in-the-wall "honey and its derivatives" shop near the plaza — demonstrates the proper blend of manure, black dirt, and vegetable matter for the tree saplings, and the group wheelbarrows the mix to our sixty holes. While the majority work the field, a smaller group slices a rainbow of veggies and fruits, making salad and juice, while minding Clea and the smaller children. The bigger kids either work beside us or pick *guapurú* in our grove, the sweet purple fruits of this native tree growing, curiously, directly out of the silky-smooth trunk and branches. Kusi jokes and smiles through the morning, flirting, I take note, with Thiago, who talks about climate change as he plants a *pacay* tree. A Polish neighbor, Rudo, shares tips on grafting and pruning. As the day passes, we shape the orchard through pooled knowledge, experience, and muscle.

At sunset, avocado and macadamia nut, tangerine and fig, mandarin and guayaba, apple and peach, root in for their first night in the ground. We circle around an apple sapling from Bergwald — a place Melissa and I are now preparing to leave, our moving boxes stacked under Mick Jagger and Keith Richards. Ludwig and Anna couldn't make the *minga*, but Ludwig gave me this apple treelet, gently scolding: "Get it in the ground!"

Kusi starts to sing. It's an indigenous chant to Pachamama similar to the one we sung at the *ch'alla* at our building spot eight months ago, where there's now a nearly finished house. I don't understand all the Quechua words, but I know this song is not just "about" but evokes what we're living right now: the search for balance, a sense of cooperation instead of competition. I realize that it matters more than ever to sing together. *Vivir bien* is at once more threatened and vital than I'd thought, and our gathering of dozens represents millions. We're not a lone glocal tree up a rockslide road. This song implicitly rejects an ecocide fomented by the neoliberal economic model and connects Suraqueta to the two million "antibodies" that author Paul Hawken talks about in *Blessed Unrest* — worker cooperatives and women's circles, NGOs and eco-villages, Transition initiatives and organic farms.

Two weeks later, beneath a *carnaval* tree on our hillock dropping its final yellow flowers, Rulas hands me a set of shiny keys. "It's difficult to give a house I've made away," the craftsman says. "Each one is more beautiful than the last." It's silent after Rulas departs. Melissa, Clea, and I cross through an arched double door into our home. "*Casa!*" a sixteen-month-old Clea exclaims. Eternity's beams a tree-of-life canopy overhead, we follow Melissa up a staircase curving into rounded adobe to the mezzanine, where Melissa pauses at the high window, in our eaves, overlooking Suraqueta. Amid the elation I feel over hearth, kin, and community, I'm also unsettled. What appears through the window as idyllic is actually disputed. I thought we'd cut cords by leaving New York, but I realize that on these wild acres in a contested town, the journey begins now.

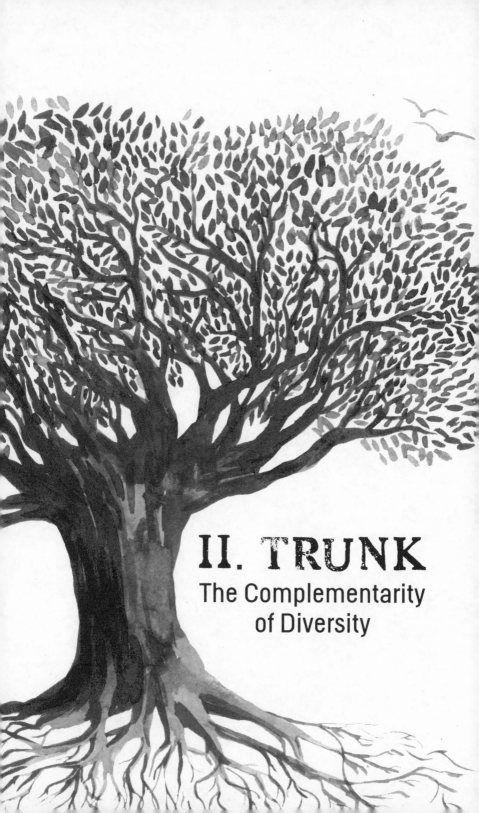

II. TRUNK
The Complementarity
of Diversity

Six

In July 2014, we move in to our new house, and a very nice family of wasps does, too. They build their adobe home into an exterior wall of ours, just below the recycled wine bottles we put in to add colorful passive light. Ahh, and is that a giant blue morpho butterfly over there, winging through the *tulas*? And, ooh, a *jitusipa* moth is curling its mauve wings into a snake-form for camouflage! Our bug-love is a carryover from Manhattan, where Melissa and I would watch the first fireflies warm Central Park in spring and gaze at monarch butterflies migrating down Fifth Avenue in fall. Romantic entomology may be a snap in Manhattan — if you tune out dull bedbug anecdotes — but it proves more difficult after we leave Jörg's antiseptic house in town for an outback eco-*casa* where humans, perhaps since Inca times, have not dwelled.

We begin to notice small roaches inside: shiny-café slivers, long skittering pinkie nails. And it's not long before they bloom into a minor plague.

Two things are clear. First: They all must go. And second: The Dalai Lama never kills insects. "Mosquitos?" he said when Melissa and I attended a talk of his two years ago. "I give them a little of my blood. At most, I shoo them away."

We abide, little Clea watching us cover each roach with a plastic cup, slide a paper under, and shuttle our brother into the *guapurú* forest just behind the house.

They become unshuttleable dozens, but we're loathe to spray Mata-todo ("Kill everything") home insecticide. So, with apologies to the Dalai Lama, we distract Clea and wincingly snatch the suckers off chairs and sinks. A pinch, a corpse.

One morning I wake up, stretch, and find myself staring into the eyelets of a roach on my pillow.

Melissa and Clea — who sleeps with us — lie on the other side of the roach on our still-on-the-floor mattress. Melissa's eyes open. In revulsion, she rolls away, startling the nursing Clea, who begins to howl, sending the roach skittering onto my shoulder.

I reel; *la cucaracha* hopscotches down my arm and into the laundry pile.

Straightaway, Melissa orders a bed frame from the local carpenter, thereby elevating us from the floor to keep the roaches out of our bed. We also install an insect guard on our external doors.

Meanwhile, new visitors arrive to the garden where we grow our food. Technically termed "fat ugly terrible gooeys," these green, sloth-slow addicts suck at our peppers, beets, and *achocha*, an Andean cucumber, which I'd planted months before our move so we'd have food waiting for us. Not wanting to use "*el remedio*" (impressively Orwellian, it means: the cure) prescribed by Truman's agronomist progeny, I follow the permaculturally correct "handpicking" method, squeezing a hundred gooeys between my fingers. It's gross, but avoids grosser organophosphate and pyrethroid pesticides. This saves maybe two-thirds of our veggies; the rest, a tithing to Pachamama.

But before long, a militia of leaf-cutter ants spies our orchard.

They strip nearly every leaf of the pomegranate and avocado saplings we'd planted in the *minga*. I watch them march up the thin trunks and carry down leaf-shreds.

Half-panicked, I call Kusi. She arrives on her motorcycle, studies the problem. "*Se necesita el remedio*" — You need the cure — she pronounces.

"We're organic," I tell Kusi.

She nods, barely suppressing an I-humor-gringos smirk, then she musters up a local solution: She and I cut the tops and bottoms off discarded two-liter plastic bottles and insulate our trees with them. The ants seem flummoxed.

Roaches at bay, fat-gooey-bugs diminished, and leaf-cutters stymied, Melissa and I are lulled back into insecto-romanticism. Bolivia, after all, is one of the world's fifteen ecologically "mega-diverse" countries — for example, the insect variety where we live is ten times that of the US Northeast — and nights on our farm-in-process bring us into philosopher David Abram's "more-than-human matrix." Our porch doesn't overlook a swimming pool and manicured terraces anymore; now it's a swath of natural hill, forest, and creek in a *guapurú* grove in a barely light-polluted part of the planet, beneath an Inca complex, bordering on a national park the size of three Yosemites. One evening, mountain air in my nostrils, I listen to Clea baby-talk about the bizarre bugs we're looking at as they alight around the porch light and the glass doors. A phosphorescent beetle perches on her wrist. "*Gentle*," she councils me, when I touch it. She and I hold ladybugs, crickets, and beetles; she gets used to them on her hand. Our goal is for her to feel webbed into nature, appreciating its creatures. This appreciation, of course, comes with firm boundaries; she knows that spiders, bees, and wasps are "no-no-nos."

One evening the following week, while I'm cooking dinner, Clea pees on the kitchen floor. Though I initially cringed at this practice, we learned from Bolivian friends sensitive to the cost and environmental impact of diapers to — yes — let her do this. "Nake-nake time," or going around in her birthday suit, is Clea's normal, and she's not yet potty trained. So I mop up the pee and spray the spot with a vinegar solution.

Clea points toward where she peed, exclaiming: "No-no!"

"It's okay. *Bebe* can pee. Daddy cleaned it." I drain pasta into the sink, wondering why she's suddenly so hygiene-oriented.

"No-no, *Papa*!"

I bend down and fold her into my arms, "Yes-yes-*yes*, honey," I console. "Look, all clean!"

Papa — finally — looks. Not at vinegar-nullified pee. It's something black and bushy.

"No-no-*NO!*" Clea pronounces definitively, indicating a tarantula.

I evacuate Clea. While Melissa distracts her, I heatedly shoe-heel the invader and compost the cadaver.

That tarantula is a mere tip-off for the coming crusades. Insects on our wide swath of land, it turns out, predict rainstorms before we notice the humidity changes, and seek refuge. Trails of black ants steal through the kitchen. Smaller reddish ones stream into the foyer. The miniroaches, only partially thwarted by our door guards, reappear. Spiders — those "no-nos" — trek up the stair railing.

Now I'm truly pissed. Handpicking becomes butchery. This is *our* house and we shall reclaim it. Melissa and I squash spiders and snuff out *cucarachas*.

Still, they come.

"Maybe they're crawling up through the pipes into the bathtub," Melissa theorizes.

Our bathtub pipe goes fifty meters downhill into the gray-water-composting banana grove Thiago designed for us. Impossible.

I investigate the corners of our house; all of the adobe appears sealed.

Riled, I once again seek out Kusi, finding her harvesting figs on her farm.

Kusi listens attentively. Then she smiles and says: "*Nosotros compartimos una casa con las arañas*" — We share a house with spiders.

This is no Park Slope bumper sticker decreeing: "Coexist." Kusi, out of the necessity of subsistence living in the subtropics, has *had* to come to terms with bugs.

Naturalist Charles Cook observed that "the idea of regularly acknowledging our indebtedness to the natural world and giving thanks for the many gifts we receive from it, or considering other species to be our close 'relations,' which many indigenous peoples still do, couldn't be more alien to most of us." But for Kusi, and so many others in Suraqueta, this could hardly seem less alien.

Back on our land, I muse on what Kusi said. *We share a house with spiders.* The Greek word *eco*, I recall, means "house." Is she suggesting that we share this larger house — our environment — with even the creepy-crawlies I once sentimentalized and now abhor?

I don't have more time to think about it. Part of my paid work in Bolivia is teaching two-week "sustainable development" travel courses for master's students at NYU's Center for Global Affairs, and the inaugural group is arriving. Students are to get an overview of Bolivia's economy, culture, and related dynamics and debate various theoretical frameworks of international development in the context of urban and rural site visits. I head off to meet sixteen students in the country's capital, La Paz.

One lecture is presented at the Bolivian foreign ministry by Carla Esposito, the forty-ish head of the diplomatic academy. This high-level official in President Morales's government asserts, "We must dethrone humans."

The students and I have attended other talks, ones more critical of the Bolivian government. So, as we listen, we are aware that, on the one hand, some parts of the government, like Esposito's, talk about Pachamama and attempt to push legal boundaries to protect her. But at the same time, others within the government push for standard northern industrialization, building dams in the Amazon and expanding the coca frontier and oil exploration into protected areas.

To illustrate her startling thesis, Ms. Esposito sketches two diagrams on a blackboard. The first depicts a large *Homo sapiens* at the pinnacle of the pyramid, with all other creatures arranged below. The second, by contrast, shows a human figure in the middle of a web, with a deer above it, a whale to the left, and to the right? I squint to see it.

A spider!

Esposito's sketch echoes Kusi's observation. *We share a house with spiders.*

Her lecture further explains Bolivia's indigenous response to the climate crisis. Bolivia's 2012 *Ley de la Pachamama* ("Law of Mother Earth") gives the planet rights similar to human rights.

That night in our hotel, my students asleep, I'm wide awake, thinking. I recall naturalist Gary Snyder's idea of wildness as the "knife edge" of nature. He argues that wildness is neither Eden nor Hobbesian savagery. It's a place, to those enmeshed in it — including my family in our recent occupation of the experimental farmstead — that demands constant vigilance, economy, and awareness.

In contrast, I also recall Liberia, one of the poorest nations in western Africa, where I worked briefly in the mid-2000s. The swanky five-story US Embassy in Monrovia had such sophisticated filtration for their HVAC system that it gave the impression of imported *air*. Visitors and employees walked through a pressure-sealed chamber before entering an atmosphere apart from Africa.

And at a meeting I once attended at the Carnegie Council for Ethics in International Affairs in New York, an executive from Hewlett-Packard, keen to extend Google's chip-in-the-brain beyond our species, held up a nickel-size metallic device and enthused, "We'll put one of these on every dolphin in the Atlantic. Then we'll be able to track them and thereby save them. Part of a single global brain." Heads in the audience nodded at the prospect of this marvel. The polished executive paused, then offered,

"Someday, we could even put a tinier one on every blue morpho butterfly."

Are these anecdotes, extreme as they may seem, really so different from what's standard today? We use sealed-off vehicles to travel from air-conditioned and heated houses to similarly nature-divorced offices within a culture of increasing surveillance. My family, I realize, moved onto our acreage with an anthropocentric worldview, one putting humans at the world's center, packed in our duffle bags, and our chosen paradigm supports the destruction of nature. Kusi and Carla — and insects — are guiding me into depths beneath the surface of Western environmental philosophy. If I follow Snyder's wisdom and desire untouched wildness for blue morphos, perhaps I must grant black widows their freedom, too. And how do I become wilder, more on the "knife's edge," in tune with flashing trout, swallow-tailed hawks, and, yes, all manner of bugs?

WEEKS PASS. My students, exhilarated by their Bolivia experience, are gone, their papers graded. Melissa and I reinforce the corners of our door guards, thereby blocking a main insect access point. While there's no longer an Earth Day parade through our kitchen, bugs still reside with us, and we're okay with that. Beyond my midnight musings about canned air and blue morphos, it's straightforward: After living with insects for months, we've become habituated to their presence.

One day, Kusi comes by with a container of gray-brown bugs. "Watch," she says and, to my chagrin, releases them into our garden.

Within fifteen minutes they're eating the green-fat-ugly-gooeys that have been devouring our vegetables. "It's permaculture," she says, adding that it's about getting the insect array back into balance.

"No more *remedio*?" I tease.

She smiles, explaining that a Bolivian nonprofit has been training her in nonchemical techniques. The same practices, she adds, that her grandparents knew but her parents forgot. Part of Suraqueta's designation as an "eco-municipality" means it's part of a new central government program investing in organic farming. This includes training outreach to farmers and a recently completed organic-produce processing center. I enthusiastically connect the dots between La Paz, where officials want to dethrone humans and expand the legal rights of Mother Earth, and our own eco-town as a physical space to ground such Sweet Life principles.

But, even amid optimism for the kind of life I want for my family, Monsanto and Dow AgroSciences have a firm foothold in Bolivia. There's *chicha americana* and a discernible buzz over the country's very first major shopping mall, to be built in Santa Cruz, a dazzling air-conditioned building. Living *better* — a large part of what I call "the Dream" — not just living *well*, continues as an economic philosophy pushed by my native northern tribe.

While Mother Earth laws, a philosophy of the Sweet Life, and towns like Suraqueta that incubate biocentric practices are inspiring, they are not enough. Without a *felt* inner choice to turn away from anthropocentrism, such ideals are easily smothered. For me, deepening into living well has to do with "our" house — Melissa's and mine — becoming Our house, collectively, inclusive of the insects, animals, and plants that share this land, which is also, so to speak, their land. As the weeks pass, *con insectos*, I follow Kusi's counsel to plant new trees only in the *mengua,* or waning full moon, and I find myself feeling for the first time like an insect. Like a soil molecule. Less mind, more sky.

ONE FULL-MOON EVENING while bathing Clea, Melissa discovers a scorpion under the rock we've carved to channel water in the gap between faucet and bathtub. She lifts the dripping Clea out and calmly tells me about it. I put down a book, go into the bathroom, and lift the rock.

The scorpion has ducked back underneath. Now its poisonous tail arches upward, and I feel something strange: gratitude. I'm glad, I realize, to share a house with bugs. They're here to keep us on the "knife edge of nature" — alive — partly by grounding us in the daily possibility of death.

I retrieve a shoe to crush the scorpion. Killing this one won't end all scorpions. My act complies with the Laws of Mother Earth. It's the same heel brought down each moment in this Great House.

I raise the shoe.

Then I lower it. I get a piece of paper and a plastic cup, trap the scorpion, and go out into the moonlight. I pass our thriving *achocha* patch, traverse the fledgling orchard, and plunge into the thorny *quiñe* forest. There's no path here, the known long gambled away. I feel the branches scrape my arms; one scratches my neck, drawing a line of blood. I stalk, deeper, and the scorpion millimeters from my hand is a knife. Finally, in a remote corner, far from human hearth, I put down the sheet of paper, lift the cup. The scorpion, shining with rich red life in the moonlight, scurries Home.

Seven

We're not the only *Homo sapiens* on our hill.

We, and our bugs, inhabit a Suraqueta frontier. Though just seven minutes' walk from the town market, our hillside neighborhood has been slow to settle because of poor road access. It is whimsically called Soto Pollerudo, or "the full-skirted *soto*," after a mythical tree whose trunk is said to have protruded like a *pollera*, or layer-cake skirt. Not only do rains turn Soto Pollerudo's clay roads into tire-spinning pudding, but the creek we cross by foot each day on the way to town swells in the rainy season, forcing cars into a long detour. Agriculture once took place here, but the town's expansion stretched into the more accessible Campeche, Vispera, and Barrio Nuevo neighborhoods. However, as land prices have risen, people now defy the mud and arrive in Soto Pollerudo.

During our first months on the land we watch two new adobe homes rise. The homes appear agreeably distant, since we're blessed with a five-acre buffer, but I'm nevertheless astounded that three houses exist where a year ago only *quiñe*, parrot-call, and meadow claimed the land. The first house shelters a young family of revillaging Paraguayans. Balu and Jaime move in with their Clea-aged daughter, two horses, and a throng of chickens. Balu tends their garden, her dreadlocks falling over homemade dresses taut with a pregnant belly, while hubby Jaime — earlobe-plugged, long-bearded — silversmiths necklaces on the porch. The second house belongs to a Frenchman named Michael and his wife, Lucia, a Bolivian from the country's north; their two young children straddle Clea's age. The couple abandoned careers in France —

Michael as a policeman, Lucia as a tourism professional — and they're starting up a health-food store near the plaza while settling into Soto Pollerudo.

I find it primal how our three families, all with kids under five, staked out boundary land, constructed earth homes, and laid water pipes. *Species radiation*, biologists call it, the way animals spread through a given habitat, taking possession of fresh territory until stymied by a counterforce. No other species, of course, can stop people radiating through Suraqueta, as they — *we* — are attracted by a year-round growing season, glocal culture, and other habitat features. The ferrets and iguanas, the badger-like *tejones* and wild guinea pigs, abundant on our land during construction, have ceded ground as we've opened trails, planted crops, and adopted competing fauna: a mud-colored puppy named Adobe and a black-and-white feline called Boots, a charming hunter. Previously displaced from the larger acreage of subdivided land with its ten homes on our border, the native species moved further into the steeper, still-wild portions of upper Soto Pollerudo.

But if iguanas can't halt radiating *Homo sapiens*, others of our own species seek to provide a counterforce. Let me introduce the *vallunos*.

Valluno means "valley dweller," and it refers to folks native to the valley region west of Santa Cruz, which includes Suraqueta. *Vallunos* have their own culture and identity, which in part defines itself by what it is not: *colla* or *camba*, two other regional identities. These three identities are often reduced to stereotypes, and they are engaged in a major ethnic rift in Bolivia. Perhaps the fiercest rift, using for a moment the common generalizations, is between the more reserved highland *collas* — hard-working, quinoa-growing peoples from the Andes — and the more fiery lowland *cambas*: papaya-plucking, leisure-loving people from the Amazon. Smack between these two sweeping cultural categories lie the *vallunos*, many of whom consider themselves superior to both *collas* and *cambas* because, like a long-aged and complex wine, they possess an inimitable, thousand-year blend of cultures: indigenous lowland Chané and Guaraní (from the eighth century on), upland Quechua of Inca pedigree (apogee: fourteenth century), blue-eyed Spanish colonials (from the seventeenth century on), Inquisition-fleeing Sephardic Jews (from the seventeenth century), and Turks, Greeks, and Croats (from the early twentieth century). These *vallunos* are now spread through a territory that encompasses San Juan in the east, Comarapa to the west, and Vallegrande to the south, and they have long controlled Suraqueta's cultural, political, and economic life.

Lately, however, tensions have risen as the "wrong" *Homo sapiens* radiate into their territory, and xenophobia has grown as the *vallunos'* historic power base erodes.

Melissa and I recognize two prejudicial targets. First are Cochabamba-area immigrants, the so-called *collas*, mostly farmers and merchants who are typically darker-skinned than the more blended *vallunos*. Second are the *jipis* (from the English "hippies" and pronounced HEE-pees), a derisive term for the barefoot-and-bearded artisan travelers from Colombia, Argentina, and elsewhere who pass through Suraqueta. But *jipi* has become a fungible category of humans upon which to heap derision, and the venom this term carries has been spreading, for several reasons, to all foreigners.

A recent incident exemplifies the clash of cultures. Local leaders, hoping to keep a Suraqueta cultural festival *jipi*-free, prevented a longtime resident, a Latin American musician of the rubber-tire-sandal persuasion, from performing that day. To protest his exclusion from the event, the musician interrupted a *valluno* leader's speech with a bit of loud acoustic guitar playing. The ceremony continued, but the *jipi's* disrespect was not forgiven.

Valluno powerbrokers thereafter twisted the arms of the Santa Cruz police, who summoned a drug SWAT team to raid the musician's home, confiscated marijuana, and tossed him in jail for five months.

Economics is another source of the swelling xenophobia that further fuzzes the line between pot-smoking traveling-through *jipis* and the here-to-stay foreigners. Elite *valluno* families, who have controlled local government for as long as anyone can remember, also dominate the town's shops and services. But this economic hegemony is splintering. *Collas* buy up agricultural land to create new farms, and they rent space downtown for profitable businesses. Foreigners from thirty countries radiate into tourism niches, cracking a globalized code that traditional *vallunos* cannot. Lisa and Jeff from Republika, for example, curate a Trip Advisor–anointed pub experience. Frank at Road Runners speaks English and German, thereby capturing high-earning tours for Amboró National Park and Inca ruins, both online and in person on Calle Bolívar. And foreigners like Lisa and Frank — damn *jipis*, mutter some townspeople — introduced a new phenomenon: branding. *Valluno* businesses do not use advertising; their owners paint, by hand, simple block letters identifying the name or purpose of the business on the exterior of the business's adobe building. But the foreign invaders create hip start-up logos and web pages to seduce travelers on their mobile screens and on the streets.

Another contributor to Suraqueta's increasing cultural tensions is the unwelcome arrival of workaholism in a town of *osiologos*. Leisureologists linger on the plaza. They spontaneously visit friends to chat for hours, preferably over *guapurú* wine. They savor siestas after protracted lunches. In this small village, surrounded by the rainforest-influenced Slow nature, leisureology *is* life. So why, the locals wonder, are these newcomer foreigners rushing across the plaza, eyes on gadgets, rudely answering phones in the middle of pleasant conversations? Why do they toil through the lunch hour? And why, in Pachamama's name, do they expend effort affixing LONELY PLANET CHOICE signs to their businesses?

Melissa and I, conscious of this attitude, maintain Sunday technology sabbaticals, minimize laptop use in public to be less conspicuous about work, and keep our phones internet-free so flex time doesn't become all-the-time. We've also learned from honeybees to flow, and from Suraqueteños like Ludwig and Rulas to resist making our noncareers into careers.

Still, busyness, the ill-famed B-word of the landmass to the north, is deeply ingrained, a tough habit to kick. I've got deadlines before my upcoming work trip back to the United States. I'm uncomfortable leaving for six weeks, just as we're settling into our Soto Pollerudo home; I'm torn about the carbon footprint of my air travel. But I've got an NYU commitment and a new book to launch. There are financial issues, too. We leveraged cash to build our house. I haven't been in debt since my early twenties, and I don't want that hole growing any deeper. I thus abandon our homegrown version of leisureology, overwhelmed with a farm-in-training, a kid, and our household, in addition to a class to prepare, bookstore talks to craft, and travel logistics to arrange. My agitation strains my relationship with Melissa and erupts in impatience with Clea.

IN PART TO DISCONNECT FROM THIS TURMOIL, Melissa, Clea, and I take a trip to the neighboring village of Paredones to participate for one day of a weeklong permaculture training. Kusi picks us up in her battered, natural-gas-converted Nissan pickup, and we head northeast along the old road to Cochabamba. The sparsely inhabited neighboring valley becomes increasingly lush as the dirt gravel road drops a thousand feet from our own more Mediterranean climate into deeper tropics. Kusi detours onto a dirt track toward the Barrientos approach to Amboró National Park, and we cross two rivers, the second of which she is barely able to ford without flooding the chassis. Within twenty minutes, we arrive at a forested hamlet with forty families: Paredones.

Recently grid-connected, Paredones features no restaurants or shops, to say nothing of the theater and Turkish food and espresso one finds in Suraqueta. But mixed in with thirty mostly Quechua farming families, who arrived here in the 1980s from the Cochabamba area, are a handful of more recent expatriate and Bolivian back-to-the-landers. There's a Dutch émigré named Hans, a baker of vegan breads, who lives in Paredones's *Origenes* (Origins), a tiny off-grid and even off-road eco-community of three, a twenty-minute wade up the Achira River. Over yonder is a Chilean baker family of five, homesteading in Paredones and selling their homemade jewelry in Suraqueta. And let's not forget Lech and Tina, a green-eyed young Polish couple homeschooling their ten children near the tarps under which they dwell; they sell natural creams and tinctures in Suraqueta on Sundays, the day the family walks three hours to town.

Finally, there's Karina and Hilvert. They're the friends we've come to visit. She's an ecotourism expert from La Paz, while he's an Amsterdam-fled anthropologist. In their midthirties with two young children, Sol and Luna, they recently founded Quinta Conciencia, an experimental permaculture farm, spiritual retreat, and hostel. Crossing the footbridge over the river to Quinta Conciencia with Kusi, we're greeted by Karina. As Kusi and Karina cheek-kiss, I sense a tension in Kusi. The two Bolivian women — though both midthirties, compelling, bright, and attractive — could hardly be more different. Karina has a wide face with high cheekbones and hair below her waist; Kusi is thinner and short-haired. Karina wears long skirts and smart-looking tops to Kusi's military khakis. And Karina is a wife and mother, grounded in family and community, whereas Kusi, despite telling me on many occasions her deepest wish is for a partner and children, remains single. Envy, perhaps, is the source of the friction.

Beyond Karina, we walk into a *scene*. Fifty people are divided into four buzzing action-learning groups. Thiago, a wad of coca in his cheek, digs a natural wastewater treatment pond with one group, and Kusi sidles over next to him. A visiting Argentinian professor helps a dozen folks build a DIY solar-heated water shower. Another instructor teaches organic gardening techniques. I step out of my shoes and join the last cluster, mixing straw into a wattle and daub to build a green-roofed children's playhouse. A giggling Clea and I stomp the mixture to the rhythm of a live accordion accompaniment. The day is renewing, as Melissa and I move from group to group, reskilling. As we work, Melissa and I catch up with Karina and Hilvert. Former city folks who had a hip, ecologically focused café and cultural center in La Paz, they decided, two years back, to revillage. They bought these five acres and are raising their kids here. Beyond maintaining chickens and a huge decades-old orchard, Karina and Hilvert use Quinta Conciencia as a teaching base. They offer sweat-lodge ceremonies, women's retreats, and practical trainings like this one an extraordinary three times a month. People stream in from Santa Cruz, La Paz, and other countries to eat the vegetarian food Karina makes, connect with nature, and absorb the realities of rural life.

Besides Paredones's seclusion and miniature size, two other things distinguish it from Suraqueta. First, the xenophobia ratcheting up in Suraqueta seems absent here, partly because basically everyone is an immigrant — *collas* and *jipis* all, with very few *vallunos* to be found. The foreigners are on the have-not-so-much side of the economic divide, as the Bolivian farmers cultivate prosperous, river-irrigated fields. If there's a Paredones potentate, it's the local Ulloa family, with the biggest holdings; it's become

a local sport, Hilvert tells me, to observe the relative impressive-
ness of the annual Ulloa New Year's firework display in Paredones
and thereby gauge the size of the family's agricultural harvest that
year. "We're the 'poor' ones here," the Dutchman says, telling me
about a government official who recently came to offer subsidized
micro-irrigation. "Our whole community gathered, and the official said each family has to pay six hundred dollars toward a small
irrigation system. We sure could have used one — it would have
made our farming easier — but we didn't have the cash, nor did
any of the other expat families here. But at the end of the meeting, the Ulloas, naturally, and also *every single one* of our Bolivian
neighbors counted off the cash and secured a system."

A second difference from Suraqueta is that there's no assault
on leisureology here. The émigrés stare not into smartphones;
they open no sculpture galleries. Under a philosophy of *integración*, many of the expats send their kids to the tiny two-room
schoolhouse, play soccer in the Friday games on the town "plaza"
(a cow field), serve their *jornales* (communal labor quotas) to
repair a bridge or clean the hamlet's water tank, and enjoy lingering lunches and siestas. Karina and Hilvert's house isn't, I self-
consciously notice, a feng shui eco-*casita* like ours. Their dining
room is an outdoor patio between a freestanding adobe kitchen
and a separate building with two rooms for sleeping and a bathroom. It's modestly cobbled together, a series of add-ons whose
piecemeal construction correlated to the previous Bolivian owner's cash flow.

At the end of the day, I pass a yerba máte cup-and-straw back
and forth with Karina under the old grapevines trellised beside
the peach and mandarin orchard. I tease that I'm jealous, wondering aloud how she and her family manage so many trainings
each month, plus two kids and this farm, while retaining perpetual calm. I say that I want to root into life here the way she has,

but I feel overtaxed under the weight of family, land, and work, including my stress-inducing upcoming US trip. "I'll never get it all done," I complain, draining the máte.

Karina pushes a strand of her long hair behind an ear, a healthy glow in her dark eyes. She says: "What's finished is done."

I pause to take this in. Melissa, some fifty feet away, lifts Clea up to pick a mandarin. *What's finished is done.* That wasn't what I expected to hear from Karina. After all, her family cut cords in a manner much more profound than we have, so I thought she might suggest dropping my US commitments to focus locally.

Seeing I'm puzzled, Karina smiles and adds: "It's our Bolivian way. When you're finished with one portion of a bigger task — say a half-built chicken coop — then it's *done*. It's not incomplete. It's not pending. It's entirely vanquished from your thoughts until you take it up again."

MIAMI.

As the plane descends over the city toward the airport, I gaze down into part of what we left behind when we moved to Bolivia: multilane highways and a thousand condos lining human-made islands. We land, and I rush to catch my Baltimore-bound connection, struck by a profusion of name-brand clothing and a multifold jump in visible gadgetry, compared to Bolivia.

Later, the African American cabdriver who takes me from Baltimore airport to my hotel near Johns Hopkins University, where I'm to speak the next day, tells me, "There's been 268 murders in Baltimore this year," and "it's racist that everyone says 'black-on-black' murders because it's white supremacy that put us in the ghetto." At mostly white and, in my Bolivian-adjusted eyes, decadently lavish Johns Hopkins University, a large police presence guards the fortress walls. Hopkins students pay $60,000 annually for tuition, room, and board, and they seem more professionally dressed and hurried than I remember from my days as an undergraduate at Brown. Today's undergrads can be nothing less than efficiency-maximizers, it would seem, since it's unthinkable to squander *time* when each Ivory Tower hour is so pricey, and education must be geared toward high-earning occupations to pay back college loans or to satisfy parents sweating to pay the tuition.

The day after my Johns Hopkins talk, my culture shock deepens as the Amtrak train deposits me in New York's Grand Central Station. Many people look so harassed that it appears there's a wolf behind them instead of a dollar in front. I time a forty-three-minute dinner with an old friend. ("Gotta scoot," my companion says, hopping in an Uber.) I break our Bolivia technology rule and get an internet-connected phone; it seems inconceivable not to have one as I lecture and hold meetings in Boston, Denver, LA. Granted, I'm trying to squeeze a year of engagements into a six-week trip, but my lightning pace feels eerily normal here. The decisive irony is that part of my stressful sojourn is focused on launching my latest book, *New Slow City*, about groping toward a peaceful life-pace. I chastise myself with self-loathing because I'm currently such a poor ambassador of the slow-and-simple message.

Yes, I find incredible encouragement as I travel around the country, visiting Transition Towns like Montpelier, Vermont, and Portland, Maine, touring the Village Homes ecological co-housing experiment in Davis, California, and meeting the Columbia, South Carolina, couple who have downshifted to twenty-hour workweeks, self-provisioning their own food and doing their own auto repair. Yet, it's obvious how much harder it is for these cultural rebels than it is for us in Bolivia, where the leisureologist lifestyle and Law of Mother Earth culture is the mainstream instead of the fringe. In the Q&As after my talks and readings, *stress* — the same stress I once struggled with in Manhattan and describe in *New Slow City* — bubbles up as the main issue for others. A kind of "whiff 'em" ethos reigns, as a single mother of two in Albuquerque calls it: "WIIFM," she explains, "or 'What's in it for me?'" I recall how, underneath even the current xenophobic upswell in Suraqueta, there's a bedrock people-are-people-through-other-people tenet in Bolivia, and how I had to learn, while constructing the house, not to kill the relational for the transactional. In America, I sense how increasingly powerful *Homo economicus* — humans reduced to their economic role — has become. Lifeconomy. An economicalife.

In San Francisco, after a book talk and two interviews, I'm feeling strained and exhausted. Regardless, I'm in front of the laptop at my hotel about to pull a late-nighter to prepare for another talk the next evening. Then I remember Karina's words under her grape trellis in faraway Paredones.

What's finished is done.

I stand up and look out my hotel window. A billboard for Home Depot reminds me to NEVER STOP IMPROVING.

A truth dawns. NEVER STOP IMPROVING is not just one corporation's slogan. It's America's. As much as I might cringe to confess it, it's mine, too. It's the voice that says: *You are not quite good enough; you can always be better.*

Years ago, in Liberia, I heard a story about a pair of African porters hired by a Belgian trader to help him prospect gold deep in the forest. After two days of brisk walking, the porters sat down and refused to budge. The trader tried several things to inspire them to keep going: belligerent demands, flattery, an increase in salary. No matter what the man tried, the porters refused to move. They told him they'd been walking too fast and had to wait for their souls to catch up.

I have a choice. Am I prospector or porter? I can work hard on the speech and shine on tomorrow's podium, and then sweat and shine at laptops and podiums for all my tomorrows, preaching a Slow Life gospel I don't happen to practice. I can let the Dream guide my efforts to critique the Dream, make a career out of my supposed anticareer yet again.

Or I can embody the shift.

I can... STOP IMPROVING. Allow what's finished to be done. Be satisfied with exactly what is, right now.

I stash the computer and head out into the city night. The air smells like eucalyptus and brackish water. I hoof it all the way to Golden Gate Park, where I bushwhack off the main path to the base of a Monterey cypress tree. I will improvise tomorrow's speech. Right now, I need to sit in the light of a waning moon and wait for my soul to catch up.

"WHAT SHOULD I DO TODAY?" I ask my family and pets. It's a Wednesday morning. I returned from the United States the previous week.

"A grown man," asks a smirking Melissa, "is asking his children...what he should *do* today?"

I shrug and lean into our front porch hammock. It's an odd question, but it's what surfaces. A curious, temporarily speechless audience of five females gathers around the hammock, looking at me: Melissa, Amaya, Clea, Boots, and Adobe.

Past those ten eyes, I gaze over our lush land. A proposal for my day finally comes. "You should get the pizza," Amaya suggests.

That's the full extent of *her* ambition for my day: Daddy getting the pizza from a family-owned shop in the market for tonight's dinner — a twenty-minute task.

I look to Clea for counsel. She's completely naked except for her beloved bright-red boots, and she has an I-don't-give-a-shit look on her cute two-year-old face. Planning is a non-concept for her. Nor are Boots and Adobe any help. Boots purrs and licks my hand while Adobe cocks her head to the side, seeming to side with Amaya: *Get the pizza.*

Despite my San Francisco epiphany, my brain still says IM-PROVE. Brain says: Shoe-up, lazy man. Grab a machete, and head into the *guapurú* forest to clear the overgrown trail to our camping area and weed the untidy tree saplings on the south border. Then plow through the eco-psychology articles on your reading list, sketch a lesson plan, and nail your fifteen-hundred-word authorial quota. Only then, says my brain, will you deserve that pizza.

I stage an intervention:

Me: Hi, brain.
Brain (embarrassed): Oh…hi.
Me: *You* do those things. I'll not.
Brain: I will…but that means you have to, since I am you.
Me: If you are me, then you're not doing them, either.
Brain: But…Noooo!
[Door slams in brain's face.]

My brain thus silenced, for the rest of the day I'm lulled into a kids-and-pets view of the world. Amaya and Clea embody the Sweet Life far more fully than I: They're *here*, and therefore always beginning. We splash in our creek pool, stroll together to the Suraqueta Refuge to chill with Cheetah the howler monkey, and hone the fine Suraqueta tradition of plaza-dallying.

"*Qué valluno!*" — So *valluno* of you — Kusi calls out, spotting me loafing on a bench after lunch. I ask her about the "manhunt" and she tells me she's, as I suspect, giving it a go with Thiago. Hours pass thus. Amaya and Clea play with whatever configuration of kids happens to be on the plaza at a given moment. I tête-à-tête with our neighbor Maximo, who in addition to selling honey and pollen at his erratic-hours shop is, in the mornings, an elementary school teacher. In our rambling conversation, and with input from other locals, I learn about Che Guevara's capture of Suraqueta in 1967 during his ill-fated Bolivia campaign.

Joining in the lilies-in-the-field antiambition of the pueblo this one time doesn't, of course, end my outsider status or the town's persistent xenophobia, but it feels like a baby step toward *integración*. "Will you watch Juanita while I'm at the market?" a dad-friend asks, and I do — a cinch when Juanita's playing with Clea and a half dozen other children under the plaza's sundial. Then, at day's end, it's finally time to debench and take care of my task: Together with Amaya and Clea, I get the pizza.

Eight

"*Papá!*" cries a two-year-old Clea, one warm evening outside our adobe home. I look into Clea's blue eyes. A second pupil — a white one — glows there: the full moon.

"*Luna!*" she exclaims, pointing up at the moon rising over Amboró National Park's mountains. My urge to look up is overcome by Clea's splendor. Her face is obliquely round; the curve of her nostril, round; her eye, round, with a plump moon joggling on her eyes' surface. Something raw in me wants to paint a moonlight circle around it all, enclose it in an *O* from a time before humans invented letters.

Aymara herders south of here still chart the night course of their salt caravans by studying the stars in a llama's fat wet eye. To gaze at things obliquely, wrote philosopher John O'Donohue, is to at last see them.

"*Papá?*" whines Clea, a little anxious now. Her tearing eyes smear the moon. Melissa and I, deepening into leisureology, have been affirming her when she notices natural phenomena — bubbling water, wildflowers, a *sur* wind, the moon — and she has come to reserve her peak enthusiasms for the animistic. So now the baby mammal beside me — barely verbal, wildly present — wants to connect with her dad by seeing the moon together, perhaps even in the same way.

I leave her eyes reluctantly, following the folds of her shirtsleeve to her fingertip. My gaze leaps off a ladybug-size fingernail into the lens of subtropical sky, lit by *la luna*.

"Moon," Clea says, switching to English, her tone softening.

She's calmed by our mutual attention to what is of most importance.

"Moon," I whisper, but the utterance feels counterfeit. ·

"TEACH A CHILD THE NAME OF A BIRD," writes Jesuit author Anthony de Mello, "and she'll never see *that* bird again."

De Mello means that language, by labeling phenomena, exacts two injuries. First, it obscures uniqueness: the mystery of this bird, this night's moon. And second — in an apparent contradiction — it also fractures the unified field of mystics and physicists.

Clea's mom and I both have graduate degrees; we've been shaped by social science, by language and reason. We're not monks, not rainforest dwellers silently stalking prey. But over the course of our professional lives, we've both come to question the hegemony of the mind in modern life. We've been influenced by thinkers like philosopher David Abram and economist Juliet Schor, and by the Earth-based African, South American, and North American indigenous cultures in which we've lived. However, such idealism is tempered by certain facts. To wit: We live close to nature, but even while letting what's finished be done so as to let our souls catch up, we earn the best part of our living through words we write on laptops and use in cross-continental Skype meetings. Even as we aspire to STOP IMPROVING, decolonizing some of our detached Cartesian training, our analytical selves exert a massive influence. The important struggle to decolonize oneself vis-à-vis a very different way of being is, literally, foreign. Aspire as we might, we are a bit like fish who do not know what water is, since it is everywhere. We breathe language.

Out of such contradictions we've been fumbling, as more months pass, into a sort of biocentric parenting tool kit. "Biocentrism" means rejoining the web of nature, as opposed to "anthropocentrism," which places *Homo sapiens* at the center of the show. We've come to see the world more biocentrically in part because many Bolivians do. Pachamama, as I learned in La Paz, really is the heart of Bolivian cosmo-vision and of a new Earth-rights legal framework.

Perhaps more than parenting, it's *childing*. Clea Luz — her name suggests the Earth's clay and the sky's light — is far less conditioned than we are. A small, barely verbal child *is* nature. So we wonder: How can we create a family culture with abundant spaces beyond words? How, in such spaces, can we learn from Clea how to be part of nature's web, both as individuals and together?

One admittedly odd practice we share is swinging from tree branches. The idea occurred to me one day when Clea was a few months old. I sat her down on the grass and swung from a low bough, making sounds poorly approximate of our ape ancestors. Little Clea cooed in response as the leaves fell around her.

Since then, I've done variations of this a hundred times, and as Clea has grown, she's come to imitate me, shaking branches herself whilst screeching, monkey-like. She loves for me to place her on tree limbs, where she shouts "*ooh-ooh-OOOH!*" Before long, we're two orangutans swinging together, the smaller imitating the larger. The fun! How genuine it feels to connect with my *retoño* ("sprout," as Bolivians call kids) through leaf, limb, and larynx.

Here's another one: We sometimes use the Buddhist practice of telling Clea, "We call this a tree," instead of "This is a tree." After all, it's not a tree. It's not ink scratches, not two consonants and two vowels. This so-called tree — an olive-green *guapurú* on our hillock — is utterly unique and utterly unified with "the ten thousand things."

A third practice is a simple, profound one we learned from my sister. Before meals, one of us rings a bell and we all bring our hands into prayer position and breathe in silence. After a while, somebody rings the bell again and we look silently into each person's eyes before eating. Clea has come to lead this, insisting on the silence even when Mom and Dad forget.

Naturally, we're not dethroning language 24/7. We do set limits with Clea and communicate them with words. (*Share your toys. Yes, it's bedtime.*) But "biocentric childing" has become central to our family. It's about getting into our animal limbs. Clea weeds the garden and orchard with us. The howler monkey up the road climbs onto her shoulders, and we interact with this fellow primate without talking. Then there's Clea's favorite element...

Water.

Clea charges, one morning, toward the creek that runs through our land. She's always first to hear its gurgle, snapping me out of my mental loops. *Splash. Gush. Gurgle.* Onomatopoeia waterfalls into our vocal chords. As David Abram puts it: "Our own languages are continually nourished by other voices — by the roar of waterfalls and the thrumming of crickets.... [Language is] a sensuous, bodily activity born of carnal reciprocity and participation."

Clea reaches the water, so ecstatic that she's stripping off shirt and diaper. "*Wawa!*" she cries out, mixing two languages, her conjunction of "*agua*" and "water" conveying the stream's voice; *wawawa* splashes into a pool, leaps into a two-year-old's inner ear, ricochets off her pink tongue.

Her bare feet enter the flow. Following her, I tear off my shoes and together we *wawawaaa*.

"IF WE RAISED CLEA IN TREES, and dug for grubs to eat," Melissa says to me one day in our fig and avocado orchard, "she'd adapt entirely."

In her book *Raising Our Children, Raising Ourselves*, family counselor Naomi Aldort encourages parents to refrain from reacting when our kids push our buttons. She's got a wonderful acronym for it: WAIT (Why am I talking?).

I use it a lot. When I'm about to either put a label on a mystery or try to make a situation right, I WAIT. I sink into the sky, a breeze...and also into my inner weather. Something interesting usually happens: The moment aligns. Life doesn't need my brain.

After a year of using Aldort's practice, I realized part of why it's effective. Instead of anthropocentrically narrowing reality, WAIT-ing allows us to be biocentric: Clea and me both. It allows me to tune in to how attuned she is to surrounding sensory stimulus. She's noticing a hawk overhead, wings stiff as kites. She's stopping to pick daisies for Mom. She's here, now: a plume of smoke, the coarse lick of our kitten's tongue, a crescent moon. Clea's in a place of peace. It's not the nervous, more-is-better place that fuels overconsumption and creates the divide between ourselves and the rest of nature. Clea is nature. Or, rather, she has yet to find out she's not.

But she's learning. The Skype screen is forever blue, even when the sky is not. Mommy and Daddy bank online and press buttons on the town's first ATM, newly installed. They text and call and chat. Though they don't own a car, they do usher baby into bush taxis where she feels the power of what she calls the "vroom-vroom."

At what point does a clever little primate like Clea sense something central to the rift between humans and the rest of nature? It's this: She learns that the important information, that is, the information related to our survival and our interconnection, comes from laptops, from cell towers, from satellites. Things she may still feel viscerally, as a baby animal, to be important — the rustle of a ferret in the heather, the splash of *wawa*, the medicinal plants she picks — are beautiful, and at times useful, but peripheral. Our shelter, clothing, and food come from money we receive in exchange for brainwork. Our interconnection comes in large part from internet and phone and, yes, airplanes, too.

I'm aware that the Sweet Life pillar of the complementarity of diversity allows *all* to be — beyond a Western either/or duality — but right now I'm feeling pessimistic, which narrows my perspective. Each moment in which we do not depend upon nature for our livelihood, pleasure, and interrelation, we depreciate it in our children's senses. It's as if I'm saying through my actions: Thank you, Clea, for noticing that hawk, but we don't need to read its signs. Thank you for squealing with pleasure when you hear the brook, but *wawa* gets piped into the house. Thank you for noticing the full moon, but GPS guides us. Thank you for the pleasure you get the first time you walk all the way into the pueblo by yourself, proudly holding Daddy's hand, but the petroleum-powered *vroom-vrooms*, not your musculature, will take you life's distances.

Thank you, Clea Luz, for your mammalian instincts, but you won't be needing them. Thank you for your creaturehood, but you are a Customer. Your name is merely poetic; don't lean on nature.

AMID SUCH GLOOMY FEELINGS about the thin degree of our *actual* connection to nature, some good news percolates up. The successful orchard *minga* on our land has been repeated on other homesteads, and these *mingas* have inspired a growing community-wide enthusiasm for finally turning Suraqueta into a Transition Town (after the false start a year ago following the *In Transition 2.0* documentary screening). Led by Thiago and Melissa, Suraqueta brings in a trainer from Transition Mexico to facilitate two high-energy days called "Transition Launch." We're floored by the local interest and have to turn away potential participants because of lack of space.

In a hall packed with an integrated group of *vallunos*, recent *colla* migrants, and foreigners, and also including town councilors, businesspeople, and students, we spend the first day envisioning our community deepening itself as an "ecological municipality," but not doing so in isolation. Instead, we'll join a network of Transition initiatives around the world focused on relocalizing economy, reducing fossil-fuel consumption, and fomenting organic agriculture.

The second day, surprisingly, is all about "inner transition." We meditate and do interpersonal exercises, like Joanna Macy's "Work That Reconnects."

The reason this pragmatic international movement, which was launched in England in 2006, now focuses on our inner lives is because many initial Transition communities failed to flourish because of ego. Some people in early communities appropriated the process as *mine*. People asked, *What's in it for me?* — the Albuquerque mom's "WIIFM" — instead of, *How does our situation and change impact all of us?* This poignant second day of the training helps me realize that part of Transition is opening to what is, whether that's good or bad, whether we like "what is" or not.

In the wake of the two-day Transition Launch, six action initiatives take root, including community gardens, group purchasing, and green-energy efforts. I'm excited to feel freshly linked with my fellow villagers. Now, when we bump into one another on the plaza or in the market, we share ideas for the recycling and organic agriculture policies we're crafting together in Suraqueta, a small place where our efforts matter in concrete ways. I'm also inspired, as the moon wanes and waxes and wanes again, by a slight maturing in myself: a deepening acceptance. I recognize that we — collectively — are currently here: within the Dream of individualism and consumerism, of the dismissal of indigenous values, of overwork and status competition, of fossil-fuel dependence. Together, we can transition to another here: an emergent

Sweet Life of community, one that valorizes Pachamama, time wealth, spiritual values, a gift economy, solar energy.

It's irresistibly nonlinear. And fun. Our basic nature is communal and enmeshed in David Abram's "more-than-human matrix." Transition, in part, means stripping away that which is not us.

MEANWHILE, AT HOME, Clea is all about *la luna*! A blue morpho butterfly! The splash of *wawa*!

But she's also all about the *vroom-vroom* of the washing machine; the distant sound of a *moto* in town; auntie on the Skype screen.

This all feels less contradictory to me now. We're not perfect; we're in transition. Wildness flourishes beyond the analytical mind, yes, but also beyond using the analytical mind to make an enemy of itself. There is grace in nonjudgment. By ceasing to judge myself and our culture for destroying nature, I find myself more deeply enmeshed in nature.

The moon transitions again to full. Naturally — and not out of any rigid "biocentric" philosophy — Melissa and I pursue a joyfully vegetarian kitchen, do yoga, spend more time working in the orchard with Clea. A week passes since we've been in a *vroom-vroom*. We're increasingly eating out of our gardens and sharing surplus with friends.

And here's my little daughter, right now.

It's Thursday. She sits on the outdoor patio in the light of a nearly full moon, on our *guapurú*-tree mosaic, talking to a gray moth on the back of her hand as Adobe and Boots wrestle beside her.

It's dinnertime. The food's hot, and it's time to eat. It's *dinnertime*.

Or is it?

I WAIT. Choosing wordlessness allows the three mammals and one insect on the porch to be.

Melissa and I eat silently, the moon shining through our circular skylight. That same moonlight falls on the soft hair of our toddler, who now — viewed through the arched glass doors — looks up from moth to moon. *La luna.*

Nine

At Flor de Montaña (Mountain Flower), a recently established K-8 school down by the old road to Cochabamba, I'm transforming disassembled shipping pallets into school desks and benches. Melissa, across the playground, installs a fence to stop the hens who have been marauding the students' vegetable garden. Around us, fifty others work — parents, kids, volunteers.

"What did you do in school yesterday?" I ask the twelve-year-old hammering nails beside me. Florinda, a sixth-grader at Flor de Montaña, answers, "Agroforestry, plus recycling, Quechua, and meditation."

Okay, so this isn't just any school. As part of the burgeoning glocal-Transition-eco-municipality, a group of Suraqueta parents founded the school two years ago after trying unsuccessfully for years to reform the local public school, which persisted with memorization and rote classroom learning. Flor de Montaña, however, is still on shaky ground. It hasn't received legal recognition due to an entrenched educational establishment not wishing to recognize that there's another way. With no building of its own, the cooperative rents this small complex. The families of the thirty enrolled students pay an average of $50 per child each month, though some children attend school on need-based scholarships. Plus, with limited funds to recruit and pay teachers, clean the school, or purchase furniture, parents feel overextended by constant *mingas*, and a chaotic feeling of impermanence pervades the school.

Still, creativity is obviously blossoming among the students under Flor de Montaña's hybrid Andean-Amazonian-Montessori-Waldorf curriculum. Then there's the massive turnout for this *minga*. Hans, the tall Dutch bread-baker from Paredones, wanders through the group selling loaves of his bread out of a basket as Clea, playing with a group of toddlers, kicks a green balloon toward me. I smile. This is the school we'd like our "mountain flower" to attend someday.

As I cinch two boards with an L-joint, my mind slips back to a conversation with Melissa the previous night, one we've had many times, essentially a struggle with our culturally ingrained NEVER STOP IMPROVING habituation. Shouldn't we do more? Launch a nonprofit to amplify *vivir bien*? Find new ways to channel the privilege of our graduate degrees and work experience toward solving the dual environmental and unhappiness crises?

As we talked, I felt increasingly phony, as if these were the words of a prior me, still stuck in my larynx. I sensed Melissa's unease, too. Our ambition software was saying: *Come on, put an extra twenty hours a week into an NGO start-up. Your white privilege requires you to strive to better the planet for others.*

Our Bolivian counterprogramming, meanwhile, protested: *Why strive individually when the Sweet is in community at a* minga, *with carnaval trees, with Amaya and Clea and wawawa?* STOP EFFING IMPROVING.

Eventually, our words sputtered out.

"Do you hear that?" Melissa asked.

I listened, heard only silence. "What?"

"That was the sound of the last of our ambition draining out."

It took me a second to absorb this. Then we both burst into laughter. The release felt wonderful. We hugged, knowing that we *have* what we'd been looking for and don't need more. We have a house and land, connection to walkable, creative community and to Pachamama, a blossoming school in Flor de Montaña, sufficient work and income, and we give "service" simply by contributing within a healthful antibody to ecocide. As difficult as it would be for our old NYC selves to grasp, power lies in the nonaction of being. Being happy with what you have. Not striving for More. Our conversation felt like clipping a final strand of the umbilical cords connecting us to the Dream.

As I finish hammering together a fine little table at the school *minga*, I sense my family deeply decolonizing the Dream and feel the Sweet Life at last in our grasp. Or rather, that we are now inhabiting its aromatic garden.

As I admire the furniture I've helped craft, I overhear Kusi saying something to Thiago. Something about a rape. "*Qué terrible*," Thiago responds.

I notice one protruding nail and pound it flush. "What happened?" I ask, figuring they're talking about urban crime in Santa Cruz.

They both look at me, strangely. "You didn't hear?" Kusi finally says. "A woman was gang-raped a few blocks from the Suraqueta plaza. Last night, after leaving a local bar."

I'm dumbfounded.

"She was raped for over an hour by three locals. They also beat and robbed her."

I call Melissa over, and the details emerge. The woman is Grace, a forty-one-year-old teacher in Santa Cruz who shares a rental house in Suraqueta, where she escapes to each weekend. As usual, she'd gone out with friends on Saturday night until 2 AM. She walked her customary diagonal path across the plaza from the bar to the church, where she was spotted by three Suraqueta males — two young brothers, aged sixteen and eighteen, both high school students, and a twenty-five-year-old local gym instructor.

Witnesses later reported that the men had been drinking heavily. They followed Grace past the church, down to the stream, and up past a hidden concrete basketball court a half block from her house. There they grabbed her, dragging Grace to an unlit corner of the court.

I take Melissa's hand, knowing it could have been her. How is it we've taken our security for granted, walking alone at whatever time of night without a thought of delinquency? Then I'm irritated that everyone at the *minga* is painting classrooms and making furniture after such a tragedy.

I thought we'd escaped this kind of danger. In Manhattan, a poster on the exit door to our apartment building read, "Close and lock this door!" Beneath these words, a fearful and angry tenant wrote a warning about a street rape that had occurred in the apartment foyer next door. But that was New York, which has hundreds of murders and thousands of reported rapes each year.

"And you know where Grace is from, right?" Kusi asks. She's looking at the ground, apparently unable to make eye contact with Melissa and me.

Melissa shakes her head. Kusi says: "*Es americana.*"

We fortify. After this crime, everybody in town seems to build ramparts. Melissa no longer walks alone after dark. Our front gate, normally open, is now nocturnally padlocked. Though it shouldn't matter that the rape survivor is American, it feels more personal. She's from California, we hear, and a math teacher at one of the elite schools in Santa Cruz. "Suraqueta isn't a bubble, Bill," says Salome, noticing my gloom one day. "We're connected to the world."

A week after the crime, we meet Grace for the first time, in a café off the plaza. She's clean-cut, determined, and hardly speaks Spanish. Grace has applied thick makeup to hide her facial bruising. I'm surprised she's back in Suraqueta. Sure, the three perpetrators were apprehended and are currently held in the Vallegrande prison two hours away, but why return to the place of such trauma? It turns out she's back to tell her story to try to bring justice. "Not just for me," she says, as a group gathers around to listen. Someone translates into Spanish. "More importantly for other women." She passes around photos taken right after the crime. They show her bloated, blood-covered, black-eyed.

As the weeks pass, however, a disquieting shift occurs. Town opinion swings toward defending the boys. Who is this blonde *gringa*, anyway? It's odd enough that she's forty-one and still unmarried and childless. What kind of woman would be walking alone late at night, in a short skirt?

Meanwhile, it turns out that this is not the first rape in Suraqueta; it's the first time an American has been raped. One of the perpetrators, the twenty-five-year-old, has previous accusations against him, but the less-well-heeled, less-vocal survivors were either paid off or shamed into silence. More stories surface of rape and child abuse. A local women-led group uses the moment to organize a demonstration on the plaza. The intent is to advocate for a center in town for the protection of women, offering legal counsel and educational programs.

Melissa and I attend the demonstration, along with about a hundred others. The crowd is almost half expat, an unfortunately imbalanced proportion. The mood is calm; vigil-like speeches seek not to cast blame but to acknowledge the problem and move forward with the proposed solution. At one point, a woman visiting from Santa Cruz says: "We need to solve this. Suraqueta can't be known as a town of rapists."

This quiet remark, almost an aside, enters the town rumor mill and undergoes revision, till people are saying that frothing-at-the-gum demonstrators chanted "Suraqueta, town of rapists!" at the vigil. Calls to free the accused rapists increase, and a counter-demonstration is organized by the conservative town civic committee, which they call a "march against crime and drugs" —

drugs that surely delinquents like that short-skirted *jipi* imbibe unaccompanied late at night.

IN THE MIDST OF SUCH TUMULT, Melissa, Clea, and I take an overnight trip to Santa Cruz to see Amaya. We hope our getaway will be a respite from the fervor, but the front page of the Santa Cruz newspaper *El Deber* shouts about *femicidio*. Femicide. Women-killing.

Not long ago, a Santa Cruz female was raped by one of the security guards at her office building, and police discovered her corpse in the trunk of a car the man had stolen. And before this, Santa Cruz's mayor had made derogatory comments about women and also touched the leg, on camera, of a young female journalist. The clip went viral and was followed by cries to impeach the mayor.

Since then, marches against *femicidio* have sprung up across the city. Civil society and the media, like never before, are confronting *machismo* — bigotry — and violence against women. Yet this movement forms only part of a grinding shift of even larger cultural tectonic plates.

In 1970, Santa Cruz was a sleepy, family-oriented town of a hundred thousand people. Now it's swelled twenty-fold to two million, and *Forbes* has anointed the city a future Latin American economic powerhouse, with the potential to grow to an incredible eight million people by 2050. (The current population of Bolivia is ten million.) In 2001, when I first visited Santa Cruz, it tallied *half* its present population. I remember my intrigue at its unique local foods, like the delicious *cuñapé* cheese bread and dried-meat and plantain *mojadito*, and the long siestas and extended family lunches in *quintas* (rustic country homes) on the weekends. There were few signs of contemporary marketing, since this demographic was too slight and too poor to interest multinationals.

But the Dream has since landed in the sprawling metropolis where my elder daughter lives, and the Sweet Life is collapsing at an exponential pace. Fast food trumps traditional food, and work hours increase as leisureology gives way to consumerism and escalating lifestyle expectations. It's part of a modern conundrum: The same corporate-owned media that helps break apart misogyny by exposing femicide also breaks apart community and feeds WIIFM. Multinationals now encourage Santa Cruz residents to *buy, baby, buy* in order to overcome an unhappiness they didn't know they felt until the marketers revealed it to them. And the race to earn more is accompanied by the inevitable leap in suicide, rape, and armed robbery, which has jumped four-fold since my first visit.

I take a *micro* (half-size bus) to Amaya's house and pick her up, while trying to push such dreary thoughts out of our *papa-hija* (father-daughter) space. At the city landmark statue of El Cristo, we pass a femicide protest, and the mood in our *micro* goes solemn. I won't tell Amaya about the Suraqueta rape, not wanting to dampen her affection for her second home in a town she loves. I do not know how to talk with a ten-year-old about something so hideous. Silently, Amaya and I join the other passengers by quietly watching the protest as we race down Avenida Monseñor Rivero toward Hotel Milan.

There, the mood shifts as Amaya hugs the proprietress, a warm, old-fashioned Bolivian *señora* who has known her since she was small — then she dashes up the stairs to our always-room, number 106, in the second-floor back corner, and right into Clea and Melissa's arms. When the hugs and updates time-out, we head outside, walking Calle René Moreno to Victory Café. On a second-story balcony of the centuries-old building, we sip espresso and juice. Next to us two elder gentlemen play backgammon. At other tables, a woman pages through *El Deber* and a young couple, touching foreheads, whisper endearments and giggle. Clea slurps her passionfruit juice to empty, then she strides purposefully across the balcony, through the café, and directly into the tattoo parlor next door.

From our angle at the table, Amaya, Melissa, and I can see Clea. Tattoo parlors, like much else in Bolivia, retain a pre-Dream innocence. The pair of on-duty hipster tattoo artists — seeming to think nothing of a toddler in their studio — chat and laugh with Clea, who reappears on the Victory balcony ten minutes later with a "tattoo" on her tiny hand, a red flower and bumblebee in ballpoint pen.

We leave Victory, ambling together across the plaza to purchase a two-boliviano bag of wheat kernels from a shoe-shine man, and Clea and Amaya perform their ritual pigeon feeding, the birds — white, gray, azure blue — landing on their hands and devouring seed.

I take a photo that I will later — in more difficult times — gaze at often. In it, four pigeons, startled by church bells, explode from Amaya's right hand. Seeds spray onto cobble. Clea looks up with astonishment at her sister. Amaya's auburn hair flies back in the wind of pigeon-wing and her eyelids seem to fly back, too, her eyes madly joyful, everything ascatter. Behind Amaya, in the photo, a background to this bliss, is nothing Dream-tainted. There's a unionized, white-capped coffee-cart guy making the rounds; intact colonial buildings like that of the Victory, unmarred by logos; Cruceños feeding pigeons; the innocuous Hotel Milan; the cathedral's timeless tower clock doglegged to a perpetual five-sharp.

Even in the moment, a part of me suspects something I'll come to feel deeply — that this is not life, but rather an edited reality as subjectively framed as the photo itself. Here is what I leave out of the frame by, metaphorically, "gazing upward":

the Burger King a half block away; the new mall rising along the way to Amaya's house; the rising suicide and crime rates; femicide.

Pigeons fed, I take Clea and Amaya into the plaza's cathedral to light candles for my mother, their "Giggi," who at seventy-six is suffering from arthritis so painful that she has to use a walker for the first time. We each take a candle to the Virgin of Guadalupe shrine. There, a young woman with long, straight black hair cries softly before the virgin, and her pain could be many things, but I'm thinking again of femicide and of Grace.

Amaya and Clea abandon me at Guadalupe, heading out to another of the cavernous cathedral's candle-ringed shrines. I look away from the crying woman and see Clea imitating her big sister, who places her candle at the chiseled feet of a medieval saint. Though I'm a lapsed Catholic, this ancient space feels peaceful, embracing. Clea and Amaya sit in the pews on either side of me, their bodies hugged into mine.

Feeling Amaya's warmth, I recall the first time I hugged her, in a hospital not far from here, surrounded by palm trees whipping furiously in a *sur* that had blown up from Antarctica. One of the four doctors attending my daughter's birth handed the newborn to her mom, who then passed her to me. I felt the purest love stir inside.

But I wasn't to dally. In Bolivia the baby belongs not only to Mommy and Daddy but to a web of extended family. From the beginning, Amaya's mother and I had decided that we weren't meant to marry, nor would we try to create a "traditional" family, but what might look like a "broken home" from a Western viewpoint would turn out to be just the opposite in practice. I passed Amaya to her maternal grandmother, who passed her to her Bolivian grandpa. Then she was passed to Tio Eduardo, Tia Alison, and Tia Alejandra. Each person kissed her forehead. She was part of *la familia*. We then ate quail eggs and drank Champagne, pouring the first few drops onto the floor as a gift to Pachamama.

My own parents became "Mama Anna" and "Pop Bill" and got to know her on their many visits to Bolivia. And I can't count the number of her Bolivian relatives and the abundant neighbors and friends who loved her as much as any relative. "*Donde esta nuestra Amaya?*" — Where's our Amaya? — the neighbors would say when Amaya was a year old. Someone would pass her over the little fence and she'd disappear into their house for hours. I'd hear my daughter squealing with laughter.

Santa Cruz felt safe then. But now, in this church, Amaya under my arm, I wonder if all the "safe" places are gone.

I get up and genuflect on the way out; the girls imitate the gesture.

The next morning, while Melissa runs an errand, a pillow fight erupts in the Milan. I'm not sure how it starts, but for over an hour I repeatedly whack *mis hijitas* in the face with padded missiles, toting up fourteen direct hits to Amaya's zero, and she is laughing more hysterically than I've seen her in months. Each time she fails to defend herself. I thrice proclaim the pillow fight over — that it's time to go take Amaya home — but our trio continues to whack, wrestle, yell "sneak attack!" and deliver *triple* pillow barrages until I finally, in tears of hard laughter, announce the conclusive end.

Amaya fills her backpack with her school uniform and books, her nightgown and toiletries, and we taxi toward her home off Santa Cruz's seventh ring between Grigota and Piray, her street just paved last year and surrounded by dirt roads on all sides. Amaya lives in a part of the city just beyond the Dream, a simple one-story house, old with memories, featuring a kitchen, three bedrooms, and outdoor courtyard surrounded by acerola, mango, carambola, and other tropical fruit trees. Adding to the life of the house are six cats and two dogs, Candy and Brownie, both poodle blends.

"You seem tired," I say to Amaya, who's limp in my arms, her eyes half-closed. Clea's already crashed in my lap. "Must have been too much pillow fighting."

"Daddy," she says through her exhaustion, "you can *never* have too much pillow fighting."

She nuzzles into me. *You can* never *have too much pillow fighting.* We're on Avenida Beni between the fourth and fifth rings, racing Amaya homeward, past new fifteen-story apartment buildings and jugglers and begging "pavement Indians," the lost Guaraní and Chiquitanos wrested from their lands by soy and timber companies. Beauty-pain shot through everything, my daughters snuggle into what I hope they feel is safety.

BACK IN SURAQUETA, the "march against drugs and crime" is tense and divided between two dissimilar groups. On the one hand, among the hundred-plus folks marching to the plaza are advocates, both Bolivian and expatriate, demanding policies to halt violence against women. On the other hand, and leading the march, is the town's old guard, calling for order, including eliminating the *dis*order of loose women drinking in local bars, calling for all establishments within a hundred meters of the plaza to be shut down. Those from the latter group make most of the speeches, which center around the breakdown of traditional values leading to crimes like this rape. The cause of this breakdown is identified: *los jipis,* a term now used to refer to all the foreigners in town. Pieter and Marga. Ludwig and Anna. Bill and Melissa?

Afterward, astonishingly, one of the accused rapists reappears in town. We'd thought they were being kept behind bars until the trial, but word has it that someone paid off a judge for a temporary furlough. The general sense of fear in town thickens. *Los jipis* might be perilous, but no one wants these *maliantes* walking around either.

To work off tension, I go for a hike alone in the countryside, aware that being male allows me the freedom to do this without fear. As I ruminate along a creek bed, I stumble upon something unexpected.

Rusty metal drums. A parched cloth that appears to have been soaking.

Putting the pieces together, I do a 180 and walk away as calmly but as fast as possible. It's abandoned and small-scale, but it's a cocaine lab: the metal drums are used to soak the coca leaves; the cloth is used to filter the cocaine base. What might have gone down if I'd meandered into an operation in progress? Some friends of ours in Cochabamba, an American family, just announced they're considering moving back to the United States. "Bolivia could become a narco-republic," the husband told me. Certainly, Bolivian president Evo Morales's policies haven't made Americans feel welcome, which is understandable considering that America's 1980s and 1990s "war on drugs" in Bolivia turned out to be a war on Bolivia's poor. The DEA eradicated vast acreages of small-holder coca plants, much of it for a legal local coca-chewing market, bringing violence and upheaval to thousands of indigenous and migrant Bolivians. These people are now Morales supporters.

The following Sunday, Melissa, Clea, and I are with some Swiss friends, Jürgen and Anja, discussing these same cheery topics: the rape case and the abandoned cocaine factory I stumbled upon.

"I wouldn't invest too much here," Jürgen says. The fifty-something Swiss has lived in Suraqueta for three decades. "Thirty, forty thousand dollars? Fine, but no more. If they decide to expropriate everything foreigner-owned, I don't care, person-ally. I'm light and can always move to Chile." Anja adds: "The *campesinos* were right here, at that door, several years back, yell-ing for the gringos to come out and face justice." She pauses, then says, as if she still can't comprehend it: "They meant *us*."

Her normally cheery countenance darkens. "We hid," she whispers. "The mob had come up from the roadblocks on the highway."

I glance over at Melissa, our cloaked child in her lap. Anja continues, "That's when our son decided '*Das reicht!*' (That's enough.) He left Bolivia, took his family to safety back in Europe."

"But you stayed," Melissa says, frowning.

Anja shrugs, her face one of astonished resignation. "We'd been here twenty years at that time! We were used to it. But for our kids?"

The conversation stops. A clumsy hush falls over the room as Anja notices... *our* kid.

In the awkward pause, I reflect: We're not even expats any-more. We're immigrant landowners who have discharged all of our savings and more, via a loan, into a house to build a life in a place where we are now unwelcome.

I'M IN THE HAMMOCK one cloudy afternoon after lunch when Melissa approaches and asks: "Can we talk?"

Trepidation. Not her usual conversational preface. I nod.

"Umm..." she says, looking not at me but at our banana trees. "The UN wants me back."

My tongue goes inert. Melissa continues: "My old boss needs me... in New York." She adds: "Just for three or four months."

A long pause. "When?"

"In a month."

"But what about *this*?" I say, getting up from the hammock, my arm sweeping out to encompass the land and community into which we're supposed to be Sweetly weaving.

"It's not like I'd be going back for good."

"'Consultancies' have a way of extending into jobs. And, anyway, you'd go alone? With Clea? I've got students coming down."

We talk. And then talk more. Melissa is not particularly keen to return to the go-go Manhattan we've left, or keen to extract Clea from *wawa* and *luna*, from Boots and Adobe, only to plunk her down in concrete-jungle day care. However, with cocaine labs, a questionable rule of law that may turn against our investments, and rapists at large, it's obvious why the offer attracts Melissa. Plus, it's been two years since she left the UN; this could be stimulating for her, and the income would defray our debt.

In Santa Cruz, during our recent stay at the Hotel Milan, I had watched a *CNN en Español* report about the tens of thousands of South and Central Americans trying to get into the United States illegally, on the trail of the Dream. The same factors drawing Melissa north draw them, too: a promise of higher income and of escape from rising urban crime and dodgy rule of law. But where they imperil their lives for weeks crossing first into Nicaragua, then Honduras, then Guatemala, and finally Mexico on "death trains" interspersed with treacherous nighttime crossings on foot, Melissa can jet over those borders in seven hours. I squirm at the paradox.

IT'S A FOGGY EVENING, and Melissa, Clea, and I are at La Cocina, chatting with the owner, our Turkish neighbor Serdar. In between bites of falafel, my wife and I discuss the first of the two topics we've been studiously avoiding. Topic Number One: whether she should go back to the United States to work. Topic Number Two: rumors that the Suraqueta old guard are scheming to use the rape-case fallout to purge the town of *jipis*. Related gossip has it that a group of "hippie foreigners" has raped a Suraqueteña girl, but no evidence exists specifying either the victim or the perpetrators.

As for Topic Number One, we both feel the job opportunity is too soon and too jarring, and we worry about the impact on Clea: eleven hours a day. That's how long Clea would be in child care in New York, factoring in Melissa's commute. In Suraqueta, we work from home, and a babysitter watches Clea in our house — she plays in our garden and woods, sometimes goes down to the plaza for a spin, and sees us intermittently during the workday.

Then I notice silence overtaking the normally bustling La Cocina. I look up. Serdar opens his eyes wide, in warning, and directs an eyebrow toward the street.

I see police. They're herding Thiago and other expatriate friends toward the police station.

Within moments I realize the rumors of foreigner-purging are no longer rumors. The sting is on.

Clea starts to say something loudly in English and I cover her mouth to muzzle that unwelcome language. I pull her face into my chest to hide her light skin tone from the police.

Melissa leans into her food, also overcome by a camouflage instinct. *We're legal, right?* I can't help wondering. I try to remember if we have our papers on us. My mind swirls. As soon as the immigration agents pass, we'll leave our food uneaten and escape through the back door of the restaurant, taking unlit backroads up to our land.

Two additional police disappear into the neighboring Tierra Libre restaurant, in search of foreigners. My heart races.

I'm about to lead Melissa back toward the kitchen when a pair of eyes lock onto mine. A man in plainclothes steps toward us.

Ten

Bone cold. Severe fluorescent light. The odor of dozens of fearful immigrant bodies in a small detention room.

A clench of indignation: *I'm not free to leave.*

The mobile police squad, brought in from Santa Cruz by the *jipi*-averse old guard, works with purpose, the officers seemingly immune to the frigidity, the hard light, the stench. The unit has a pair of laptops, and they're now electronically fingerprinting our Polish friend Rudo, checking his residency card against a computer screen.

Melissa, in frosty silence beside me — a sleeping Clea huddled into her for warmth — seems to share my feelings. My agitated mind goes to Hans, the baker in Paredones, who lived in the eco-community up the river from Hilvert and Karina. One day, Hans vanished. Deported. "Problem with his residency status," people said. No more delicious five-grain loaves in our kitchen. The noncitizen was boarded onto a Frankfurt-bound airplane.

"We should talk to our lawyer," I say to Melissa.

She frowns. "What lawyer?"

Right. No lawyer. And we don't have Clea's papers with us. How flimsy a pretext do they need to extradite someone, as they did with Hans? In America, I felt ire whenever I heard reports of how appallingly Mexicans and Salvadorians are treated in US holding centers: detained for excessive amounts of time, denied legal assistance, deported. I didn't think I'd get a taste of it in Bolivia, given our relative privilege. And even now we are still in a more powerful position than most undocumented Latin Americans in the United States, who often lack cash, connections, and

English, but I am suddenly aware how sweet the taken-for-granted jewel of citizenship is, the inherent right to be in a place.

I remember Romina, who did our land-transfer paperwork a couple years back.

"I'd like to call my lawyer," I say to one of the officers, showing him my cell phone. He shrugs.

Romina answers. She's not a lawyer, but her husband, Antonio, is a Santa Cruz policeman, and the couple have a weekend cabaña in Suraqueta. Thankfully, that's where they are now. Romina says she's appalled and will send Antonio down to the station immediately.

Meanwhile, more bodies are packed in. No more seats, so the new roundups stand in the corners. Salvador is here now, too, with three or four Argentinians he and Salome are hosting at their house this weekend.

Waiting. I'm concerned about giving our fingerprints. It seems they are using a manufactured *jipi*-rape rumor for this roundup, so what's to stop a mistaken or contrived link between one of our fingerprints and that alleged crime? In my NYU Bolivia course, I teach that, according to Transparency International, Bolivia has one of Latin America's more compromised judicial systems, but I never expected to face this so directly.

Then a strange phrase comes suddenly to mind: *I walked backward into America.*

Years ago, when I lived in a twelve-by-twelve off-grid cabin in North Carolina (which I describe in my book *Twelve by Twelve*), I had a soft-spoken Mexican neighbor, José, who told me one day:

My cousin convinced me that we could make money in America. We traveled north from Guerrero. We crossed the border at night, through the mountains, the desert. We spent three days in the desert. At one point "Immigration" had raked the desert sands to a smooth surface. Perfectly flat and smooth. Why? So they could count how many wetbacks had come in that night! So do you know what I did? I walked backward into America to make it look like I was returning to Mexico!

Have Melissa and I followed José's south-pointing footprints *out* of America and into this holding pen? Clea suddenly wakes up, blinks into the severe fluorescence, and bawls. Melissa tries to comfort her, but Clea sobs on. Romina's husband, Antonio, arrives. He greets us briskly, then approaches one of the officers, whom he obviously knows. A hushed conversation.

He comes back to Melissa and me. "*Es abusivo*" — This is abusive — Antonio says, but there's nothing he can do. We should give our fingerprints and "*esperamos*." That Spanish word fits the situation perfectly, meaning either "to wait" or "to hope." Or both.

COLLAPSE. That's the book I've been reading, its apocalyptic title reflecting my family's mood. The author, geographer Jared Diamond, examines past human civilizations and small colonies alike, evaluating the factors that led them either to fail or to succeed.

It's the day after our detention. Immigration eventually questioned, fingerprinted, and released us. On the walk home, Melissa, more New York–resolute than ever, vented: "If they don't want us here, *fine*." Today, still badly hungover from the experience, I am on our hillock reading *Collapse*, feeling oddly akin to the Newfoundland Viking families Diamond describes. Like them, Melissa and I have brought Clea to what each day appears an increasingly inhospitable place. To wit: A handful of premodern Norwegian "Norse" Vikings made it all the way to Newfoundland, but they survived a mere decade under Native North American antagonism before abandoning the colony. In contrast, according to Diamond, other Viking settlements succeeded. Their Greenland colony lasted an impressive four centuries before environmental degradation and Inuit invasion rubbed it out. And a third Norse colony, that of Viking Iceland, flourished exquisitely; a millennium later, their direct descendants govern one of the highest per capita GDP countries in the world. But my imagination leaps over Diamond's statistics and alights on specific people. Viking people. Redheads like myself, with their Norse brides, cutting the umbilical cord to their home in Scandinavia and heading to locales thousands of miles away with their seven-suitcase equivalent: livestock and a few practical and sentimental belongings.

I gaze up from *Collapse* and look over our south fence toward the new Soto Pollerudo adobe homesteads, toward the Paraguayans and the French-Bolivians. It strikes me now how much like Vikings our Paraguayan neighbors appear, with Balu's wild long hair and a pregnant belly, and bearded Jaime's earlobe plugs and seafarer's gaze.

I wish I was feeling Greenlandic or Icelandic Norse today, but I'm in a Newfoundland state of mind: collapsed. None of the three groups of Vikings knew which destiny they faced as they staked claims. Like us, either they learned to assimilate to difficult geographies or they failed.

I WATCH FROM OUR TOWER WINDOW as white-stockinged Boots stalks something by a rock pile below, then gives up and slinks down our dirt lane with Adobe in russet pursuit. Canines and felines thrive when wild. Daily, the pair roams our full acreage and beyond. Now, they stop at the creek, both taking sips. We don't put out water bowls for our pets, saving effort and getting them — fauna — to the creek, into natural range. Watching them quench their thirst, then vanish through the barbed-wire fence, I think back to Greenwich Village, to our micro-apartment. A few buildings down, at the corner of Cornelia and Bleecker, lived a neighbor who retailed "dog therapy."

The man, a busy Midtown veterinarian, taking what I then saw as an unscrupulous cue from Mark Twain's Tom Sawyer — who convinced others to pay for the privilege of whitewashing a fence — had actually convinced folks, not just to walk his dog for him, but to *pay* him to walk his dog for "a dollar a minute," so the sign read in a little kiosk outside his building. "Credit cards accepted." The vet did not lack takers. I'd spot them touching their plastic to his smartphone. Other days I'd see harried Manhattanites in the Washington Square Park dog run, with the vet's therapy pooch, a distinctive-looking, long-necked borzoi named Rhett. One particular Friday, while heading back to our flat from my NYU classroom, I spotted Rhett in the dog run with a brunette, late-thirties businesswoman, still in office garb.

She unhooked Rhett's leash. I expected the dog to bound into the chaos of the other dogs, but he remained with the woman at the center of the swirl. Fifty dogs in motion and therapist Rhett nuzzled the woman. She bent down, her cheek brushing Rhett's.

Something glistened. Fell to the ground. The woman was crying.

In an interspecies take on Freud's "talking cure," she whispered feverishly to Rhett, whose nut-brown fur soaked up more tears. The sun slid behind the apartment buildings stacked to Washington Square's west, staining the arch crimson, and still the beast absorbed her ache. My veterinarian neighbor's dog rental was evidently no scam, this eco-therapy as valuable as a psychiatrist's couch. Nevertheless, my annoyance bled through the touching moment. In what corral did this woman live? What profane polis, this, where both owners and dogs are caged all day in offices and apartments, only to emerge — not into the Sweet Life of our larger body, Pachamama — but into another pen? Then I realized, at the time: *I'm penned here, too.*

In Bolivia, I'm no longer penned that way. I'm surrounded by raspberry trees (yes, there is a tree version — not just bushes), now two meters high, and by *pacay* and *níspero*, and beyond our orchard, by the pines and Amboró's cloud forests. A slate sky today, and what feels like an extra layer of silence placed on top of the usual silence, a misty morning on the porch of a round house my wife and I designed, built with father-and-son carpenters out of adobes from our own soil, sunbaked in their place. But are we penned in other ways, even here? Not just by the holding pen at the station, but by walls of xenophobia, femicide, and narco-crime, and the colonist's self-loathing. A door opens north, Melissa holding the coveted key.

Collapse.

Two millennia of ruins speckle Suraqueta: Chiriguano and Chané, Inca and Spanish. Aside from the clay roofs and arcades of the four-hundred-year colonial pueblo — the inhabited skeleton of a defeated Spanish crown — the most conspicuous ruins are Inca, principally the UNESCO World Heritage site above the town. El Fuerte is, at 220 meters across, the largest-surviving carved rock in the Incan empire, as well as that empire's easternmost fortress. When the Spanish invaded in the 1600s, El Fuerte's Quechua-speaking (Inca) descendants either fled or melded into Suraqueta's hybrid *valluno* culture, leaving behind not just El Fuerte but stone agricultural terracing and Inca roads that still weave through town. Upon those thousands of miles now lies the contemporary road to Cochabamba and La Paz, then on to Cusco and Machu Picchu in Peru. I stumble upon pre-Inca remnants, like the millennia-old, barely excavated ancient ovens a twenty-minute walk above Suraqueta in the barren Campeche hills. Even our own land entombs mysteries; while machete-ing *quiñe* shrubs one day below our hillock, I discover the foundation of what suggests a mysterious wall. Melissa thinks it's part of a Spanish fortification, since a battle is said to have been waged between Spanish royalists and Bolivarian separatists right on our hillock in 1819. But might it be Incan?

Recent ruins, too. Sitting a twenty-minute walk uphill from our land is the remains of what could almost be a Hugh Hefner mansion. The three-story faux-adobe palace is abandoned, its swimming pool and artificial ponds caving in. Cows manure the floors. I ask around, but nobody knows the conclusive story behind what's called "*la casa de* James Bond," or more simply "James Bond." Beyond James Bond rises the adobe vestige of a far humbler house. On a walk one afternoon, I ask a local farmer who used to live there. "*El Ateo*" — the Atheist — he replies, adding, in a chiding, reap-as-ye-sow tone, that *El Ateo* spurned the pueblo and God, thus "of course dying childless, alone, and destitute."

To the west of town is another house carcass: that of the half-finished-then-abandoned home of a Canadian Jehovah's Witness named Jesse. I knew Jesse peripherally ten years back while I was on a writing fellowship at Suraqueta's now-defunct Casa del Artista. Jesse was even more Viking-chic than the Paraguayans: tall, with freckles and red hair — so red it was orange — and a long glowing auburn beard. I remember spotting Jesse in the La Chakana café on the plaza in a shockingly yellow polo shirt, hunched over a laptop, placing Facebook ads for something as he talked, loudly, on his cellphone in a Canadian accent. "*My workers…*" he said several times, emphasizing proprietorship as he sputtered about Bolivian ineptitude. Jesse lasted only a couple years in Suraqueta, having met, per one teller, "a beautiful Bolivian girl, much younger than himself, and not a Witness." He abandoned the house, decamping with his striking fiancée "to Argentina or Chile or…" The teller gestured vaguely to points beyond.

Jesse is gone but Witnesses remain. On a long afternoon walk — Melissa and I know it may be our last together, since she flies to New York in four days — we pass a group of thirty missionaries fanning out in pairs to distribute Spanish-language *Watchtower* magazines. A man in Sunday starch thrusts a copy at Melissa and invites us to "come talk about the Bible" at a weekly gathering. Flight patterns. I'm starting to recognize them. Like the perennial Southern Hemisphere summer migration of thousands of Israeli backpackers through Suraqueta — our town a point on their worn path between Rio's carnival and Machu Picchu — so these Witness flocks alight in Suraqueta each year, leaving behind a few who, between migrations, occasionally flutter around the plaza and trill to passersby, secure in their *Watchtower* nests.

Melissa and I walk past long-gone Jesse's ruin. I think of telling her Jesse's story, but don't. Why deepen the departure theme? It's bad enough that she and Clea are leaving.

We're silent. I'm hurting. We follow a dirt road through a compound of incongruity: four white and airy modern homes, each belonging to a different family of Danish Jehovah's Witnesses. Floor-to-ceiling glass walls and balconies face paradise. They possess a turquoise swimming pool and a private water supply in this parched fringe of town still unconnected to public water lines. During their short annual migration from Denmark, I'll spot them on dirt bikes and in cars. It's said they plan to retire here, turning the town's drier western flank into a "*burbuja de Testigos*" — a Witness bubble. In the meantime, gardeners keep the properties green in their long absences, and their bleached homes stand like future ruins.

We loop around toward Campeche, still in silence. I hold

Melissa's hand, then can't stand the tenderness and let her hand fall. I try to recall what drew us here: *suma qamaña. Vivir bien.* I remember a dimension of the Amerindian idea of the Sweet Life: Greater diversity in the life system means greater strength, and we should therefore prize the complementarity of diversity among people. How far we are from that vision! Today I'm feeling sour as the mouse in Franz Kafka's story "A Little Fable." Kafka's mouse navigates a maze toward a goal — *the Sweet Life?* — but the maze gets increasingly convoluted. The mouse finally comes to the end: a solid wall, through which there is no advance. "Why don't you turn around and go back?" asks a wide-eyed cat, who then eats the mouse up.

"Hey," Melissa says. "Isn't that Klaus's former house?"

I nod. I don't want to talk about it. Or even think about it.

"Grisly, what happened to him," she continues.

Now I *am* thinking about it. Another inconvenient bit of history I'd rather block out, maybe because it challenges what I want Suraqueta to be.

Ten years back. The knock at the door of Casa del Artista. Still in my PJs, I open the door to see four uniformed Bolivian police officers. There's been a murder next door. Did I see anything?

No, I didn't see the murder of my neighbor Klaus, an elderly, German gay man, short of stature, blue-eyed, and pleasant. For half of each year, he taught English in Oxford, England; the other half he spent in Suraqueta. Klaus and I sporadically chatted in front of his cottage. As it turned out, he liked not just men but very young ones, and he unfortunately became romantically entwined with a Bolivian teenager visiting Suraqueta from Cochabamba. Unbeknownst to Klaus, the teen ran with the wrong crowd in Cochabamba, and with an accomplice, he knifed poor Klaus to death in his home (while I slept twenty meters away), then stole Klaus's money and jeep and dumped the British man's body in the local landfill. There it was found, half-burned, in an apparent attempt to hide the evidence.

The killers were apprehended and jailed up the road in Vallegrande — the same porous prison where Grace's rapists are now imprisoned (or rather, *back* in prison after that brief, well-noted furlough out from behind bars). Then the killers "escaped" — that is, somebody paid to have them covertly released — and the youths were never seen again. Afterward, a small stream of spooked foreigners abandoned Suraqueta.

"COME BACK!" shouts Melissa into her cell phone. I'm still in Santa Cruz's Viru Viru International Airport. "They're not letting us through Immigration!"

I've rarely heard my wife so perturbed. What a shift from fifteen minutes back: our good-byes, the gloom of two plane tickets instead of three, little Clea crying for her "Papa Bear" as she passed through security.

I rush back to the airline desk. I tell the agent that Immigration won't accept our notarized letter giving my permission for Melissa to travel alone with Clea. We thought it would satisfy this legal requirement, intended to prevent child-snatching, which is sometimes committed by a parent. But Immigration is saying the notarization won't do. Our letter has to be signed by a specific Santa Cruz judge. That's impossible at this point. The flight is about to board.

"Maybe you can go through and give your verbal permission," the airline's agent says. I get back on the phone with Melissa. Nope.

The Bolivian agent attending to me, perhaps a parent herself, flashes me an empathetic look. "Give me a credit card," she says, selling me a ticket on the same flight. "Pretend you're traveling with them, then don't board. I'll refund your ticket."

I agree and race to a distressed Melissa. We all go through security, the flight already boarding. Rushed hugs and they board without me.

The jet rolls back, taxis, and glides skyward. I'm empty.

In a dull haze I retrace my steps with another airline representative, thinking of José's words: *I walked backward into America.*

I walk back into Bolivia. The Immigration hall, bustling just a while ago, is now empty. An official frowns. "Why didn't you board?"

I've been coached by the airline agent to feign ignorance of Spanish. Not hard. I have no words, anyway.

The official eyes me hard, a feline gaze, predatorial. Like Kafka's cat: "*Why don't you turn around and go back?*"

"He has an unexpected engagement in Bolivia," the agent says. All too true. The official maintains the stare, suspecting deception, certainly, and weighing whether to detain me or not.

Then nothing happens. He stamps my passport and hands it back. The stamp, which annuls my exit, reads: "Did not board." As I walk away, all I can think about is why the hell I didn't.

III. BRANCHES
A Unified Vision

Eleven

Alone, a too-bright morning sky. Melissa and Clea eight days gone. Suraqueta is in a drought. *Dry*: More than the weather, it's become my dominant feeling since our separation.

Tomorrow is June 1, 2015, winter's onset in the Southern Hemisphere. I flip the seasons; June is December. The intermittent airstream from Antarctica — the *sur* in shorthand — howls more frequently in packets of a few days as the sun backbends into an ever-more-northerly arc, shortening the days. Sunset occurs at six o'clock now instead of high-summer's seven. I water our parched gardens and orchard, feeling unease. Any *sur* could drop a hoarfrost and kill what we've planted.

On our thirsty hillock, I drink yerba máte through a metal straw, a local habit, Argentinian-influenced, that I've adopted. My máte is the only liquid around since our creek dried up, too. A crow lands on the eucalyptus tree below me, soon joined by its partner. Then I eye the "crows" more carefully — black feathers and the same *caaww* call, but with quetzal-like long necks and flaring yellow tails and wing tips. I wonder if a single day has passed on our land without our spotting a new type of bird. Below this avian array, which has adapted to Adobe and Boots, emerald iguanas stealth-walk among the *tula* trees, and ferrets and marmots rip a brush path that smooth-haired guinea pigs follow. One day, a *tejon* badger chews through a temporary electric wire, cutting power to our house.

In the afternoon, I walk into town to meet a newborn. Six days ago, our thirty-something British-Uruguayan couple friends, Roh and Gabriel, welcomed their son, Jack, in a home birth. I arrive with gifts: Clea's outgrown set of reusable diapers, two containers of homemade soup, and lettuce and chard from our garden. Gabriel's mom, visiting from Uruguay for the months around the birth, directs me through their small, centuries-old adobe row house to a tiny, freshly painted bedroom. Cuddled in Roh's arms is an angelically sleepy sprout. The mother and moist infant seem an oasis in the drought. I feel a gut-cramp, a bodily missing of Clea and Melissa. I kiss Jack, present the gifts. "Before he was born," Roh says, "I was afraid that I'd have no maternal instincts. That I'd be a bad mom." An astonished smile illuminates her face. "But, instinct! I stare at him all day." Life. It's here in this adobe room, where her blue-eyed, Bolivian-citizen son slid into a midwife's hands.

THREE RAINLESS DAYS LATER, I'm in the market buying papaya and cacao from our *casera* Serafina, when our Brazilian acupuncturist friend, Ivete, approaches. "Hear about the EU police bust?" she asks in Portuguese-accented Spanish.

I pay Serafina, who gives me change off a coin magnet from the depths of her apron pocket. "Where?" I ask, only lightly interested.

"Here."

Now I'm very interested. She tells me an Interpol antinarcotics squad stole into Suraqueta, predawn, and captured an Austrian citizen who has been hiding out. A most-wanted drug trafficker. He's been whisked off to Santa Cruz for extradition to Austria, Ivete adds, to serve a possible thirty-year sentence.

"Did you ever meet him?" she asks. "His alias was Stephan."

I consider this. No, I never met an Austrian cocaine smuggler absconded under an alias. The only Stephan I know here is somebody else: the cheery, forty-year-old Stephan, by chance also Austrian. A loose acquaintance I first met around a friendly bonfire last year, Stephan is a clean-cut plumber in early retirement who bought a house in Suraqueta. Stephan deejays with Candida, the daughter of our friends Silvia and Carlos, and he once talked about participating in Transition.

An eerie sensation envelops me. Ivete's eyes swell as she sees me connect unhappy dots.

As the day passes, I can't quite digest this. How could this ordinary guy be a crook en route to a European jail?

The arrest of "Stephan" forces me to surface additional facts that I omit from my selectively rosy vision of Bolivia. Or rather Oblivia, as some have dubbed this obscure nation, the mysterious and mountainous "Tibet of South America" that has long been a refuge for the world's banditti. "Stephan" joins an unpalatable lineage stretching from Butch Cassidy and the Sundance Kid's 1908 shoot-out to Third Reich war criminal Klaus Barbie, a.k.a. the Butcher of Lyon, who lived for decades under the alias Klaus Altmann until his 1983 capture by a Nazi hunter. Then there's the recent, more-nuanced case of the fifty-year-old Brooklyn businessman Jacob Ostreicher, who not that long ago was front-page news in Bolivia because of the arrival in La Paz of his ally, the actor Sean Penn.

Ostreicher had been locked up for two years without trial. He'd come to Bolivia in the mid-2000s, managing land holdings in the Amazon for a Swiss company producing soy and other grain commodities. A whiff of intrigue and infamy surrounded him, with his alleged relationships with Argentinian beauty queens and Latin American mafia-style bosses. Envious of the American's apparent wealth, a network of some twenty Bolivian officials allegedly looped him into an extortion racket, which required that Ostreicher pay kickbacks to continue operating. Then the payoff-pyramid toppled. Ostreicher and the twenty officials were arrested, and millions of dollars' worth of the New Yorker's assets were seized.

Enter Sean Penn. Ostreicher, like Penn, is Jewish, and Penn

teamed up with a Jewish advocacy group in an international campaign to free the businessman, claiming false charges. Penn met with Evo Morales, but the president refused to release Ostreicher. Penn then threatened to launch a global exposé of Bolivia's prisoner-rights record, riling Morales. But Penn's visit apparently helped; Ostreicher was moved from Santa Cruz's unsavory Palmasola prison to house arrest in Santa Cruz. From there he fled Bolivia in an illegal border crossing into Chile one night, raising perennial questions both about the compromised state of human rights and the judiciary in Bolivia and about the privilege of a wealthy American like Ostreicher to enlist the likes of Sean Penn to get him out of Palmasola prison and into the convenient position of "house arrest" from which he was able to flee. Others without such connections have no choice but to languish in Palmasola prison.

Before the escape, Ostreicher was quoted as saying: "I'm afraid of spending the rest of my life in Bolivian prison." Stephan need not fear spending the rest of his life in Bolivian prison, either, and I've had another wake-up call about this odd paradise I call home, the knife's edge of living in community.

MY LAUNDERED CLOTHES HANG on the line beside our droopy banana trees. They're slicked by the happy surprise of a drizzle, the first in a week. But the sprinkle stops in minutes, and the hot sun redries them again. The strong notes from mariachi trumpets drift upward from the wedding in town below. A parched and cold northern breeze lifts my hair; Adobe gnaws at fleas. Why, I wonder for the hundredth time, have I brought my family to Suraqueta? Why not stake out our life somewhere else a little more familiar? The breeze blows in Georgia, too. The dog and cat, now warm against my thigh, exist in New Hampshire. Clothes hang on lines in California. Landscapes color lives near my sister

in Vermont, near my parents in North Carolina, near Melissa's
folks in New Mexico.

A teal butterfly with translucent wings passes above the
leaf-cutter ants, as they march off in a neat line carrying pieces of
the sole jasmine plant on our property. Our British neighbor Eva
gave us the jasmine as a housewarming gift, but with a caveat: The
scent is gorgeous, but ants routinely devour them because they're
a foreign species here. Jasmines are expats. After the housewarming, we transplanted the baby jasmine at the base of one of the
soto-wood posts supporting our veranda, placing a native-adapted
honeysuckle at the base of another post. I compare them now.
Whereas the honeysuckle spirals fragrantly up the pole, lush with
orange and white flowers, the struggling jasmine is a third its size.
"Since we'll not use pesticides," I said to Melissa, before she left,
"we have to remove that stricken jasmine. Maybe plant a second
honeysuckle?" She was silent, gazing out into clouds stacked over
the plaza, not meeting my eyes. I knew Melissa hankered for jasmine scent on her porch. But when, the following day, we walked
past Eva's house and saw her jasmine, years old but still bare, having been regularly vanquished by leaf-cutters, my wife sighed and
said: "We'll plant what works here."

Will we *work here*, I wonder? Boots meows, rubbing against
my leg, hungry, and I wonder if Bolivia will abide our continued
presence. I scan the land. Garbage bags lie on the shed roof, safe
from marauding dogs. There's been no municipal trash pickup
for weeks — the town is behind on salaries. Last week I convinced
a friend to drive his truck up here; we loaded a few weeks' worth of
trash bags from the shed roof and the final debris from our house
construction. For over a year those beam ends and barbed wire
rested there, protected by my sloth. Weeds covered the pile, eventually requiring a machete to expose the materials to be carted off.

The thriving honeysuckle reminds me of Pieter and Marga's lush organic farm, of Ludwig and Anna's flourishing Bergwald, while the ants carry away parched jasmine cuttings as if stripping away Melissa from me.

A tree holds up the world.

Chief Gaspar, a thousand miles distant in the Bolivian Amazon, told me about this tree. The tree that holds up the seven skies. I know part of what motivates me toward *vivir bien* is shame.

"Andrew Jackson killed the Indians! Andrew Jackson killed the Indians!" That's what I used to hear, in second grade, through the walls of my elementary school classroom, the teacher in the adjacent classroom leading her students in a resentful righting of history. My more traditional teacher cursed her under his breath, feeding us the approved version of President Jackson, but this interruption made me realize that no one ever told us what the indigenous name of my school — Nassakeag Elementary — meant. Nor the name of our town (Setauket) or our river (Nissequogue) or any of the hundreds of Native American words around us on Long Island, the dead words of a vanquished people.

Ten years ago, shortly after getting our bee-filled truck out of the Amazon mud, I met the very last speaker of the Guarasug'we language, someone from the small tribe neighboring Chief Gaspar's Chiquitanos. Today, Guarasug'we is another of the world's extinct languages, and every two weeks we lose another indigenous language to cookie-cutter globalization, to the Dream. All along, I have hoped that the Sweet Life — which grows out of Amazonian and Andean indigenous traditions in "glocal" fusion with modernity — would be a resilient, local-adapted hybrid. Chief Gaspar's wisdom, and indigenous culture, would not be lost but rather fused with that of Kusi, Thiago, and others, putting marrow into the bones of, not just a single Transition Town, but

an entire contemporary nation, a "plurinational state" with official indigenous languages and a framework Law of Mother Earth.
That was the vision. But now the Sweet feels more elusive
each day.

THREE AM. Unable to sleep, I'm reading Rick Bass's 1989 memoir *Oil Notes*, which washed up in the Republika travelers' book
exchange. In it, Bass is a young petroleum geologist sniffing out
oil and gas reserves in Mississippi, Alabama, and Oklahoma. He
zealously pursues oil — unseen, a mile down in the Earth's crust,
250-million-year-old deposits of rotted ancient forests and ponds
and dinosaurs that have decomposed into "fossil" fuels. But as this
determined engineer obsessively surveys the 1980s American South,
when there was far more guesswork and instinct to finding oil than
there is today, it becomes clear that he's really searching for something else. Happiness. And Bass keeps finding happiness, not in anchor winches and diverter valves, but in things like rain thrumming
on a roof in rural Oklahoma, or two abandoned puppies he adopts,
or a catfish café in Mississippi where he one night has an epiphany,
realizing that his girlfriend will leave him someday because of her
independent spirit and out of wanderlust for Nepal and India.

Melissa and I spent a couple of years scouting for land in
Suraqueta until we found ours. We took a year to plan and build
our house, plodded through the blood tests and notarized marriage certificates and long lines and fees to win our residency. Out
of love for Bolivia, we brought our offspring here. And we've done
so to be close to Amaya, to forge eco-friendly community, to find
vivir bien, out of passion for this far-flung yet rooted life. Like
Bass, we're ultimately searching for happiness.

Melissa and I have for quite a while been skating around the
idea of another baby. But in more difficult moments — miscom-
munication, quarrels, shredding by leaf-cutters — the possibility

won't come up for months. "It could be an anchor baby," Melissa said at one point, only half-joking, but aware of the misfortunes awaiting foreigners who don't have the cover of citizenship — Ostreicher, imprisoned; Grace, embroiled in a legal case against her rapists; Klaus, murdered. A Bolivian child, I think a little morosely, would give a layer of legal protection to ourselves and our land.

THE REPORTS I GET BACK FROM MELISSA via email and Skype: All is exceedingly well. "It still feels unreal," she says one day, "to walk out the door at 7:30 AM and not see Clea for another eleven hours." Melissa's mom takes care of Clea in the morning, and a nanny covers the afternoon. Clea rides her new scooter in Prospect Park. In a photo Melissa sends, my baby bear wears a blue helmet on her head as she scoots beneath brownstones. Clea had a fever for a week, then recovered. She's speaking better English now. Watching Curious George cartoons with her cousins. "Screens are impossible to control here," Melissa says.

My wife occupies a private office on the seventeenth floor in midtown Manhattan overlooking the East River. She has a title, business cards, and an institutional email address. "Newfound freedom," she says. "With Clea in child care, I can go get a coffee whenever I want. Imagine." Over two years of no regular child care and little separation between the two has made this shift all the more powerful as Melissa experiences life as a "working mom." Last weekend: Her grad school friends visited from DC. This weekend: She's in New Hampshire with college pals, while my sister and her family scoot down from Vermont. Melissa tells me how her current three-month consultancy position is becoming a full-time post, for which she'd be a shoo-in. Everyone is asking her the same thing: Will she apply?

"What do you tell them?" I ask her, not sure I want to hear the answer.

"I tell them that…" — she pauses as she chooses words — "our life is too…good in Bolivia." In her video-streamed image, I try to see in her eyes what she may not be telling me. Sunlight, from Queens, streams over her shoulder. "And how are things in Suraqueta?" she asks. The name of our town echoes awkwardly in her office.

I parse words, too, telling her about Roh and Gabriel's new baby, the need for rain. Like her, I'm screening my feelings. I don't mention that Grace's rape case seems more tenuous than ever. I don't mention such things because I'm terrified of America's splendid gravity, and I cannot admit what I feel: That we came to Suraqueta for Transition, for the Sweet Life, not for ants eating our plantings, killer wasps, and poisonous snakes. Not for cocaine labs and a questionable rule of law that may turn against our residency and investments. Not for undercover drug-lord plumbers and death-to-Yankees sentiments. Not for killing drought.

"Hold on," Melissa says, thumbing a phone in Manhattan. She looks busy, needed, connected. Happy. I look away from the screen and out the window to the jasmine bush. Freshly stripped of its leaves and flowers by the ants, its trunk appears weaker and more exposed than ever.

Twelve

A four-in-the-morning inchoate fear: *I'm forty-four years old.*
In a dream I'm talking to someone who's twenty-four, and
I wake up shocked that I've lost something prized. But what? Two
decades are missing.

I get out of bed, look out a window over the moonlit pueblo,
as I've been doing almost every night lately as insomnia deepens. Suraqueta appears gossamer in the distance. In the daytime,
sounds, movements, and colors swell and breathe. But at 4 AM
the silence is national park–like, with maybe a hundred lights in
the dehydrated village beneath, humanity beside the point against
mountain and sky. I shiver — a touch of fever? — and climb back
into bed, burrowing into my down comforter.

A half hour later, still unable to sleep, I light a candle to read.
But my absorption in my book competes with this: *forty-four,* a
thirsty tree root, tunneling toward unfound moisture.

ONE EVENING, just after sunset, Thiago stops by. Bumpy days for
him. He tells me he was in bed Saturday and Sunday, unable to
eat, feeling depressed. "*Pero hoy día estoy mucho mejor, che*" —
But I'm much better today, man. He talks about how he knew he
had to get out of bed this morning to do urgent Transition tasks,
and that set a new tone in him. Thiago's routine has become a
coca-leaf-chewing and merlot-drinking combo in the evenings.
While this provides a euphoric energy and keeps him working
until two or three in the morning, he's then too fried to either
work or sleep and ends up awake until daybreak. I ask him about
Kusi, and he replies, "*No quiero hablar de ella ahora*" — Better not
to speak of her right now.

Within our curved, candlelit living room walls, we talk about the Transition Thursday lunches, an upcoming "inner Transition" retreat, and the success of *minga*-esque work exchanges among family plots. These efforts reflect a viable Transition intention toward resilient globalism. Yet, in a sense the initiative has plateaued, largely because of the corrupt local political context. Transition depends a lot upon links with municipal government to spark momentum for desirable goals like organic agriculture, clean energy, and "glocal" economy. But Suraqueta is still in many ways feudal. Beneath the cultural intolerance targeting both Bolivian highland immigrants and *los jipis*, we're discovering, is an autocratic power base. One key municipal official, for example, is a businessman who lives, not here, but in Santa Cruz, and he has consolidated local support — as rumor has it — through vote-rigging in some of the outlying municipal villages. He is said to control the town council through payoffs and does little but line his own and his acolytes' pockets. A citizens' political movement dovetailing with Transition is emerging to try to bring in new leadership in the upcoming elections, but many Suraquetenños see the situation as hopeless. The current political elite is deeply entrenched. Should he come up short in the next election, he could simply skew the vote again, continuing to exploit ethnicity to spread fear, treating *colla* Bolivians and *jipi* foreigners as what amounts to second-rate citizens.

Such talk further depresses Thiago, so I suggest we switch to lighter topics. I feel feverish and headachy and only want to rest, but I cook him a meal. Later, lacing up his shoes on the porch before heading down the path through the orchard into town, he says: "*Gracias*. This helped."

MY FEVER WORSENS. Muscles ache, phlegm clogs, throat stings. "It's the *chikungunya*," Maximo tells me, adjusting his olive-green *valluno*-style cowboy hat. I've come into his shop for honey.

An odd word I've never heard before — turns out it's Bantu for "to become contorted," referring to the bent-over posture of those groaning under the disease's joint pain. Maximo tells me that only one in a thousand people die from it, but that the joint pain, headaches, and fever can last up to a month. His advice: Rest and wait it out. The nagging sickness will go away on its own.

Maximo segues away from my personal case to the global context. "This is not only the driest winter in memory, but also the third in a row without a frost," my neighbor says, walking over to me with a half kilo of honey he harvested. I take note of his slight limp. "Global warming is killing us. Our entire animal and insect array is changing."

I cough. My lungs feel more heavily coated in mucus than I've ever experienced before.

"Animals are opportunistic," Maximo continues. "As Suraqueta warms, more poisonous snakes slither up from the lowlands. Many of the bees have left; that's why my honey shelves are so sparse. And we have two new species of mosquitos now, which could mean new diseases."

Maximo adds that "a week of frost would kill off all the mosquitos" and send the serpents slinking back from whence they came, but this fails to comfort me. I ask him where the *chikungunya* comes from. He says the *Aedes aegypti* mosquito, which is too tropical for mountainous Suraqueta, so maybe I was bitten on my last Santa Cruz trip. I slog home, feeling wretched, and am bedbound all day. How unnerving to have a disease with a name in an indigenous African language. That night I unwisely watch *Under a Sheltering Sky*, coughing in my bed along with John Malkovich's character as he dies of a vicious Saharan plague.

Happy memories, though, do hover like *la luna* above my sickbed. Clea. Our time together before she left, six weeks ago.

"*No hay guapurú*" — There's no *guapurú* — she told me, as

we walked past that lone fruit tree on the hillock on our way toward the wooden gate and town. She and I spent weeks stopping, daily, at that tree to feed, sitting beneath the fleshy branches and popping *guapurú* into each other's mouths. The honeyed fruit, unexportable because of its short shelf life, is indescribably delicious, unlike anything I've tasted. Then one day the tree stopped giving, but Clea continued to pause at the *guapurú* to look up, touch the tree, and note her favorite fruit's absence. The dozenth time Clea paused under the tree, pointed up, and said, "*No hay guapurú,*" I realized my daughter now knows, not only that her food comes from the earth, but that just as importantly particular foods do not always come from the earth. With little off-season produce available in town, she eats of Pachamama and begins to understand her cycles.

In the evenings, especially, and sometimes during my four-in-the-morning restlessness, Clea surfaces. How she plays with Adobe and Boots under the single light on our porch at night, occasionally opening the door to come in, half crying and complaining that Adobe's been too rough. Melissa goes out and mildly disciplines Adobe, then comes back in, leaving our daughter outside to further nocturnally bond with the animals.

And there's another evening routine we've oft enacted, where I'm in the hammock and Clea switches off the porch light.

Darkness. Silence. We listen.

Crooak, calls a frog from the little pond behind our banana trees. "*Frogs!*" Clea always exclaims in a loud whisper, running full-speed over to the hammock, clambering onto my body, and wiggling her chest into mine for protection. Then we listen together. The frog's patterned call stops intermittently, and when it does, she breaks our embrace. "No more frogs," she says, matter-of-fact while doing the Bolivian *no hay* (no more is available) gesture, a rapid side-to-side hand motion. Then she climbs down, switches on the light again, and turns it off to repeat the routine. I don't remember exactly when she invented this game, but it's play born of life on the land: Allow darkness, listen for perilous wilderness calls, run to Papa Bear.

ONE DAY, A NEIGHBOR, the slight, thirty-something Rafaela, approaches me at our gate. I'm soaking up the sun, hoping the vitamin D might help my fever. "Don Bill," she says, "could you sell me a tiny piece of your land?"

"We're not…planning to sell our land."

"Yes, but we need just a tiniest corner anywhere, to build a house."

I feel awkward. Rafaela is the *cuidante* — live-in caretaker — for the large white house of the near-always-absent Katie, a wealthy woman from Santa Cruz whom I've never met. I've known Rafaela superficially for years, since my stays in Suraqueta in the past. I know Rafaela's two adolescent daughters — from a hundred *holas* whilst passing them walking on the road to town — and her partner, Porfirio. Friendly and a little timid, Rafaela hasn't been able to afford the kind of small lot she's talking about, one on which, if she follows local custom, she'd pop up the simplest of cinder-block rooms at first and then add space as money comes in. I dodge the subject.

In two days, however, we cross paths on the parched dirt road down to the pueblo and she asks again. I tell her we're not planning to divide the land; we bought all this degraded pastureland to reforest it, giving a gift to the village of more green space, watershed, and "bird habitat."

"*Y mi habitat?*" — And my habitat? — Rafaela says.

I feel a sudden upswell of heat, the *chikungunya* causing my bones to ache. "We're a very tranquil family," she adds.

We're right on the edge of my land, along the pine- and eucalyptus-lined north exposure. In this conversation the land feels particularly massive. Outsized. Easily shared. *Suma qamaña*: Living well…*together*.

Yet, serene as her clan may be, once a deed is transferred, the owner can build however many floors they wish, play music at whatever decibel, and sell it off to whoever they please. And it's one more human footprint in natural habitat that supports marmots, parrots, Clea's killer frogs, and I'm also aware, my own family's quietude.

"And Katie?" I ask, referring to her employer of many years, whose tract above is larger than our own.

Rafaela shakes her head. She doesn't say anything, but I've been in Bolivia long enough to read the implicit message. Rafaela has already asked for a sliver of land and been denied, probably for reasons similar to ours.

That night — 4 AM and feverish — I think of something Clea said just before leaving. Melissa had been coaxing Clea to eat her food by saying: "We're lucky to have food when many in the world have much less."

Clea thought about this, then said: "One potato." Thereafter, she began referring to those with less than us as "one-potato people."

One evening she came up with a two-year-old's solution. "They can *cut* it," she said, miming cutting a single potato. Then she paused, realizing that, even sliced, it would still be one potato, until her eyes widened. "The one-potato people...they can come to *our* house! We have bananas, and *salad!*" She looked out the window at our garden's plenitude, continuing to list all the food we could share with the one-potato people.

At four-thirty, I squint into a garden too parched to feed the one-potato people, realizing that tonight is darker than usual. *Power outage*, I realize. No lights below, no moon. Pitch-black. Vulnerable.

"First, secure your borders, Billy boy!" Pieter chided, during his and Marga's first visit to our land, before we built this house.

They gifted us, from La Vispera's excess foliage, seven hundred spiny agaves and a thousand thorny "Moses beard" sprigs. While Rulas was laying our *casita*'s foundation, we planted them around our entire perimeter in a permaculturally correct "live barrier." The spiky plants have, over the ensuing two years, grown along each side of our simple, rustic barbed-wire cattle fence to make our property livestock-resistant. And people-resistant.

Have I planted a live barrier inside myself as well? I feel — 5 AM now, ill — as individualistic as ever. This is not Sweet. I am separated from my US kin, from my wife and younger daughter, and also from most people in town.

Just recently, I was lecturing to US college students in a sustainable-development module I've designed for Santa Cruz and Suraqueta. I was talking about Transition in Suraqueta and remarked that, despite the current upswell of xenophobia, many expatriates — and I was very conveniently thinking of myself, our family — have made strides toward integration into the local context. Even as I spoke, I realized this was magical thinking.

Lisa, a sophomore, raised her hand. "Do you *really* know," she asked, "what local people say about you in their homes?"

I admitted I didn't know. Couldn't know. In part because that's not where I ever am.

Lisa became more fired up: "People at the bottom of the socioeconomic ladder are *always* aware of the privilege of those on the rungs above."

The one-potato people.

People like Rafaela and Maximo.

I recall a recent conversation with Maximo, our neighbor and go-to honey *hombre*. Whenever we see each other, we stop to chat, usually about the drought or fruit trees or bee counts. Maximo's been building his own house below our property, bit by bit over the course of years. He'll teach part-time at the tiny elementary school, sell honey, and drive his little Nissan taxi six months and save up enough for an additional room. Meanwhile, our fully completed house shot up in eight months, courtesy of a bank loan. Maximo lacks credit history to access such a loan and continues to live with his two daughters — it's not clear to me where their mom is, but he's raising them alone — in a brick-floor house beside the construction site.

A couple weeks back, while downtown, I hailed the beat-up Nissan Maximo was driving. The good-looking, cowboy-hatted man braked, smiled, and extended a hand through the window for a shake. He looked like there was something he wanted to ask me, but my gringo-mind was all agenda. I asked, "What kind of roof are you going to put on your house?"

His perennially roofless house, I'd just noticed, looked like it was finally about to be capped.

His smile faded. He considered the question. "*Calamina brillante*" — Glaring tin.

A frown dug into my forehead. Did he realize ceramic *teja* tiles cost the same as tin and preserve the use of local materials? Before I could school him, Maximo continued: "I'll use *teja*, of course."

Of course. Maximo was kidding about the tin, and I felt embarrassed about my transparently self-interested agenda: Secure our view over picturesque Spanish roof tiles, instead of tacky metal.

Maximo's motor was still running. I'd stopped his taxi unnecessarily, and now I was wasting his gas. I asked him what he'd meant to ask me.

"How's your hand?" he said.

I looked at it. Wrapped in gauze. Oddly, I'd almost forgotten about the injury. I realized that what I used to see as hardship had become normal, ordinary, for the subtropics: stepping on *quiñe* thorns, diarrhea, even *chikungunya*. Several days before, while harvesting corn from our garden, I gashed my hand against the husk grain. Maximo saw me with a blood-soaked arm and drove me to the hospital, which — in this densely settled town — is just a ten-minute walk from our land.

"Four stitches," I said, aware that his thoughts, like mine, had been focused on my well-being.

My mother injured her leg, so she and my father canceled their planned stop in New York to visit Clea and Melissa. Her bursitis flared up so badly that she could hardly walk, not to mention get up three floors to Melissa's Brooklyn rental apartment. I miss my parents, and a streak of guilt creeps in that I'm not closer to them. I know they're fine and in a magnificent retirement community; I know that I see and will see them as regularly as possible. We have good phone and email conversations. But I picture Mom icing her leg four times a day, going to physical therapists, torn about her desire to go to New York to be with Clea and yet unable to do so.

A dark, fevered sky. The dried-up root of *forty-four, no longer twenty-four*. My aging mother, five thousand miles away.

Out the window I watch what Melissa and I call "the fireflies," the slow and silent ribbon of headlights, two miles distant. They are vehicles traversing *la carretera antigua* — the old highway — to Cochabamba, a city two hundred miles away. Suraqueta lies along this early road: Once Incan, it connected El Fuerte to Tiwanaku and Machu Picchu; then Spanish, linking colonial Santa Cruz to Cochabamba and La Paz. In 1956, the Bolivian government finished the new highway to Cochabamba on the other side of Amboró National Park, to the north, and our more mountainous road fell in stature. But it's still the only road connecting Santa Cruz to the country's judicial capital, Sucre.

The headlights appear, then snuff out as they wind a bend or go behind a cluster of distant eucalyptus, then blink on again like fireflies, revealing the fact that our circular adobe nest lies on a migration path. Thousands of people pass through Suraqueta each day, along the Old Road, which goes nowhere near the plaza or our home, passing instead through a rougher neighborhood hidden by a bluff, and one we rarely tread: El Surtidor. Its unembroidered name means, simply, "the gas station," and to 95 percent of wayfarers passing through, Suraqueta is gritty. The fluorescent-lit Turista restaurant and the Cerveza Real beer distributor along the roadside; a quick stop for a pee or to buy a bag of coca leaves. Our hillock, creek, and orchard; our eco-house and the quaint plaza; Bergwald and La Vispera — all of this is entirely invisible to highway passersby, to whom Suraqueta is similar to dozens of other pit stops, placed 20 kilometers (12.5 miles) apart. That's where the Spanish Crown put them; a day's journey for the army and its horses. The intercity commerce streaming through Suraqueta's Surtidor neighborhood each day remain invisible to us, as we graft our persimmon trees, socialize with friends at the market, share meals with Amaya and Clea.

But a sliver of this traffic does peek up over the bluff and enter our world. Some come for local trade from nearby towns and hamlets — mandarin juice and beer from Alto Florida, honey from Paredones, potatoes from Piedras Blancas, wine from Valle Abajo, brie from Vallegrande — and other traders arrive from Santa Cruz with bales of used clothing, soft drinks, and electronics. But the larger portion of this sliver are tourists. Suraqueta receives some sixty thousand of them annually. Cruceños, residents of Santa Cruz, flock in when there's a scorcher weekend in their tropical city, and every hotel bed in Suraqueta fills with them on the major holidays, as do the weekend cabins a hundred Cruceños own here.

Then there are the international travelers. Foreign tourists to Suraqueta, due to mudslides on the way in and the lack of upscale services, are not high-enders wielding *Fodor's* guides. A town story captures this: A well-heeled gentleman from Buenos Aires is said to have arrived in a limo in Suraqueta one day with his private guide. Dressed in a snappy shirt and fedora, he got out, took one walk around the plaza, and then quipped: "I believe this is not my place." Having spent just five minutes — old-time Suraqueteños say with a grin — he returned to Santa Cruz. No, most of the foreign tourists are either *jipis* or youngish *Lonely Planet* globe-trotters.

The former are bare-bones jugglers, musicians, and jewelers. Suraqueta is known, in artisan circles, as a place with cheap dives, pristine nature, and fellow *jipis* with whom to play *charango* (a small Andean guitar) and recount tales around a bonfire. The latter, more abundant group is typified by the late-twenties, unmarried professional couple from Europe, poking around and staying at Andorina Hostel or Bergwald, a little too cool to be visibly sporting the *Footprint Bolivia* or *Le Guide du Routard* that is surely in their backpack. Suraqueta isn't firmly on the "gringo trail" — places like Mendoza in Argentina and the Sacred Valley of the Incas in Peru receive manifold Suraqueta's numbers — and these travelers seem to want to keep up the understatement. Once they've dropped their packs, many end up extending their planned two days to a week in order to trek to condor nests, tour El Fuerte, relax in hammocks, and enjoy the village vibe; then they join the "fireflies" in one of three nightly buses along the Old Road to beautiful Sucre, ten hours away, and then perhaps to the Uyuni salt flats and the Chilean coast.

Excepting holidays, a mere 2 percent of the town at any given point is a tourist. Sometimes I'll stop to admire a sandy-haired Swede, or a cheery flock of Spaniards, their presence texturing

Suraqueta. These are lives you see but once…except for the very few travelers who stayed, like Pieter and Marga, Anna and Ludwig, those who could envision a life in Suraqueta.

"I'm never going back to Australia," says Jeff, a bearded-and-tattooed, midthirties Australian. We're at Republika, the bar he and his wife, Lisa, own. I've known him casually for a while, but this is the first time we've really talked.

Though he has appealing new Bolivian microbrews in from Cochabamba and Sucre, my *chikungunya* rejects them; it took all my energy to get myself out of bed to try to be social. I pick at a veggie burger from the neighboring La Cocina and sip a bottle of Fuerte mandarin juice from a friend's organic farm. "Lisa may go back, probably her last time, next year," he continues, in a soft-spoken manner, "before Eleanor turns two, while her ticket is still free. But that's the end."

I press the cold juice bottle on my fevered forehead for a moment. "What makes you feel you'll never go back?"

The music, Latin rock, suddenly seems loud, and Jeff turns it down. He says: "I look at how much more relaxed our life is here, compared to our friends in Australia. The rules and regulations and building codes and red tape and permissions gone. This is a free place." The bar is almost empty, just a few small clusters of expats and tourists scattered through the three large rooms and the upstairs patio deck. I recall the still-festering post-rape sentiments of some conservatives in town who are trying to shutter some of the successful foreigner establishments, especially near the plaza.

"It's been six years since I've been to Australia," Jeff continues, "and I'm happy to never go back. I mean, there are my friends, but with Facebook and everything, I'm chatting with them every day, so it's almost the same. We want Eleanor to go back and study, get a university degree in Australia. And then come back and take care of us in our old age!" He winks.

My fevered, 102-degree thoughts go to Brooklyn, where Clea is probably asleep. My family has lived in Suraqueta for almost two years; I've already been stateside for a work trip, and Melissa has all but moved back. Yet this other immigrant couple, Jeff and Lisa, along with their one-year-old (born here, a Bolivian citizen, an anchor) are already projecting *seventeen years* in the future, sure they'll be here then. They're an oblique mirror to our situation, a "first world," young family becoming Bolivian.

Jeff tells me about the first time he saw the land they now own: six forested acres, twenty minutes from town in the hamlet of Palermo, a place where they eventually want to practice permaculture and build their house, plus maybe tourist cabañas for income so they can get out of the bar business — they knew this land would be the place where they would spend the rest of their life. He and Lisa had traveled around the world for several years looking for a place to plant roots. "We had these shiny rocks in our packs. We'd leave them in the places that we really loved during our globetrotting years. And you won't believe this. We left two stones in Suraqueta: one on what's now our land, and the other on the plaza, right at this corner where we now have the bar." Jeff's eyes shine.

The door swings open, and in walk Thiago and Kusi. They're apparently still together, despite Thiago not wanting to talk about her the other night. They order beers and sit down next to me. "I'll probably take San Pedro with Karina and Hilvert on the winter solstice," Kusi says. "You want to join?" San Pedro is a hallucinogenic plant, similar to peyote, containing mescaline.

It feels strange. Two swinging singles popping into Republika, inviting me to trip with them. I'm a dad. I'm settled, with a home, a family. So why am I feeling single? "*Chikungunya*," I say. "And anyway I have a friend from New York coming for a visit."

"Bring him," Kusi says.

"Ahmet? He's a Manhattan banker. Don't think he'd be down with San Pedro."

Kusi nods. I picture her hanging with Thiago at his group house, nothing like mine. (*Ours*, I think, catching myself.) Their floors need sweeping, and a sense of transience reigns. Thiago resides with two hip itinerants — an artisan and a filmmaker — their living room an impromptu yoga studio where Thiago gives classes. Kusi asks me, "Do you have an American flag?"

I pause, then shake my head. "Why do you ask?"

"*Es el cuatro de julio, la próxima semana*" — Next week's July fourth. Kusi adds, "My niece needs to bring one to school for a project. She's learning about America."

I look out the window. The Fourth of July seems so far from this Southern Hemisphere winter, from the Bolivian flag flying just outside the bar, over the plaza, in its three colors. Green for trees, the fertile flowering of Pachamama. Gold for the wealth of the country's minerals. Red for the bloodshed in *initiation*, freeing a people and building a country. Though I am a foreigner, I feel a tug toward those colors, toward their ideal of a Sweet Life.

"Hey, maybe your friend can bring a flag down?" Kusi says. I nod.

Thiago says his bag is packed. He's off to Santa Cruz today to board a plane to Colombia for two weeks for a large, Latin America–wide gathering on permaculture and eco-villages. "Not sure when I'll be back," he says. "Maybe in a long while, if things get interesting." He smiles. So does Kusi. I feel the amiable-breakup-vibe. I know Thiago is looking to meet his permaculturally correct match; he wants nothing more than to marry, settle down, and have kids on his Suraqueta acres. But yoga and organic farming classes don't pay the bills here, and the pool of ladies — Kusi, evidently, there within — has proven inadequate for matchmaking. Thiago starts talking about the possibility of moving on from Suraqueta.

My bones ache, the *chikungunya* burning. I need to go home. But where is home? I'm unconnected to neighbors like Rafaela and Maximo, nor do I feel at home in this predominantly expat bar.

I get up to leave. Jeff is talking to another customer about Lisa's possible trip Down Under, before their daughter turns two.

"A visit home?" he asks Jeff, who's drawing a beer.

Jeff says: "No. Australia."

Thirteen

Maximo's natural-gas Nissan motor whirs as we jolt in bush-taxi manner along a ruddy dirt road. A Turkish grad school friend, Ahmet, sits beside me, has just flown in from New York and looks ecstatic as we see, far below, a tiny Suraqueta set against Amboró's forested mountains. The town vanishes as we crest the lip of an incline and plunge into Vallecito, a neighboring agricultural valley. Gone are Suraqueta's cobblestones, Republika, and La Chakana café. Gone is Casa Guapurú — the name we've given our house because it's nestled in an old *guapurú* grove and because its canopied circle of beams evokes a tree. Gone a glocal civilization of Small. We pass numinous ancient hamlets — Empinado, San Juan, Chakra — towns that never became towns, Armistead Maupin's "half-made places" with their drowsy plazas, Pachamama rendered against their unfinishedness in sandstone ridges.

In part to make amends for my unfortunate assumption about his roof, and also because I'd like to throw my neighbor business while getting to know him better, I hired Maximo to drive Ahmet and me directly from the airport to our remote camping spot. He stops suddenly. "*Momentito*," he says, getting out of the taxi and disappearing with his machete into the dry forest.

Around forty, of medium stature, and with a minor limp, Maximo's modest appearance belies an oversize presence. He re-emerges from the thicket with two long, straight poles — *chacaltilla* wood. In no time, he's strapped the poles to the roof, and we're off again. As he drives, he explains that he'll use the poles and one of his pigs for *chancho al palo* (pig on a stake) for his daughter's birthday next week.

"My first wife went alcoholic when the girls were small," Maximo says. "She disappeared, lunatic, into the city. I've raised my two daughters alone."

I look out the window, wilderness speeding by as we climb a steep, narrow road taking us toward the waterfall where we'll camp. Maximo continues: "My daughters are teenagers now, the elder one off in college in Santa Cruz, but she wishes me 'Happy Mother's Day' every year."

Ahmet, in his decent Spanish, says, "You mean Father's Day, right?"

"No," Maximo says. "*Mother's* Day. Because I was their mom, too. I'm proud of that."

He adjusts his olive-green cowboy hat and continues, "I cried every time my daughters would talk about a boyfriend. Jealousy is my greatest vice. I still cry, but I don't feel as jealous anymore." Maximo continues to talk, openhearted and tough, his an untamed lexicon: *went alcoholic, jealousy, I cried.* I wonder if my academic training and cultural conditioning keep me from the direct and fresh human communication that's so common here, and if that could be part of what separates me from Maximo, Rafaela, and many others in Suraqueta.

It's midafternoon when Maximo drops us off at a thickly forested cove thundering with a waterfall hidden from the road. Promising to be back in three days, Maximo departs. Ahmet, a confident backcountry camper, suddenly looks edgy. He lets out a whistle: "This is...raw."

Though my *chikungunya* has receded enough to camp, I'm still feeling its effects. And what about snakebite, when we're a day's hike from the nearest clinic? There's no cell coverage here. Perhaps we should have kept a vehicle with us. Ahmet, apparently deciding to shake off anxiety by moving, drops his pack and walks toward the falls. I follow. The sound swells, blotting the other senses. As I break out of the forest curtain, I spy Ahmet staring up into the waterfall amphitheater. We don't talk. Can't, in this roar. We've entered what I call the Dark Bush, both a place of genuine wilderness and a state of consciousness beyond the Dream. We strip, wade into the catchment pool, and swim. After floating on our backs, we get out and walk back wet and naked to the gear, dry off, pitch the tent, and head off on a hike.

Above the falls, the forest breaks up into clumps of drier trees, cacti, and succulents as the terrain steepens and grows rockier. At the top of the sandstone mountain, I pick up a rock and smash it, Bolivia's infinity in every direction. I wrestle up a bigger one, hurling it down the steep ground into stands of palm and mahogany, into the cries of macaws down by the river. Not a hut in sight, and the sole sign of humanity is a hardy black *vaca andina*, a cow that can live for months — alone — back here, its owner intermittently appearing from the tiny hamlet of Empinado, five kilometers away.

I grunt to lift chunks of rock and smash them, harder now.

"Powers, take it easy," Ahmet says, watching me hurl rock.

I continue busting stone, as something burns within me.

"What are you doing?" Ahmet says.

Shattering chikungunya and loneliness, I think. *Shattering doubts about my family's solidity.*

Ahmet picks up a split piece of a rock I've hurled, tells me to check it out. Orange and burned-red sediment in perfect vertical lines. Eons of deposits in the cross section. "Cool," Ahmet says, picking up a rock and launching it.

We throw stones in proxy for a conversation I can't begin. We're panting, smashing more rocks, and I lift a particularly heavy one and heave. Its pastel layers jump forth in a dozen ensuing pieces. I pick up a brick-size chunk and throw it down again, then I stomp on what's left: sand. "Ten million years to make this rock," I say, "and seconds to destroy it."

Ahmet leans over, hands on his knees. Spent. "Why did it bother going from sand to rock, just to be sand again?"

"In other words…what's the point?" I bend down and pinch sand, letting it snow onto my palm. As my stomach grumbles, hunger eclipses eternity. "Shit, I forgot the cook pot."

Most of the food we have — pasta, rice, oatmeal — requires, well, *cooking*. And I forgot a certain Iron Age implement needed to do that.

"No worries," Ahmet says, amazing me again at how he never blames others. "Don't you remember the dude Maximo talked about on the way here? *Carlos*, I think he called him. Carlos Peralta."

WE RETRACE THE DIRT ROAD we came in on. Maximo had pointed out an indent in the forest, and soon we discover it: a toolmaker-trod path to the farm of Carlos Peralta. Soon we pass banana trees, then the intercropped "sacred trio" of corn, squash, and beans, the squash suppressing weeds and the beans poling themselves on the corn stalks. Then mandarin and apple trees. And asparagus-kale-spinach-endive-achocha-beets. Grains, too, remarkably. "*Wheat?*" Ahmet says, picking a shaft and biting off some kernels. "Is this guy even grain self-sufficient?"

We ford a river and follow a footpath toward the comforting cluck of chickens and bleat of goats — and an adobe cottage, topped with carroty *teja* roof tiles.

The whole way Ahmet's been verbally flipping out about the off-grid, homestead aplomb of this libertarian-self-sufficient-holy-crap-amazingness. Now we're at a gate and there's a man — stocky, black hair, a *campesino*-style hat. His back is to us.

I'm about to call out, but hesitate. If this were Tennessee, there'd be rifles. Carlos Peralta did not withdraw to the Dark Bush for spur-of-the-moment social calls. He did not relocate to the Pleistocene to open a gringo-friendly cook pot dispensary.

But the sun is about to set. If we're to eat, we need a pot. "Don Carlos!" I call out.

The man spins around, his face alarmed. Instinctively, I try a disarming introduction: "We're friends of Maximo!"

The old man puts down a bucket and, wordlessly, walks our way. Though his creased face looks like gingerroot, pegging him in his seventies, his young man's gait gainsays advanced age. Nervous, I breathe more quickly now, and the air smells like a farm. He's still silent and serious as he stops a few meters from us, on the other side of the gate.

Suddenly, his stoic expression melts. "I knew you were coming!" he exclaims, his smile sparking, eyes large. "The giant hummingbird told me so."

Ahmet looks, blankly, at him, then fires a *Guy's a nutter?* glance at me. Behind the man a simple adobe home rises, capped with two solar panels, below it a profusion of fowl and beast: ducks, geese, chickens, goats, sheep, and puppies, issuing a cacophony of calls.

"*Siii*," he says. "I told my wife: We will have visitors today. Whenever the giant hummingbird appears, you see, this happens."

Not a nutter. Just biocentric.

"You're Carlos Peralta?"

He nods, pushes open the handmade wooden gate, and welcomes us onto his portico. Grandly draping a llama-wool blanket over the hand-cleaved board he's got balanced on two plastic buckets, Peralta insists we sit. Coffee? We accept. Before long, his wife appears with four steaming mugs. Maria, we discover, is forty-eight years old to Carlos's spry seventy-nine, and they have eight grown kids, all of whom have since de-bushed for Suraqueta (two of them) and Santa Cruz (the rest).

Despite the size of their farm, and the fact that, with the children gone, they have nobody to help with it, the couple exudes lightheartedness. How big is their property? "Four hundred and fifty acres," Carlos Peralta offhandedly replies, as if it were

Ahmet's Manhattan apartment building's crabgrass welcome mat of a lawn. The couple beams, responds to each of our questions in a few cheery words.

> Ahmet: Does the government help you?
> Carlos: They do nothing for us, and we don't need them. We grow, graze, and hunt almost everything we need, and barter our excess for the rest.
> Me: How often does the giant hummingbird appear?
> Carlos: The last one was two years ago, preceding a pair of French campers, tall like you.
> Ahmet: Solar power?
> Carlos: We have two panels, but only use one. Four light-bulbs are enough.

The conversation, on their end, keeps coming back to a single topic: How happy they are that we've come. Maria says, "And if you'd come an hour earlier, you would have missed us! We were up there, scaring *jochi* (large rodents) from our corn." She indicates a sloping swath of lush corn in a clearing maybe a mile away, under a distant ridge. I picture them clearing and planting that acre plot by themselves, tending it, shooing away these corn-eating pests, reaping and storing their crop.

The sun sinking over the corn ridge, Ahmet navigates to the practical reason for our visit. "Don Carlos," he says, "we were wondering…if you might be able to spare something that would be useful to us as we camp."

"Of course!" Peralta and his wife cry in unison.

I jump in, using the roundabout Bolivian communication style: "A trifle that would work a miracle. We forgot to bring…a cook pot."

Carlos leaps up and leads us to the back wall of his home.

Beside the freestanding adobe baking oven and the wood-burning stove that acts as an outdoor kitchen hang, on a wall, pots of various sizes, all of them charred black. Proudly, he announces: "Take as many as you like, *amigos!*"

We suggest leaving collateral. Money or an ID card? The couple has no idea what we're talking about, the idea of a guarantee as foreign to them as hummingbird envoys are ordinary. We're sent off with grins and a pasta pot.

That night Ahmet and I get hammered. Smashed as hurled sandstone. We finish the first bottle of tannat wine while cooking up the pasta in Carlos Peralta's pot. Then, by campfire, we drink the rest of two additional bottles, which were meant to last the three nights. Maybe the booze will finally squelch the *chikungunya*, I think. Maybe it will squelch some of the shittyness I feel.

Later, wads of coca leaf in our gums and a slurred moon above, I ask Ahmet about Melissa.

"We haven't connected," he says. "She's busy, I'm busy. A couple of emails, though. She seems content at the UN, and in Brooklyn."

I look, glumly, into the fire. Ahmet clarifies: "But probably because it's a nice switch-up for her. You know that I thought you were crazy to leave New York for a village in Bolivia. But now I see why you did. I'm on a treadmill in New York: work, spend, repeat. There's no free time, the kids are overscheduled, yada yada. And it's so tense I've even changed my name. I go by 'Al' now." He explains that, with all the anti-Muslim sentiment in the States, "Al" is just easier, especially with blue-blood clients at work. "You'll get used to it," he tells me.

After a pause, he says: "Your town is awesome, your house... and *this* incredible place."

I tell him that he's been here only two days. That there's an underbelly. That the xenophobia he feels in New York exists here, too. But he shakes it off. "Powers," he says, "it's like this article I read, about 'progress' being a zombie category, neither dead nor alive. 'Development' has been declared dead over and over — because it's fucking up nature and, you know, everything's-amazing-and-nobody's-happy. But we don't know what to replace 'development' with, so it keeps zombie-ing on."

The forest shimmers in moonlight. We sip and chew coca. I remember the American flag Ahmet — *Al*, I remind myself — brought down. The mixed feelings I had when I held it, ran a finger across its stars. I make a mental note to pass it on to Kusi. "I feel like this jasmine plant at our house," I finally say. "Stripped of the sweet."

The water crashes, the gulch we're in as empty and echoing as Carlos Peralta's cook pot. I wish Clea wasn't in Brooklyn, that she was instead splashing here, *wawawa*. "Sorrow," Al finally says, his voice half-lost in the falls' din. "Maybe it's what's left at the bottom, a residue after the joy's boiled off. Sorrow is old joy."

I OPEN THE TENT FLY, the next morning, and find Al gone.

Eventually, I spot a skein of smoke on the mountainside beside the falls. Squinting, I see a hominid tending fire. Hungover from the wine, I wend my way through the thick jungle and mud, a place so different from yesterday's sandstone ridge and the plummeting depths, and finally reach him.

"How did you find this spot?" I ask. He's on the outer lip of a half-moon grotto. Monkey's tail cactuses droop from above, a phosphorescent green hummingbird darting in and out of rock fissures.

Al shrugs and grins. "Breakfast, brother?" he says, and hands me coffee.

We're silent. I'm muddled from the booze, but also better somehow, as if last night's alcohol seared out a bit of the *chikungunya*. Al is making oatmeal in Carlos Peralta's cook pot. It becomes a meditation focal point for me. The cook pot. Blackened on the outside, clean shiny tin on the inside. A lime-green parrot feather floats down, hovers on the pot's steam, then falls at my feet. Above, parrots squawk and fight and play and mate in another cave, several cliff-protected stories above ours.

Thus passes the day, two hungover old friends in a half-moon cave. A swallow threads through an air pocket in the rocketing falls. We talk for hours, catching up as the air's aroma thickens with warming flora, then nap in the mouth of the cave.

In the late afternoon a human silhouette appears on the riverbank below, and before long, Carlos Peralta joins us. For two hours we chat and drink coffee, an inexhaustible smile on his lips from his arrival through his departing words: "*A casa!*" — Homeward!

The next morning, Al and I rise early, and after a chilly dip in the falls, Al says: "Let's go someplace nobody's been for centuries. Or maybe ever."

The sun rising, we bushwhack down to a stream and trace it upriver, swimming the unpassable stretches. Al identifies our ambitious goal, the place-where-no-human-has-trod — a palm gulley jackknifed between schist bluffs.

However, as we arrive at the edge of a black stone towering over two beautiful swimming pools, our gringo-ambition to achieve those goals vanishes. "Another time," Al says. We've been talking less, easing into Carlos Peralta's cook pot, the great gorge of Pachamama: *nada*. Nothing.

Nada is beautiful. *Nada* is easy. It's two good friends occasionally swapping a word or two — a koan from Buddhist teacher Pema Chödrön, a note of the sun's kaleidoscopic gleam on water — and otherwise being without jobs or calendars or anything much besides our limbs, hearts, and a cook pot.

Later in the morning, Al suggests solo time ("We'll meet back at the tent at sundown"), then hikes west. I decide not to have a destination. Well rested from the previous day's leisure, I walk upstream, then spot a condor above, its wingspan maybe ten feet. The condor rides an air pocket north, and I track it.

An hour passes, then two. My mind clicks off, and I'm a *Homo sapiens* bipedaling a condor pathway.

Ascending now, up increasingly steep and rock-strewn paths.

Ascending. Sandstone crumbles into a gravelly riverbed beneath. Millions of years of mauve stones reverting to sand.

And then I can't go forward. Or backward.

AFTER MY YELLS FOR HELP echo into nothing...after I flush out the chartreuse, orange, and charcoal-colored duck and breathe in its ripe pungency...after I concede that the path is too steep and brittle in both directions, and that Al, seasoned hiker though he may be, has not a clue where I am...after hours pass and I accept that my water's almost gone and frigid night will come...after all of this, I surrender.

Carlos Peralta's cook pot is larger than I. Pachamama is larger. I'm not in control.

Capitulated, I sit cross-legged and remember something Kusi said the other day at the bar. "Our Pablo Neruda and your Henry Miller. Did you ever think about how different they are?"

I shook my head. Kusi went on: "The difference between them is the split between 'living well' and 'living better.' Neruda gazed at the world, awed! — 'Give me silence, water, hope / Give me struggle, iron, volcanoes.' Neruda let the world be, whereas Miller devoured it."

I gaze toward the black schist bluffs behind which the condor I'd been tracking has long disappeared, remembering how much, back in high school, I loved reading Miller. Loved how he devoured Paris, consumed it experientially, squeezed every sensory experience and emotion in it. This drive to possess resonated with my NEVER STOP IMPROVING upbringing.

I got to this brink of death by needing to devour. I had to improve, experientially, tracking a raptor to death's edge.

A tear surfaces, hot; it traces a line down my cheek. I need Melissa. She balances me and understands something I'm just beginning to grasp right now, in this surrendered state: To *devour* is to Dream that something could be mine. A sweeter life rests on that which Dreamers most repudiate — the daily presence of death. I own, perhaps, my next breath. But that's it. Maximo, Kusi, Carlos Peralta, and Pablo Neruda walk, like many Bolivians I know, paths that lead nowhere. *Día de los Muertos* — the Day of the Dead — is more than a two-day celebration in Suraqueta's cemetery each year. It's now. And now, and now.

I sink into the afternoon, watching the sun move across the sky, my molecules merging with the landscape as if I were already decomposing into Pachamama. I start to feel a little ashamed at how, in a sense, I've abused the land we steward, "our" Tierra Guapurú, as we've come to refer to our land. I *devour* it, while Melissa lets it be. The Henry Miller in me catalogs everything as I survey the paths on our land, observing the slightest growth of cactus fruits, parrot roosting patterns, the presence of iguana scat. I devour our five acres, not just by imprinting permaculturally with a *quiñe*-slashing machete, but by wolfing down the beauty of its every inch, viscerally digesting it. Melissa, in contrast, doesn't cock an ear to each distinct creek note, doesn't inhale the eucalyptus's breath. She doesn't maximize communion with Pachamama through the relative reflexology of each rock underfoot, doesn't feed mindfully on edible mushrooms under the pines while recording wind patterns toward ideal wind- and fire-break placement. She instead lives her life on the land in Nerudian beauty, delighting in the discovery of a new orchid that placed its seed in the fork of a tree, appreciating moon phases, and remarking on the day's hummingbirds. The land is, at core, a space she traverses to get to town or to the orchard. It's the area in which we dwell, and it is everything except "ours." The sun is about to set. I breathe, feeling a certain courage. I realize there's a unified field I'm in now — what indigenous peoples call *la Pacha*. I've been divorced from it in the months since Grace's rape, since Melissa and Clea's departure, and in my hard drinking and angst in the conversations with Al. I've been totally in my head, in "first world problems" of ego and identity and their ensuing fear. In this place, death's precipice — a place where so many wise, expansive Bolivian friends live because death-life-death are the very steps of "walking questioning" — it's obvious I've been living in a tunnel. A dark place, where I try to grope from point to point with little candles of positive thinking or hopes or pleasures, when there's this overwhelmingly broad, rich, and mellifluous *tree* of life aboveground, arching into sky.

At dusk, I hear a human voice. Al.

I rise, and soon see his shape upon the ridge.

Before long — assessing the landscape from a broader view — he finds a series of footholds to reach me. A friend's grip, and I'm led to firmer ground.

Fourteen

"'What's the biggest thing in the world?'" Maximo says, in the bush taxi back toward Suraqueta. "That's what I asked my first-grade students the other day."

Al and I have been quiet for a long while, both stirred. Me by near-death; Al more generally by the Dark Bush.

Al asks: "How did they respond?"

Maximo laughs. "'My Dad,' answered a small boy in the back." I smile at this, thinking of Clea's 'Papa Bear.' "Another student said: 'An elephant.' 'A mountain!' answered a third student."

The taxi planes over a dry riverbed. Maximo banks left to avoid a fallen rock, then picks up his story: "Finally, one of my quietest students said: 'My eye is the world's biggest thing.' When I asked her what she meant, she replied: 'My Daddy, an elephant, a mountain. They all fit into my eye. So my eye is the world's biggest thing.'"

As Maximo says this, the light vivifies. I absorb what that six-year-old said as we crest the lip of the Suraqueta Valley, and magnificence explodes. Amboró's cloud-forested mountains upsurge over a dwarfed Suraqueta, as a flock of a hundred green-and-red parrots streak the blue sky. Grand Canyon vast, yet it all fits in my eye.

We arrive at Casa Guapurú, drop our gear. Maximo takes out his machete and hacks off two *tipa* branches, from a tree I liberated when I took out some spiny *quiñe* plants. He instructs me to boil it to help with the *chikungunya*. Then Al and Maximo hug, clapping each other's backs. "Happy *Mother's* Day," Al says, grinning. Maximo smiles back.

My friend and I spend two more days together, then we walk his bag down to the shared taxi depot. He's off to the Santa Cruz airport to board a flight to New York for a meeting, a fact he laments. I thank him for rescuing me; Al scoffs it off, and says, "Powers, I was thinking of Maximo's tiny philosopher. Even more than the eye, the imagination is the biggest thing in the world." Al hoists his backpack into the taxi's trunk. "Volcanoes, continents, galaxies…what doesn't fit into my imagination? But what's most messed up about it all is how I let *them* shrink it. Or maybe how, with all the 'shoulds' I've constructed in my life, I actually *choose* to shrink it."

No hay cambio. There's no change.

"*Joven, no hay!*" my *casera*, Serafina, tells me at the market when I try to give her a twenty-boliviano bill for cacao and co-conuts. Ninety-five bolivianos in coins is selling for a hundred boliviano note in Suraqueta, a 5 percent premium on copper over paper. People are paying more in bills to get physical coins.

Hay cambio. There's change.

Walking through the pueblo, I notice it has spawned new businesses. Jürgen and Anja have inaugurated their café-cum-tour-agency on Calle Bolívar. Some other friends, Sandro and Ligia have revamped the old Tierra Libre restaurant into a tapas joint. When I pass by to retrieve the silver bracelet I left with Sandro to be soldered, he and five others are plastering, painting, installing lighting. And an enthusiastic Cruceña has opened a shop near the plaza where she sells art that she makes on-site: colonial-style painted vases, bells, and dishware, fired in her kiln. On the plaza, a new café, La Caffette, is unveiled; it belongs to a retired Suraqueta family that lived for three decades in Montreal, and they've come home to bake croissants on weekends and brew up top-notch cappuccinos. Our "Viking" neighbors, Jaime and Balu, are no longer hawking their jewelry and leather goods from a blanket on the plaza. Now they have their own small shop near the church. Transition entrepreneurship, informal economy power. Nary a chain or a franchise until you reach Santa Cruz.

Hay cambio. Three political parties effervesce, seeking to challenge the questionable incumbents running as the Alliance Party candidate. The first is Los Verdes ("green" being the color of the Santa Cruz state flag, not the ecological Green Party), a regional party associated with pro-*valluno* and pro-*camba* sentiment and neoliberalism. The second party — called Citizen's Unite — is based out of Suraqueta's rural *valluno* stronghold and becomes one gathering point for anti-incumbent sentiment. The third party makes the biggest splash. Evo Morales's MAS party selects as its top candidate a soft-spoken Quechua farmer of Cochabamba-area origins, raised here in a rural hamlet of Suraqueta, named Enrique who promises a robust ousting of the old guard; this causes *valluno* Suraqueteños to fire back with anti-*colla* fervor.

Suraqueta receives a generous baseline of $1.3 million a year, mostly through a national hydrocarbons tax, plus the ability to fairly easily triple that sum through supplemental national government and foreign aid projects. The three new parties pledge to direct these sums, at last, toward the public interest. The forerunners in the political race are the incumbents and the neoliberal Verdes candidate, but these are followed closely by Enrique's MAS.

Suraqueta has never had a town hall not filled by its economic elite, and the fact that MAS is even a close third in the race suggests Bolivia's national political revolution has finally come to Suraqueta. Long-oppressed *colla* immigrants, nearly all MAS supporters, become odd bedfellows with the other outsiders, including some foreigners, as they seek to challenge the established order. However, the incumbent leadership, astute in their political maneuvers, knows they can exploit the fragmentation of anti-incumbency sentiment across the three parties. After all, the party only needs to win a plurality. The party with the most votes wins, even if it's just 20 percent. So the incumbent party tap into their deep campaign war chest to outspend the others. His campaign posters dominate town walls, as his commercials do the airwaves. His campaign hires a Santa Cruz studio band to regig popular Bolivian songs to encourage a vote for him. One of his many hired jeeps traverses Suraqueta nonstop for weeks, blasting these songs through mounted loudspeakers, the upbeat jingles attempting to disrupt all memories of decade-long corrupt leadership. These pro-incumbent melodies even surface in my dreams. The ritual in Republika is to rise and hoist mugs beer hall–style and ironically sing the tunes each time the jeep passes.

"The incumbents can't lose," one Transition *amigo* says. "Over the last years, they've built such a powerful base of local allies — teachers, bush-taxi drivers, farmers — that they have their vote secured. People here like the status quo."

Nevertheless, *hay cambio*. Town conversation spools out around the various party platforms. And Bolivia, bigheartedly, allows foreigners to vote after just three years as residents, so even *los jipis* will have a say. "In England, I always felt like a random demographic," one friend tells me. "But at this small-is-beautiful scale, I can affect who wins." Melissa and I fall shy of the residency requirement and can't vote in this important local election.

No hay cambio. How strange scarce coinage seems. In the north, the predictability of currency makes it as unappreciated as paved highways, potable drinking water, central air.

Now, when our tap is dry for a day, I savor its gushing return.

When our internet stumbles on cloudy afternoons, how pure and blue that Skype screen seems when it finally punches down from its satellite, especially after the fortifying unconnected hours spent in nature in its absence. When pocket change ebbs, how satisfying the palm-weight of boliviano silver; the coins jingle as they pass from my hand to Serafina's, replaced by a ripe mango.

I AMBLE ALONG OUR NORTH FENCE LINE, watching the sun settle into its afternoon arc over the valley near Mairana, a fool muttering into a digital recorder. I often prewrite while walking, knowing that transcription encourages streams of prose to channel and pool. I'm feeling better, Maximo's *tipa*-leaves remedy seeming to do wonders for my *chikungunya*. I hear a motorcycle, then Kusi appears. She cuts the motor and smiles into the dense silence. I've known Kusi for a decade now, and how I enjoy my friend's Sweet ways. Though reedy and slight, Kusi — along with Maximo and the Dark Bush's Carlos Peralta — is huge in that she's lightly conditioned by empire.

For two days Kusi had been trying to get back to Suraqueta from Santa Cruz but couldn't. "The road through Laja," she says, "was blocked by a landslide. You know…the place with the falling-down house with the pigs." I don't know the place but, as per local convention, nod as if I do.

The road to our house has been muddy, too. Kusi is the first to traverse it after a cold but welcome Antarctic *sur*. Then, in a seeming non sequitur, she says, "*Es paraíso*" — It's paradise.

Our cut-off, stuck-behind-rockslides place is…*paradise*? I gaze around at this, the driest spot on our property, with the sand-tolerant succulents and a few cacti. Steeply sloped, covered with boulders, concealed from the rest of our property, it's thirsty. Counterintuitively, our creek jumps down through this scrubland, leaving moisture in eucalyptus and ferns. The leaves above dapple sunshine across a faultless late afternoon, fresh winds having blown away the *sur*.

Creek warble, sky beam, joy on my friend's face — I know how much Kusi loves Suraqueta. Then she says something I don't catch.

"*Qué dices?*" I ask.

Her words have united: "*EsNuestroEden*" — It'sOurEden.

IN *POETICS*, Aristotle observes that all art, at its best, resembles a statue of a person. An Athenian statue does not have three biceps, nor a single thigh. Each feature of the statue resonates toward the whole…toward the One Thing.

I'm slicing *quiñe* one afternoon, and it slices me back, my forearms and shins streaked with blood. Beneath a million thorns is the Athenian statue of our homestead. I upgraded from my machete yesterday, purchasing "*una osa*" — a female bear — a vicious-looking bear-claw-shaped metal knife on a stake. I'm hacking a path to a prize beyond this parched and thorny tangle of *quiñe*: below the hillock, an atoll of yellow *carnaval* and spry *tipa* trees. This island is far thicker than any other such cluster of trees on the land, and I wonder why, imagining it to be linked to an earlier human settlement. Like a mother bear, her cub endangered, I rush at *quiñes*, but not out of rage. I crave the uncovering of a meter-wide trail that leads only here. A falling *quiñe* comes within feet of my soft eyes — how fragile the world's biggest thing. I'm more cautious after that close call, but I continue bear-clawing toward hidden wealth, a someday grove for Amaya and Clea.

OUR SOTO POLLERUDO–FRONTIER NEIGHBORS, the Bolivian-French couple, Michael and Lucia, invite me over to their son's second birthday party. I arrive to a happy mix of children playing outside and Michael's brother, Arnold, holding forth to a group in the living room on a story he's reading. The tale is from an obscure book, which washed up in the Republika book exchange, by a seventeenth-century aristocrat and rebel. "She'd curate gatherings of people from around the world at her castle, and they'd talk philosophy, read poetry, imagine," Arnold says. Light shines in, painting the adobe walls gold, casting the shadow of a *noki* tree onto coffee-colored floor tiles. Outside, a double rainbow hovers above the El Fuerte ruins. Michael and Arnold's eighty-seven-year-old father — an artist who recently sold his house in France and moved to Suraqueta to paint and be with his children and grandchildren — sits beside me, gazing toward the rainbows, seeming to reflect on his son's words. I wonder if Suraqueta, and other secret melting pots, are today's "castles." Here, thirty nations interact; Transition simmers in Carlos Peralta's pot of artistic, social, and economic flavor.

Al, before he left: "Maybe our imaginations are the world's biggest thing."

Kusi, of Suraqueta: "*EsNuestroEden*" — It'sOurEden.

Today I settle on: It'sStory.

Legends flourish in Suraqueta. There's the tale of the undiscovered tribe, still in Amboró National Park, living in primordial accord. There are legends of Incas who dwelled here before us, of those who built the skilled agricultural terracing visible at El Fuerte. Their biocentric legacy lives on via the yearly winter solstice ritual, where a thousand people raise palms to the first ray of morning sun at the ruins above town. Such legacy stories and practices flow into today's "glocal" narrative; when I ask a bush-taxi driver about the upcoming elections, he complains that "the candidates aren't talking enough about environmental protection." Both MAS and Los Verdes advisors, separately, invite me to brief their candidates on "eco-municipal" practices of sustainable tourism, organic agriculture, and local economy. After all, such elements are in the Story.

I ask myself, *Do you believe in Suraqueta? Could a new and ancient Bolivian Dream unfurl?*

I STOP BY KUSI'S HOUSE — she lives with her extended family — to drop off the American flag.

Kusi welcomes me into the dim adobe anteroom. White-washed adobe walls, wood beams holding up a high ceiling. Our house uses the same traditional building materials, but there's history here: family portraits on the wall, antique wood furniture that looks out of the 1920s. We walk into a sunny courtyard and sit on a bench beside Kusi's eighty-seven-year-old grandfather, who's cleaning, with a brush, several baskets of potatoes. Kusi tells me he harvested them this morning from their plot outside town. He's quiet, focused on his work, and wears a brimmed *valluno* hat, a button-down shirt, and dirty jeans. Eventually, Kusi's tall fourteen-year-old niece joins us. It takes me a minute to place her. The lipstick, the twinkling braces...she's the teenager who, while on a walk one day when we still lived at Bergwald, tossed that red Pilfrut yogurt bag on the ground.

Her name is Esmeralda, and she accepts the American flag, then lets it unfurl. Kusi asks me to tell her about it; tomorrow is July Fourth. As I talk about stars and stripes, thirteen colonies and fifty states, I notice, hanging unobtrusively off an outdoor portico beam, a Bolivian flag in its red, green, and gold, and I feel caught between two worlds. Kids — others of Kusi's nieces and nephews — gather around to hear about the flag, about America, then disappear into the anteroom and onto the street beyond. An hour becomes two, and at a certain point Esmeralda leaves with the flag. As we're helping clean the potatoes, passing a yerba máte cup-and-straw around with Kusi's grandpa, the sun hitting a harder angle to the west, I realize that the Sweet Life is in one

dimension very *ordinary*: being in a naturally antique house that
STOPPED IMPROVING a century ago, allowing silence as we mellow
into the sound of potatoes being scrubbed, noticing the courtyard's passionfruit tree catching a slight breeze. At one point I ask
her grandfather: "*Que es 'vivir bien' para Usted?*" — What does
"living well" mean to you?

He nods, smiling, not quite getting me; Kusi repeats the
question.

The old man continues to scrub a potato, and I'm all but
certain he's forgotten the question when he answers, in a slow
Spanish: "Living well? It's this: Eat well, sleep well, love well."

I'M ONLINE LESS. I clear *quiñe* and write more. Are the two all
that different? Wielding a bear-claw toward One Thing.

"Am I a Luddite?"

Barefoot and alone one afternoon, I hear this question,
Hollywood voice-over clear. I whirl around. Nobody there, of
course, and I laugh.

A family of German classical musicians lives in Suraqueta,
our erstwhile neighbors from Bergwald. They make their kids
"earmuff" whenever they pass a house or vehicle playing contemporary music. I once asked the dad about why he has them
cover their ears, and he told me, "It's self-explanatory if you think
about it." I recall, too, how author Charles Eisenstein's brother
reads nothing written after the year 1900. And how farmer and
writer Wendell Berry reads little that's current because he doesn't
want it to affect his voice. I recall Kusi's family courtyard, similarly buffered from "modernity." While I happily use blenders and
bush taxis and the internet, I'm a sensualist in love with the feel of
wind on skin and creek on feet, with the sight of a vulture soar-
ing, right now, skimming our orchard's canopy, nearsighted in its
carrion quest.

If I look sideways at my family's plunge into the Sweet Life enigma, I see children and dogs running down our dirt road. I hear friends' laughter and *no-hay-guapurú* and *wawawa* and Story simmering in Carlos Peralta's cook pot. I sense One Thing in eucalyptus-scented winds, in the jingle of change, in blood on a bear claw and groves uncovered.

Fifteen

"*Cuando llega Melissa?*" — When's Melissa back?

I've heard this question one hundred times over the past months. When I was away, Melissa told me she constantly fielded the "*Cuando llega Bill?*" corollary. In a small community, people miss you and wonder when you'll return. Smaller kids ask it like this: "*Y Clea?*" — And Clea? It's always accompanied by an anguished expression and stated painfully. The kids never ask: "When is Clea coming back?" That's future. When children approach me with "*Y Clea?*" they empathize with my incompleteness.

I spent forty-eight hours, all of a Sunday and a Monday, without going into town center. The walk to the birthday party at Michael and Lucia's house, including the stop at Kusi's, was the only time I abandoned *quiñe*-hacking and writing, gardening and creek-mucking. Now I walk five minutes along our dirt road, over the creek, and into the market and plaza and town, initially jarred by the hundreds of people. "*Hola, Kusi*," I call, spotting her across the street.

"*Cuando llega Melissa?*" she asks.

"Soon," I tell her, followed by a silent *I hope*. Still no date set, and the dangling possibility of her taking a lucrative post at the UN in New York. There's a "last chance" feel to her decision. Her UN contacts will only get colder, and should she refuse this offer, I wonder if there'd be another opportunity.

Another friend walks by. The ubiquitous cheek kiss. I admire her baby, which she has strapped to her back with an *aguayo* (multicolored cloth), tussling his hair, but before we can exchange a word, a Transition *amigo*, José Antonio, extends a hand, asking about Melissa, telling me about his new art studio and what he's been painting. Teo, a gray-haired Suraqueteño architect, comes by with his daughter ("*Y Clea?*" the four-year-old asks, her expression anguished), and he joins our chat about politics. The rumor is that the incumbents will boost their votes by busing non-Suraqueteño residents in from Santa Cruz to vote illegally in the outlying municipal towns. "This time we'll be ready for him," José Antonio says, "with observers at every polling place." I walk another few steps and there's Sylvia, with little Ulysses, waving and smiling before ducking into the tailor. And then Rulas Maradona wanders by, our house builder, talking about his own nearly completed eco-house.

After two cloistered days, I enfold an hour of social life into a half block. I smile, remembering how, back in New York, Melissa and I had to schedule most social engagements three months in advance.

In the evening, I Skype with Melissa. Though we've talked on the phone and emailed, this is only our second Skype call since she left. Clea is napping, and we have the video off for clearer audio.

"Ahmet — er, Al — called me," Melissa says. "He seems amazed by Bolivia. What the heck happened on your camping trip?"

A New York driver leans on a horn in the background. How to convey anything of the Dark Bush, Carlos Peralta, and my fresh awareness of death-and-*la-vida-dulce*? The dissimilar experiences my wife and I are living feel like a further layer of separation. Before I can answer, Clea wakes up. We turn on our cameras, and I'm looking into my daughter's eyes as if she is sitting beside me in our adobe "eaves," what we've come to call the second-story rounded mezzanine overlooking the *guapurú* trees and *achocha* vines. "*Papa!*" she exclaims. We play our "crazy chicken" game where I cluck wantonly, feigning blindness, until the last minute when I finally look into her eyes, and then attack her neck.

It feels like we're playing it live, such joy in her face each time the eye contact happens and the crazy chicken attacks. We do it several times. She asks me to sing "*Pio Pio*," a popular children's song in Bolivia, which I do. And then it's "Wheels on the Bus," together. Then she sings "Happy Birthday to Mommy," whose birthday has come and gone in New York without Papi. "*Casa Guapurú!*" Clea says, in the song's wake, finally tuning in to what's behind me on the screen. I point the laptop up into Eternity's beams, and I'm aware we built our canopied home in the spirit of the tree that holds up the seven skies, of *vivir bien*. At the end of the call Melissa says, "We should maybe think about Skyping more often."

There's a pause. I'm looking into my wife's beautiful eyes, perfect stainless-steel appliances gleaming behind her in the kitchen of her Brooklyn apartment and mumble: "I guess."

The next morning, I realize why I hesitate. I feel closest to Clea and Melissa when they are here, but least close to them as a two-dimensional image. Sure, Skyping with Clea and Melissa is precious, but a regular video running between two hemispheres doesn't let the heart open up to this world, here, where Clea and Melissa are with me all the time. They are here, now, in the creek gurgle, in the brush of *tula* on my arm, and the scent of eucalyptus, the young branches of which I pick and place in our shower for the aroma. They're here with me in my ache for something that seems each day less probable...their return.

La Paz. The sacred Andean peaks of Huayna Potosí, Mururata, and Illimani rise jagged into a bowl of high mountain sky. The thin oxygen tastes different from Suraqueta's earthier air. I've come to take over a consultancy Melissa and I were hired to do together, but instead I will work alone. My task: evaluate a network of nine Bolivian social and environmental nonprofit groups. I stay with a Bolivian friend in the city's southern zone for a week, riding a collective taxi to a downtown office where I conduct two dozen interviews and review scores of documents. I also make site visits. The work is familiar, enjoyable.

One afternoon on a lunch break on Plaza Murillo, I bump into the Bolivian vice minister for decolonization, the Aymaran Félix Cárdenas. Yes, Bolivia has a Vice Ministry of Decolonization. Cardenas, a very dark-skinned man with a penetrating gaze, once gave a talk to my NYU students when we passed through La Paz, and he remembers me and stops to talk. The branch of government he leads, instituted by Morales, seeks to "decolonize" society; in other words, Cardenas operates on the level of Story. In his lecture to my students, Cardenas sought to undermine Spanish colonial and Bolivian elite narratives, as well as those of the Catholic Church. ("They gave us Bibles," the vice minister told us, "and told us to close our eyes to pray. But when we opened our eyes, they'd taken our land.") He's also critical of corporate power, the big-fat-Contemporary-Dream, which he says requires even deeper decolonization.

The vice minister asks after my family and sees something in my face when I mention Melissa's absence. "You know about our Aymaran *chacha-warmi*, right?" he asks. I nod. "The couple ... *Two*," he says, holding up a pair of fingers. "In our communities, odd numbers are unlucky. *Chacha* is male, *warmi* female, but it's one single word, illustrating the unity of the couple. Our leaders have to be married; if they're not, they're incomplete. *Para vivir bien* you need your *warmi*." I know *chacha-warmi* is part of an essential layer of the Sweet Life: the unified field, or life's essential wholeness. I've also learned that, in a deeper dive into the *chacha-warmi* concept, homosexual unions contain both "energies" and are equally as whole.

It's with a mix of confusion and melancholy — and far from an inner sense of life's essential wholeness — that I complete the La Paz consultancy and board a bus to what I recall, from my days living in La Paz, as a gorgeous jungle town called Coroico, thousands of meters below the capital and three hours away. I'm going for a weeklong solo writing retreat. The vice minister's words make me miss my *warmi* more, and I'm feeling alone and raw, unsure of our future. I also carry mixed feelings about the evaluation gig. It's the kind of tangible and technical task I've been trained to do, and the results of the work could help an environmental justice defense group and an educational nonprofit improve their services in the most marginalized area of El Alto, the huge metropolis adjacent to La Paz. So why do I feel tepid about it?

The bus climbs a winding peak, before our steep descent to Coroico. Off in the distance, I spot El Alto and the bright glare of a *cholet*. The word *cholet* is a tongue-in-cheek contraction of *cholla* (a once-derogatory term for traditional indigenous people now widely embraced by them) and the French word *chalet*, and it refers to a startling new architectural style: million-dollar, multistory buildings constructed by an indigenous bourgeoisie class that is amassing business wealth in Morales's economy. *Cholets* typically feature lavish wedding/catering halls on the ground floor and family living quarters on the upper stories. The extremely ornate façades reflect the rainbow colors of traditional indigenous weavings and Andean ritual *k'oa* mandalas.

The bus peaks at a snow-strewn landscape above the tree line, then plunges into the long descent. Nearly two hours of down. My ears pop, and I shed layers of alpaca-wool sweaters as the trees get larger and the air stickier. On the far side of the deep valley I spot the hairpin curves of the now-defunct "world's most dangerous road," which I biked down in 2002 when it was the only way to Coroico. That road has been replaced by this asphalt road, built pre-MAS on an Inter-American Development Bank loan.

In Coroico, I head to my hotel, Sol y Luna, at the dead end of a mud road rising beyond the town. I get my key and walk the crisscrossing footpaths to my tiny glass cabin, called Alaya, at the secluded far end of Sol y Luna. Putting down my backpack, I'm elated as I gaze through Alaya's floor-to-ceiling windows to a Yungas rainforest rising to the visible snowcapped peaks, far above, that I passed through earlier. Coroico is totally unlike Suraqueta's mixed Mediterranean and subtropical climate; here it's the bouquet of tropical plants and their equally exotic scents, hotter, denser air on the skin, and a different buzz from its birds and insects.

Not much has changed in the decade since I last visited Sol y Luna. The fifteen beautiful TV-free cabañas and rooms, a modest outdoor restaurant, two natural swimming pools fed by rushing creeks, and miles of naturally contoured paths, bordered with agave and pines, and, intentionally, no roads into the expanse. I'm acquainted with Sigrid, Sol y Luna's owner, now in her seventies, who arrived in Bolivia from Germany four decades back. Sigrid purchased these acres and created what is not so much a business but a fenceless, mini-utopia where the "staff" live in houses interspersed with the tourist cabañas, forming family with her. Sol y Luna is Sigrid's life's work, and it remains an inspiring one, I find, as I easily slip into a daily routine of rising early, writing through lunch, then taking afternoons off to practice writer Brenda Ueland's "moodling": productive dawdling, where one's subconscious works out aesthetics and structure without the rational mind's interference.

Two days into my retreat, I wander down into the town of Coroico and feel a mounting shock. While Sol y Luna has maintained its essence, the town has not. A pueblo that, a decade ago, was tranquil and historically intact, is now filled with dozens of bland, cinder-block, five-story high-rises, without a trace of *cholet* ingenuity. Most of the traditional homes were ripped down for hastily erected apartment rentals and hotels. The ensuing multi-fold spike in human density means increased cars and motorcycles spewing pollution and causing congestion. This uglification of Coroico has caused its previously strong tourism industry to plummet. Tourism here once centered, like Suraqueta's, on using this quaint town as a base for surrounding ecotourism activities. For example, downhill mountain bike operators in La Paz used to include Coroico as part of their package and annually bring tens of thousands of primarily foreign tourists to the area. They now skip the town. And La Paz residents today seek out more tranquil destinations for their weekend trips. The collapsing tourist economy affects shop owners and almost anyone else doing business here; in the market, I notice the grim faces of the market-lady *caseras*, so different from the upbeat expressions of their Suraqueta counterparts.

In a flash I comprehend. Suraqueta could become Coroico.

In Suraqueta, only the El Fuerte Inca site has legal protection, through its UNESCO World Heritage classification. The rest of the four-hundred-year-old town's well-conserved architecture is vulnerable to Coroico's brand of Dream development.

I snap photos of the altered Coroico and email them to Transition *amigos* in Suraqueta. Thiago writes back that, indeed, architectural plans are in the works for four-story buildings near the Suraqueta plaza, with nothing available in our "little anarchy's" tool kit to stop them. Another friend chimes in that if the questionable incumbent party wins in next week's election, those buildings are sure to get a greenlight, since the developers support them. Only their ouster could protect the town's heritage. Paul Hawken's "antibodies" to an ecocidal story must at least grow from minuscule to small. A tiny, tolerated Transition group in Suraqueta is not enough — the Transition antibodies have to be at least municipal-size, and that would mean new leadership in City Hall.

I walk Coroico's loud, congested streets, the humans dwarfed by shadow-casting towers, desperate folks trying to sell a pile of potatoes or used clothing. I imagine Doña Serafina, our joyful, prosperous *casera*, as one of these grim souls should the incumbent win and the high-rises go up. At the same time, I feel guilty about my snug cabin in Sol y Luna where I have a bed, refrigeration, a hot shower, a bathroom. What a privileged position from which to judge these five-story buildings! Through my own filter, I see Coroico's architectural destruction as a lost future: what could have been a century of sustainable tourism, of folks from around the world who would have come and spent, over time, millions of dollars to experience this now-no-longer-desirable destination. I know from research and experience that, if they'd conserved the historical integrity of the pueblo, tourism would have accounted for about one-third of the economy, now a ghost income that could haunt the entire economy if the town suffers.

Then again, why should Coroico freeze its style in an earlier century? "Modernization," visually displeasing as it may be, is here, and I certainly don't know where it will lead the good citizens of Coroico. Plus, there's conceit in believing it can — or should — be stopped. I imagine the companies and families who invested in each of these buildings, their pride on the day their building was consecrated in a *ch'alla* celebration, *singani* (Bolivia's national liquor, distilled from white Muscat of Alexandria grapes) poured in the corners, creating a ritual *k'oa*, the dancing, and the sense of freedom these "million-potato people" no doubt experienced, since now they own spaces to share with family and rent out to others.

But what happens to Clea's "one-potato people"? I notice many more of them now than before Dream development struck. On Coroico's periphery, less fortunate souls live in the kind of peri-urban destitution you rarely see in Bolivia, certainly not in Suraqueta. This is closer in appearance to a Mexican border town or Brazilian *favela* (slum). I focus on one dwelling, assembled from random scraps of corrugated metal, teetering on the brink of a hill. Shouting emerges from behind the house. Two women and a man emerge, their voices escalating with a raw anger. Neighbors quarreling? A man and wife's frustration exploding?

Unseen, I watch. Three or four kids now take turns peering fearfully out the door of the shack. The woman shouting the loudest seems stressed. Stressed by being hemmed in around a single, insufficient water pump? Stressed by having nowhere even to hang her laundry? Stressed by living on the side of this mountain in these terrible conditions?

Watching this family, I understand my tepid reaction to the La Paz consultancy project. It's useful, but so grossly insufficient to apply technical fixes like program evaluations, alone. This work is deeper than aid. *It's Story.*

What story led this family to Coroico? In essence, the Dream. The Washington Consensus economic narrative insists that nations like Bolivia need to embrace "development," and in the 1990s, this Dreamer discourse steeped into the imagination of Bolivia's elites. They "liberalized" the nation's markets, causing economic catastrophe in Bolivia. In agriculture, for example, the nation was flooded with cheap industrial corn and other crops from the United States — cheap because of the use of agrotoxins and fossil-fuel subsidies up north. These crop imports were so cheap that many Bolivian *campesinos*, no longer able to make a living on their acreage, fled to the margins of La Paz and, as I'm witnessing now, to urbanizing towns like Coroico to work low-wage jobs... like constructing five-story buildings. They once were large people, like Dark Bush Carlos Peralta, like Maximo and Kusi and a thousand others in Suraqueta's still-robust glocal entrepreneur economy. But today they're Dream-chastened refugees.

With a sinking feeling, I recall a profound observation from anthropologist Arturo Escobar's landmark book *Encountering*

Development. When I taught in New York, my grad students always queried the following statement, leading to fruitful discussion, but it has never felt as portentous as it does as I watch this edge-teetering family: "The discourse and strategy of development," Escobar writes, "produced its opposite: massive underdevelopment and impoverishment, untold exploitation and oppression."

Hold on a minute. Development *causes* impoverishment and oppression? In front of me, the shanty dwellers fight more heatedly; one woman screams so loud, her voice is a force-wind of anger whipping against the other. She's displaced — and yes, *by* "development" — from her five-acre Tierra Guapurú equivalent, from Pachamama, with little choice but to flee to urbanizing spaces like this one where she's barraged, as we are in the north, by commercial and peer-internalized propaganda telling her about More. Work ever harder, longer hours and you can afford, someday, to live in a five-story building.

It's an especially dark night in spite of the moon.

All *chacha*, no *warmi*. Alone, in my cramped ego, far from *la Pacha*, or the Sweet Life's unified vision of life. I stay up late, writing. I've tabled the evaluation consultancy. Tonight I'm furious at development. That shanty-family singed me. Escobar: *Development has produced its opposite: massive underdevelopment and impoverishment, untold exploitation and oppression.*

Abandoning notebook and digital recorder, I take a moonlit walk to the town cemetery below Sol y Luna. It's tucked into a small spot on the hillside. Because of lack of space, the graves rise up like scaled-down five-story buildings, the coffins pushed inside at each level, a photo of the person in the coffin on front. Banana trees and all manner of tropical vegetation crowd into the graves, and I feel lonely. My mind, stuck in New York, jumps to Melissa and my onetime neighbor, the actor Philip Seymour Hoffman.

Hoffman owned a penthouse several blocks from our micro-apartment. We spotted him a couple of times during our Slow year in 2012. I would sometimes gaze up at his apartment, on the top story, wondering about the private life of one of my favorite actors. Because he lived so close, it was a particular shock to us when he overdosed in early 2014. Then, about six months later, actor Robin Williams committed suicide by hanging, following a long bout of severe depression, among other medical conditions. Dimensions of sadness — Dream refugees in shanties; Hollywood stars in penthouses — they can't be equated. But I wonder about how pain and loneliness intensify both in grinding destitution and blinding wealth. Hoffman and Williams achieved the Dream, and after the striving and climbing, perhaps reached into themselves and found that they were alone.

What I felt then, and what I feel now in Coroico, through the pain, is what Pema Chödrön calls *bodhicitta*, or the soft spot that we all have of tenderness, pain, and joy. All wrapped up together, that's our humanity. An acute soft spot has opened up by separating my animal corpus from my tribe of Melissa, Amaya, Clea, Adobe, Boots.

MY SEVENTH NIGHT ALONE in Coroico. I've not washed my hair for days. In silence, I cook my meals and in silence eat them. The cabin is so secluded that nobody sees me. I write.

Solitude is a tool sharpened on both edges. One machete edge slices mental concepts that conceal imagination's grail. *I'm a husband.* That concept is sliced away like so much *quiñe. I'm a father.* Slice. *I'm a professor.* Sliced. *I'm…sliced!* Alone, here in the giant ferns, amid five-story towers customized for the living and dead, there's nothing but raw presence where, yes, creativity resides.

But that same solitude — though liberating to the human eye, the world's biggest thing — wants Melissa's warmth. Sliced away by the other edge. *"Papa Bear!" comes Clea's sweet voice.*

Slice. *The joy of a tribal Transition Thursday lunch.* Felled. Gone are the voices of kin in the curves of our Casa Guapurú. Inaudible is the gurgle of our creek and the cry of parrots. Unfelt is the swing of our hammocks, the swing of our moods, together. I ache for my wife, spooning in bed at night, and Clea's little voice in the morning.

I learn the next morning that Sigrid has put Sol y Luna up for sale. The French-owned hotel, Cafetal, fifteen minutes downhill from Sol y Luna is for sale, too, as tourism dries up along with the Sweet Life that attracted these folks here. Still, the modernist towers rise. "Grow or die" is how a college friend, now CEO of a growing US company, put it to me, conveying the Dream's underpinnings. When I asked him why equilibrium won't cut it — economist Herman Daly's argument for a "steady state" — he replied: "If you don't get bigger, you're eaten. That's what *creates* the equilibrium."

Do I really know my CEO friend is wrong? Globalization has paralleled a 160-year-long rise in wages in Europe and the United States, which has grown a middle class with cars, mortgages, and pensions. Shouldn't *I* walk questioning? My friend might view the "one-potato" people not as the dying gasps of the Dream, but part of humanity's birth pains within it, the Dream yet to be culminated in a shared Good Life through the coming "smart economy" of labor-saving machines, clean-energy technologies, ever-extended life spans…cornucopia.

I'm a fool who hasn't showered, wanting to lash out, *Fight Club*–style, against progress. On a bluff above my cabin, chewing coca as the moon arcs higher into the night, I feel increasingly on my own. I'm outside of a pillar of the Sweet Life, *la Pacha*, or the unified field where wiser ones than I know that I'm the lady screaming at that shanty water pump, and I'm Philip Seymour Hoffman, too. I'm the Dream, and I'm Transition. One side of me understands the pain I feel is connected to near-religious convictions I have *against* the Dream, that this is very much a part of the Cartesian, mind-based separation from life in its fullness.

Still on the periphery of the Sweet, I wonder what it might mean to inhabit *vivir bien*, to not just experience it in flashes but to exist within its search of balance, to dwell in tolerance of diversity, including a diversity of worldviews and economic systems. I think of the initiation rituals I saw in the Bolivian Amazon, the ones that thousands of people, Chief Gaspar included, experience.

Going into the deepest part of the forest.

Being cut. Sliced open, blood drawn, scarred.

Returning to tribe as an adult, fully matured into the reality of living well.

I have not been initiated into a true adulthood, so I don't yet inhabit the tree of life, the one that holds up the world.

IV. SKY

Initiation

Sixteen

The people stream in.

I hike up to the El Fuerte ruins beside MAS farmer-unionists hoisting rainbow-checkered *wiphala* flags. As we crest the bluff over the two-hundred-meter carved rock — for two millennia a religious and political site for Arawak, Incan, and Spanish peoples — the view stuns. Three-hundred-sixty-degrees of greenery and a spectrum of wildflowers brought by returning autumn rains. MAS mayor-elect Enrique, wearing a red Inca-style poncho, stands in a silent circle with the two new MAS town councilors — one female, one male — draped in *wiphala* scarves, Bolivia's second official national flag representing the colors of "pluri-nationalism." Salvador, our architect's husband from Transition, stands beside Enrique — open to new initiatives like Transition — in this new circle of power; as the mayor's campaign manager, he's slated to be a top advisor.

I'd rushed back from Coroico after receiving a text from Thiago: The incumbent party had lost, and the MAS candidate, Enrique — open to new initiatives like Transition — had taken Suraqueta. Word of this first-ever "symbolic inauguration" of the incoming authorities also spread throughout the Suraqueta municipality's fifty satellite villages and hamlets, and a thousand people have gathered for the ceremony. A few hundred gather around me above the ruins to witness a *ch'alla* ceremony, while far below us in the south section of this ancient complex, hundreds more await to receive our representatives.

A woman in a bowler hat and *pollera* layer-cake skirt passes by, doling out free coca leaves. She smiles as I, *el gringito*, open my backpack to receive the hallowed leaf. Along with those around me I fill a cheek, and I'm amazed how many people I don't recognize, mainly the darker faces of the *campesinos* populating this vast municipality. Quechua-language chanting starts. The mayor-elect pours a bottle of the expensive local Vargas wine onto the ground. Each of the town councilors, advisors, and shamans also pour full bottles of Vargas wine and *singani* liquor into Pachamama, asking Mother Earth to sustain this new government. The story here: Criollo grapes, like the ones climbing the trellises in our orchard, grow, are tended and harvested, processed into fine wines, and are finally gifted back to the ground.

The empty bottles pile up — fifteen, twenty of them — and, the traditional coca-chewing kicking in, I marvel at how two thousand years culminate in the now. The officials before us are indigenous on a spectrum. They range from rural Quechua *campesinos*, peripherally tied to native culture, to a *valluno*-descendant teacher, who grew up in town and is less tied to Pachamama. This Earth-blessing brings these diverse politicians into the depth of their biocentric culture, regardless of their place on the "indigenous" spectrum.

The *ch'alla* ends, and the crowd claps and tosses confetti above the officials as they pass down to the fiesta below. I shake Mayor Enrique's hand, slap him on the back, and congratulate him; his glance tells me he remembers me from a Transition workshop we attended together. I congratulate the two town councilors, whom I also know peripherally, feeling related to the political process in a way I've never experienced before.

At an excited clip, and accompanied by roving trumpeters and *charango* players — and a friend who runs the local TV station, filming the festivities live for those who couldn't make it — hundreds of us walk a path through pockets of forest interspersed with other ruins, arriving after ten minutes into a storm of confetti sweeping across a wide field that was once part of a Spanish colonial fort. Applause echoes off the temples as groups of unionists shout *presente!* as the mayor's procession passes, a roll call of support, and ancient music rises as dancers in Amazonian and Andean dress twirl, soon grabbing the new mayor's hand and towing him into the dance. More music, coca leaves, wine, *singani.* Everyone is mingling excitedly, and I greet Maximo, who's with his younger daughter, Sofia. "*Y Clea?*" Sofia asks. I have an answer — at long last — to the question I've heard a hundred times. "*Miércoles!*" I whoop. On Wednesday, one week from now. Two days ago Melissa called and said, "I have tickets. Clea and I are coming home."

Rulas and Thiago, adobe-maker Estuvio and our *casera* Serafina, we all share words and smiles and hugs. I chat with a beaming Salvador, who laments about the photos I'd sent of Coroico and agrees, now that Transition is close to the government, to fight for a historical heritage ordinance to protect glocal Suraqueta from the Dream. Then the music abruptly stops and Mayor Enrique turns on his microphone.

The new mayor's voice catches in a manner that conveys how unprecedented this moment is, the inauguration of an indigenous *campesino* as mayor. Enrique, a small farmer, grew up in one of the municipality's hamlets. Oration on this scale is new to him; he stumbles through earnest thanks to each of the groups present for their help in the campaign. Then there's a pause as he searches within himself for language. A thousand souls silent. Behind him I see the path to a pre-Incan sinkhole I always visit with my students. No records exist about who excavated it or even where the tunnels beneath lead. Eighty percent of El Fuerte remains unexcavated. Perhaps it's analogous to the world's biggest thing, our unexcavated imagination.

Enrique speaks with great emotion. "All the bad governance," he declares, "will be gone."

The scent of lunch wafts over, as volunteers prepare local corn, potatoes, and *charque* (dried beef), and I feel a gratitude that's sinkhole-deep. Pouring spirits into Pachamama, this *cult* of traditional music and dance, it's none other than *blessing*. And as Irish philosopher John O'Donohue wrote: "Blessing has pure agency because it animates on the deepest threshold between being and becoming; it mines the territories of memory to awaken and draw forth possibilities we cannot even begin to imagine."

The dancing starts, and I move. The stymied, isolated feelings plaguing me in Coroico dissipate into the music of an evolving Suraqueta. Nobody here is untainted indigenous and few wish to re-create the past. A question is being danced today, in a colorful field of bio-culture, a question about how "territories of memory" might — in the end — help create possibilities beyond the Dream.

AT SANTA CRUZ'S VIRU VIRU AIRPORT the following week, Clea breaks away from Melissa and charges the customs gate. *"Papá! Papá!"* she cries, breaching the barrier to hug me like I've rarely been hugged: legs clamped to my torso, warm face embedded in my neck. Minutes pass like this, Melissa's bags still under inspection. Beside us, a young Bolivian couple cuddling their infant notices our protracted primality, and we share the smile of parents who understand this shared experience.

"I missed you, Papa Bear," Clea whispers, finally unlocking from me and falling onto small feet. Melissa pushes a baggage cart our way. We hug, and Clea tries to climb the *chacha-warmi* tree, so we lift her up. Clea hums. I laugh, having forgotten, in my solo months, this Clea-invented custom. Like the three monkeys in one of her children's books, we join in a threesome hug. We hum in unison, allowing the vibration to move deeply through our whole bodies.

IT'S A SERIES OF EPIPHANIES for Clea. After Papa Bear comes Amaya.

When I arrive with Amaya at the Hotel Milan in Santa Cruz,

having picked her up after school, we find Clea napping off the long flight. Amaya lies down next to her snoozing sister, taking her in for twenty minutes until Clea awakens, at first disoriented. Her face imbues joy and she says — lovingly, slowly — "Am*aaa*ya."

We spend a day together. The four of us hum. We open gifts: books Melissa brought for Amaya; the oversize tie-dye I bought for Clea at a used-clothing stall. We eat celebratory ice cream, play tag on the plaza, clamor in the playground, retrieve mail from our box in the labyrinthine post office, visit the Victory Café. Our "Slow" Santa Cruz rituals, all a short walk from the Milan.

Then it's time to take Amaya home. Her grandmother invites us in, leading Melissa into their courtyard to show her their fruit trees — chirimoya and *guapurú*; mango and papaya — while Clea wheels around on Amaya's scooter. Melissa produces matching raincoats for Amaya's mom and grandma, and we tell big sister we'll see her in Suraqueta soon.

Clea's next epiphany comes when, after the two-and-a-half-hour shared taxi ride to Suraqueta, she glimpses something exactly as primordial as Papa Bear and *hermana* (sister). "*Casa!*" she cries when she sees the curvature of her round house on the hill above as we drive into town.

Clea wiggles uncontrollably in my lap, repeating *casa-casa-casa*. It's sunset when we walk through our wooden gate. All of the *tulas* seem taller after the rain showers quenched Pachamama's long thirst, thriving in the space where *quiñe* shrubs used to be, the grass everywhere green, the eucalyptus and *tipas* and *carnavales*, green, wind-like sea surf in their leaves. Adobe barks at us from *la casa*, then, realizing Melissa and Clea are back, does spastic leaps. Boots joins us. I watch Melissa's awe over gardens fleshy with beets, lettuce, and kale.

Over the coming days our bodies and lives restitch. Unforced, it happens, *Mamá, Papá, Bebé*. For me a tumble from solitude into our species's communal norm.

Alone for those months — bear-clawing *quiñe*, breathing in the giant ferns at Sol y Luna — I experienced snatches of a monk's nonduality. My little body as Body. At Melissa and my wedding, my mother read aloud this from Kahlil Gibran: "Love one another, but make not a bond of love: Let it rather be a moving sea between the shores of your souls." And in Andean culture, fiancés are required to live together for at least one year before getting married, *chacha-warmi* on trial. After marriage, the Andean couple regularly joins and separates, the women having distinct, separately connected lives, particularly with a tribe of other women. Our marriage, too, is starting to contain such Antarctic *surs*. They gust in, dropping fine chilly isolation, then wail out, and leave in their wake sun and growth.

One evening Clea rolls on the grass outside with Adobe and Boots. "Her world order is reestablished," Melissa says, the sun setting over the Mairana hills. We don't need to talk about the doubts in New York. Now there are banana trees shredded by winds Melissa missed, the silence of rounded adobe walls, a firm bed and its sheets — our bed, our sheets.

"MEET THE COORDINATOR of the new Transition Education group!" Thiago calls to us from his table at Tierra Libre, where we're having lunch. He points to the long-haired, homesteading jeweler, Sandro, who takes a bow. "After a dip in energy and participation, Transition is firing up again, stronger than ever," Thiago says, updating us on the results of the communication group that met last night and on the upcoming seed exchange and *k'oa*.

The next day twenty of us gather for the weekly Transition Thursday lunch at a new vegetarian café, Melissa-Clea-Bill now stitching back into clan. As our two-year-old joins her clutch of friends playing under trellised grapes, Melissa catches up with everyone, as much around communal matters as personal ones.

Angelica, a thirty-five-year-old Suraqueteña, insists we reinvigo-
rate the town's water cooperative, owned by its eighteen hundred
users. The cooperative is now a hive of nepotism and corruption,
she says, "but we shouldn't let the new municipal government use
that as a reason to take it over. That's just too much power and
money concentrated in one place. We'll struggle hard to keep it
owned by the people."

At one point I mention the proposed municipal historic conservation designation in order to protect Suraqueta's old town.
Abundant agreement. And Yuri, a Suraqueteño trumpet player,
introduces his out-of-town visitors, announcing they'll jam out
Saturday night. A cheer goes up. "Melissa, are you restarting your
yoga classes?" someone asks. She nods. I'm asked when we're
going to do a salsa dancing night.

"Whenever," I say.

"And what should we call it? It needs a good name," Angelica
says.

"How about *salsa en transición*?" Thiago suggests, to laughter
and agreement.

Talk of politics, economics, culture bubbles in this group of
municipal officials and artists, locals and expats. This is the biggest Transition Thursday lunch we've had, and I'm amazed how,
out of scant central organizing, the "Transition" rubric is bringing
us together in both thoughtful and fun ways. Part of what's buoy-
ing it is the sense that the new local government — formerly a
distant and corrupt entity — is something we can actually *touch*.
How much better democracy feels when tangible. *Localization* is
the word for it: governance in which decisions are made as close
as possible to the people affected by those decisions.

HOE IN HAND, I walk the clay roads up along our land's north-
facing hill. This evening the sky's indigo clouds are bordered in

a cherry hue. Above, eucalyptus trees sway. For all the bad rap eucalyptus gets for sucking the ground dry, how glorious their sound, God's static.

I ram hoe to earth, opening up the *acequia* (irrigation ditch) I'd dammed a week before. It had been flooding our orchard, but it's been dry for several days, so the persimmons and pomegranate, the tangerines and macadamia are overdue for a splash. I make a mental note to re-dam the *acequia* tomorrow because I've learned the peaches quickly overwater and shrivel.

As I work, Clea and her fourteen-year-old babysitter, Marisela, are dots across our land, up on our adobe *casita* front porch. In the office-bedroom inside, Melissa must be on her final Skype call of the day; she's working remotely with the UN to wrap up New York. For her first week back, we took a technology sabbatical. Gadgetless, we tended the farm, visited friends, and reestablished Clea's "world order." Then, back into work, but not into workaholism. Our center is family-tribe-town, *chacha-warmi* spooned in bed after ninety nights apart.

I'm sweating and panting when Melissa and Clea cross the orchard to meet me, Marisela waving behind them as she disappears through a clump of *tulas* on our east footpath into town. Clea coaxes Papa Bear away from the fields, tugging me down the hill to our little swimming hole. Clea immediately gets naked, wanting, in the Spanglish she often speaks, "*papá conmigo* in the *wawa*." I oblige, Melissa soon, too, in habitat. We sing the water song: It's a never-the-same ditty about Clea and Daddy and *agua* and fun. We improvise, adding Adobe and Boots and Mommy and blue morphos to our song.

It's irresistibly revolutionary, this living Sweet, not being busy and not hurrying and rushing to change things. This is not the same mentality of planning and control and urgency, but rather the deep time that a lot of our ancestors experienced, within a context where there simply was no clock. Like Adobe and Boots and the other animals on our property, and like the trees, we don't rush today. The sunset's cherry-red now loosening from sky, we amble barefoot up to the round house because, per Clea, *Me want food.*

On the way back up, Boots appears along the path — with a headless guinea pig in her mouth.

Clea cries out, which gets Adobe's attention. The pooch comes bounding through its range, chasing Boots and her prey into our raspberry thicket.

After dinner, a sleepy Clea says: "Boots is bad."

"Why?" I ask. I'd noticed Clea had been unusually quiet after seeing the dead guinea pig in her cat's mouth.

"She…died that *ratón.*"

I repeat what we've explained before: Boots kills rodents, like that wild guinea pig, that would otherwise attract *corredores* and *chutos*, two venomous snakes that could hurt us.

"But…guinea *died.*" Clea's choked up.

Melissa hugs her. Then Clea asks, "We will die?"

The question feels like a stabbing. We're all silent. Through the window it's the gloaming now. Adobe chases Boots up the *noki* tree. The jasmine plant the leaf-cutter ants had stripped climbs the portico, almost fully recovered, with light-green leaves and fragrant white flowers.

"Yes," Melissa says. "We'll die."

Later, it strikes me how courageous it is to say this. It sounds improbable. Everything is so *alive*, with the rains back, gardens thriving, and my daughter fresh as a flower bud. "Like everything else," Melissa continues, hugging Clea, "we go back into Pachamama."

Later, Clea asleep, Melissa says: "Remember the dog corrals? In the Manhattan parks…"

We're cuddled in a hammock on the porch. I say: "How could I forget our dog-therapist neighbor?"

"Every time I passed a dog run, I thought of Adobe, ripping

through our *tula* forest, unpenned." She looks away from me and over our dark sea of *tulas*. "It's not that the New York dogs aren't content. They circle the pens in safe little packs, go back to their owner's apartment to eat canned food. The next day they circle the corral again."

Melissa's warm body against mine feels mammalian in the hammock. She continues: "But it made me realize something about the Sweet Life. It's not safe. Because it rests on death, because it's so transient. It sounds nuts, but the phrase that popped to mind one day on 41st Street and Second Avenue was: *Free dogs die.*"

I think back to Carlos Peralta's cook pot, the Dark Bush, that cliff. Maybe Melissa and I didn't have such dissimilar experiences after all.

As THE MONTHS PASS, the rainy season deepening and another Christmas approaching, our family restitches into one another and tribe, but *chacha-warmi* is increasingly ascatter. "People come to Suraqueta to break up," says our tall, bottle-lamp-creating friend Mateo. He's addressing Melissa, Thiago, and me at a bonfire in the pit beside our house on a Saturday evening in late December. We've finished dinner, and Clea is asleep on my lap.

Mateo doesn't need to explain. He means the rash of expatriate separations. First, our Turkish neighbors, Serdar and Denise, split. She left last week for Istanbul, and he'll continue to live here and run La Cocina. Their house, a two-bedroom they just finished building right below ours, is already up for sale.

Next are our Danish friends Anette and Thomas, homesteading organic farmers who make the wonderful local beer and juice we drink. They're divorcing after nearly two decades together, ten of those years in Suraqueta. She'll take over their ten-acre farm outside town, and he'll build a house on a lot they own in town, with his new partner; their teenage son will straddle these arrangements.

Now there's Mateo, looking downcast in the bonfire glow. He and his partner of eight years, Ivete, the Brazilian acupuncturist, have broken up. Of the three separated couples, they were closest to us. I remember his gusto when, while we were living at Bergwald, I first visited his flourishing recycled-glass workshop. *In Europe*, he told me in those days, *I used to feel like a piece of trash. Here I've repurposed myself.* Now, two years later, his hanging bottle lamps shimmer inside our house, but he's shuttered the workshop. *I don't love you anymore*, he told Ivete, driving her into depression and out of Suraqueta. She passed her clay-based soap-making business to a friend and flew to Portugal with a plan to do acupuncture in a seaside village outside of Lisbon. At her going-away party, she and I danced. Her hot tears falling on my arm, she blamed Mateo for doing this after so many years together. She told me she wanted to stay, and will come back someday, but for now she needs to leave a place with so many memories connected to her life with a man she still loves. Up for sale: their sixteen acres, the half-built eco-house, a beat-up van, and their dog-eared copy of *Permaculture: A Designers' Manual*.

"I'm not sure what I'll do," Mateo tells us. "Italy first, for sure, where I have a gig to earn fifteen hundred euros in ten days. Then maybe I'll work four or five months in Europe, before vagabonding in India. I'm a traveling monk at heart. At least I think so."

Mateo becomes quiet, stares into the flames. He's shed his partner, his business, and now his community. If there's a lightness in that disentanglement, it's not in his voice or demeanor. Thiago, meanwhile, happily munches coca leaves, recounting the magic of his fortnight at the permaculture and eco-village gathering in Colombia, and his inspiration over a healthy eco-municipal Suraqueta. Then he, Melissa, and I segue into details of building and creating here, in the place where we live, own property, and want to raise families. Thiago met his possible *warmi* on the road and is hopeful she might come to Suraqueta. At one point, I ask Mateo a question, but he doesn't hear me. When I nudge him, he says: "Sorry. I'm already someplace else."

A FEW DAYS LATER, Melissa and I have a simultaneous hankering for fresh books, so we gather up Clea and the four books on loan from the "Vagabond Library" — our collective shorthand for the backpacker book exchanges in La Chakana café, Road Runners Tours, and Republika — and walk ten minutes to Republika, whose branch of the Vagabond Library is a cozy, back-corner nook of the pub. While Clea plays on the old-brick floor with Jeff and Lisa's two-year-old daughter, Eleanor, Melissa and I sip beer and skim the spines of the latest volumes that have washed up. I snatch C.S. Lewis's *The Lion, the Witch, and the Wardrobe* to read with Amaya when she comes. Melissa finds a slim novel by a Georgia author, Terry Kay, called *The Valley of Light*.

Melissa, as usual more social than I am, thrusts *The Valley of Light* at me and skips out of the Vagabond niche and goes to the bar to talk to her friend Steph, while Clea and Eleanor, giggling, toss a ball for the bar dog, a black lab named Danny.

I sink into beer buzz and story. *The Valley of Light* takes place in 1948 in the American South. A young man, a World War II veteran, ends up stateside and unable to settle down. He finds a fragile inner peace as a wandering, moneyless fisherman, eating and selling whatever catfish and bass he can catch along the way.

Clea and Eleanor curl up like two kittens on the sofa next to me, falling asleep to the Andean-fusion music playing, as I deepen into *The Valley of Light*: Will the man settle down in one of the towns he passes through in North Carolina, which he falls in love with, or will he eventually vagabond onward?

Later that night, at home, I finish the short book. Melissa starts *The Valley of Light* the following day, a Slow Sunday with a rain shower. There's much planned for today, including attending a Transition-sponsored talk on water catchment by a La Paz professor at three and a tai chi class by an eighty-year-old Chinese master at five. We STOP IMPROVING and do neither of these; instead we nap and read and creek-sing when the sun peaks back out. "Me want food," Clea says at various points. Mealtimes don't matter to her; little hunger pangs do. We let her eat when she wants — papaya, mandarin, and bread from our Valley of Light. In the late afternoon, Melissa suggests a walk along the perimeter of our land, now a Sunday tradition. Sauntering, we talk specifics: the progress of individual members of the three hundred trees we've planted; the animals flying above and skittering underfoot; a firebreak we need to widen. Elation, though, is what pervades the permacultural details. We're elated by the uncomplicated act of being. Being with spouse and daughter, being with pets, being unscheduled on wild land. Being.

We arrive at our hillock, the spot where we've always talked about building our "final house." Much as we love our round house, it has just a single bedroom. There is no dedicated room for Clea, nor for Amaya when she visits, nor for guests. Melissa squeezes my hand. "We're so lucky," she says. Today's sunset is orange sherbet. Up in the round house, Melissa tented *The Valley of Light* to a middle portion where it's still uncertain as to whether the protagonist will stay rooted or ramble on. Melissa kisses me, lingering, then asks: "What about that anchor baby?"

Seventeen

Up in the eaves one morning, I hear Adobe barking below. Looking out the window, I'm surprised to see our honey-farmer-teacher-taxi-driver-*amigo* Maximo, wearing his *valluno* cowboy hat. Beside him, a teenage girl, his younger daughter, Sofia.

It's uncommon to have spontaneous visitors on our acres. We're far enough from town and up a hill; plus, after the rape incident, our gates have generally been locked, and the rest of the land is protected, not just by cattle fencing, but by the ever-taller rows of spiny Moses beard and agave.

Maximo waves up. "We jumped the fence!"

I call off Adobe, realizing why they're here: The previous week, Maximo saw me walking my mountain bike across the plaza, and he mentioned offhandedly that his daughter was excited to participate in the annual 20K Suraqueta bicycle race.

"Wonderful," I'd said.

Maximo nodded. "Except that she needs one thing for the bike race."

"What?"

"A bike."

I had offered to lend mine, and he accepted.

Now I jog down the stairs, grab bike and helmet, and wheel it out to them. Smiles blossom on both of their faces, and I feel joy in the offering. Maximo tells his daughter to ride it home — he'll walk. After I unlock the gate and we watch her wheel off down the hill into town, Maximo asks how our orchard is doing and offers to take a look at it. At the *minga*, Maximo had advised on spacing, planting depth, and irrigation. As we walk the now-flourishing orchard, he prunes the mandarin and star-fruit trees with his pocket knife and prescribes an organic cure for a fungus outbreak: boiled *paraiso* tree seeds. I ask him what he would charge to come and do it, and he says: "I'll come next week and do a half day in your orchard for free in exchange for borrowing the bicycle."

My impulse is to refuse. After all, a couple of bike-less days is nothing. He shouldn't have to pay me.

I'm programmed to say, *No, Maximo, it's my pleasure.* The mercantilist Dream, based on self-sufficiency, tells me "not to be a burden" on Maximo. Cash, in this story, is the neutral, nonbinding means of exchange. And gifts, like the bike loan, are totally free of future obligation.

But something in my Sweet Life reverse-programming gives pause. Gifts are different here. Anthropologists call it the "gift economy," where, for example, my bike — something Maximo needs and upon which his daughter will place wear and tear — is given to him, but with the expectation of reciprocation. To refuse his "gift" of orchard work is to nix an ongoing relationship with his family. By accepting, in this case something of greater value, I imply that I'll share with him later, synching us.

I choose obligation. "That would be wonderful, Maximo." We set a date.

A second spark of gift economy comes with an invitation from Suraqueta organic farmer Don Asano.

Melissa has heard that the eighty-year-old Asano has been more or less gifting organic agriculture courses (he does sometimes accept voluntary contributions) as a way of passing on his knowledge. So when we're on our weekly Friday afternoon visit to his farm — that's when Asano harvests for Santa Cruz and also opens his gate to locals — Melissa asks for a course. He agrees, saying: "Minimum three hour. Can't convey lifetime of experience in less than three hour."

So one afternoon in February 2016, Melissa and I gather a group of friends, including Karina and Hilvert from Paredones, and Kusi, and arrive at Asano's farm, five blocks from the town plaza, at the appointed hour. We're excited. There's a mystique around the generally reclusive Don Asano. A half century back, Asano arrived from his native Japan as director of Toyota in Bolivia, but tiring of corporate life in the 1980s, he gave up car hawking to farm a dozen acres he purchased in Suraqueta. At that time an economist with no agricultural training, Asano learned by doing, fashioning what is today a model organic farm. Asano pioneered a no-till method — he only moves the top five centimeters of soil — about which he's regularly invited to lecture internationally.

Exactly on time, the five-foot-four, mildly Yoda-reminiscent man appears in an outsize Texas Rangers baseball cap. He guides us past the simple adobe home he shares with his wife, past the guinea pig pens, and over to an outdoor porch strewn with *papa del aire* ("air potato," a tuber-like yummy that grows on vines). There, he seats us around a wood table. Standing before us in front of a flip chart, marker in hand, he is so short that he almost appears seated.

Then he begins to teach.

I've struggled enough with pedagogy to spot a master teacher. Asano, blending facts, humor, and suspense, has a porch-full of rapt students. Soil technique, animal fertilizers, and his philosophy of energetic harmony with nature, all of it comes alive in Spanish still stubbornly accented with Japanese. Asano poses frequent questions, drawing a quick X in the air when someone gets an answer wrong.

Soon we're on our feet and into his flourishing domain. At one point Asano kneels down, plucks a plump earthworm out of the soil, brushes the dirt off it, and...pops the worm in his mouth.

Confusion washes over the group. "What the heck?" mutters Kusi.

Asano remains down on his knees, tonguing the invertebrate from one side of his mouth to the other. Then he takes the wriggling guy out, shows it, and pops it back in.

"You see?" Asano says, worm-in-cheek.

In awkward silence, we wait for him to elaborate. He doesn't. Around us, a hundred persimmon trees with enormous dangling fruits, a football field of tomatoes, bok choy, carrots, and numerous other vegetables in perfect rows. He's holding our attention through sparking our curiosity.

Finally, brave Karina asks the obvious question: "Why did you...put a worm in your mouth?"

"Ah-hah!" Asano says, as if this were an unexpected question. He roots around, finding another one right away, and dangling it before us.

"Is that how he farms?" I overhear Hilvert whisper. By stimulating each worm with saliva?

"Please," groans Karina.

I take a stab: "Are you showing us...that your soil is healthy? Chemical free?"

Asano uses his worm-free hand to X out my answer. Amusement tempers my embarrassment as the baseball-capped octogenarian deletes me.

Nobody guesses the answer. So Asano, leaving the worms a deadpan conundrum, leads us into a greenhouse, and gingerly removes a tomato seedling from where it's rooted with hundreds of others...in yellow *sand*.

He holds the tiny tomato plant out reverently, like a communion wafer. There's silence.

"From here," he says, solemnly, "I transplant them into their nursery."

Asano shuffles through our circle into the nursery, pokes a hole in loamy dark soil, and places the seedling in, then lightly surrounds it with soil.

"But," says Melissa, asking the question on everybody's mind, "why do you germinate your seeds in sand and not soil?"

"Ah-hah!" Asano's eyes light up, feigning surprise at the question.

Kusi, avoiding deletion, correctly posits that it's to develop a strong vertical root structure, eliciting a discussion of soil — all topics that I hadn't imagined would have so much relevance in my life until I came to Suraqueta.

After bidding farewell to Don Asano, our little group spends an animated hour under a nearby *soto* tree sharing new ideas. The topic turns to local governance, and what it would take to make Suraqueta — with a fresh government and already an official "eco-municipality" — 100 percent organic. Karina enthuses about how our original Transition efforts at family-garden exchanges could go much broader. "In a recent meeting in Paredones, with the mayor and town councilors, the mayor was explaining how they needed *gente preparada*" — "prepared" or formally educated people — "so I wrote a letter to the mayor offering my support." Karina proposed to the mayor that she lead a participatory process on ecological agriculture and tourism. Her plan has been accepted; Karina will join the government. With this happy news we depart from an afternoon of Asano's tutelage — educated, entertained, and bubbling with Small-is-beautiful optimism.

A MONTH AFTER VISITING DON ASANO, Melissa, Clea, and I head to Santa Cruz. I'm to teach a new group of American undergrads in Santa Cruz the next day, and we go early to spend the afternoon with Amaya in our "gazing upward," or visually curated, version of Santa Cruz: playing tag and feeding pigeons, pillow-fighting and siestas at the old-school Hotel Milan, and visiting the post office beside the Victory Café — the sole post office, remarkably, in a city of two million — where we have a box. Wandering our way through the vast, mildew-scented halls of steel mailboxes, Clea and Amaya try to find ours amid thousands of identical ones. Before we rented our Santa Cruz box, our address was: "William and Melissa Powers, Bergwald, Suraqueta, Bolivia." Every three or four months, when the pile of Suraqueta mail got big enough at the Santa Cruz post office, a volunteer from Suraqueta would bush-taxi it to our town and deliver the mail door to door.

I hear a squeal as Clea finds our box. After the lock clicks open, a hush comes over our family. We haven't been to our mailbox in six weeks. Out of the slot, Melissa pulls three precious letters.

"Don't open them *here,*" Amaya asserts, this place too profane for the sacred act of breaking an epistle's seal. Clea perches on tiptoes, grasping upward almost religiously, wishing to hold the missives.

It's not until we're seated at a table at the Victory Café that Amaya gives the nod. We open the letters.

They're anticlimactic. One's a bank document and the other two are generic Shutterfly Christmas cards from America, our friends' family photos on the front, computer-cursive Happy Holiday notes on the back. It's the end of March, mind you. The postmarks go back to December, and I wonder about the intervening delays. Clea, at first fascinated with the cards, immediately forgets them as Amaya leads her out of the Victory and into the kids' area of a neighboring ice cream shop, where there's a room of colorful plastic balls.

Kids, however, have taken many of the precious balls home over time, and so this is no waist-deep plunge into thousands but a toe-deep wading in only some twenty balls. This matters naught to Amaya, Clea, and the other little ones who toss balls, inventing hilarious games with what's available, having as much fun as if they were backstroking through an ocean of them. And I realize, this is part of Clea's Bolivian childhood: mail four months late, a trickle of plastic balls. Slow, simple, sufficient.

Meanwhile, Clea spots something out of the corner of her eye:

a coin-activated choo-choo train. She runs over to it and climbs on, Amaya clambering in next to her. They start moving it around manually. Our Dark Bush–raised sprout doesn't know about inserting bolivianos for sound and vibration, and Amaya — after a wink from me — doesn't say anything as they happily play in it for ten minutes, then get down to hop into a little spaceship. Until, that is, two other kids come along, plop boliviano coins into the slot, and the train starts to party.

Clea steps off her now comparatively dead spaceship and reviews the revised state of affairs. She goes over and puts a tiny finger in the coin slot. A moment passes.

Then her eyes get very wide. She asks me, "Toins?"

When the other kids finish, I sigh and slide in two bolivianos.

Clea and Amaya pass three bouncing, musical minutes on the train. When it ends, Clea cries out, "Toins! Toins!"

"No, Clea," Melissa says, "That's enough. We have done it once, now we are going to go play on the plaza."

Huge pouting face. "*Toins*," she explains, getting out and indicating the slot.

Up until now, her little jar of toins in Suraqueta was just something to shake, but today she's seen the connection between them and train ecstasy. As we walk away, three-year-old Clea's in tears, saying, "Toins, toins." She's pleading, really, trying to clarify for us thickheaded adults how easy it is. All you have to do is pay.

"Oh no," Melissa says. "She's discovered the power of toins."

"Out of the past rises a dream of future" reads a banner outside Santa Cruz's new Ventura Mall, the first in Bolivia. I'm on a bus with twenty American undergraduates and the staff from their study-abroad program. Silence blankets the group as we pass alongside Ventura's five stories of towering glass. We park and go inside, the mall's innards even more astonishing. Where I'd expected a few dozen international chains intermixed with idiosyncratic Bolivian-owned *salteña* (empanada) joints and *aguayo* weaving shops, we instead walk past the first of two hundred stores of every conceivable American and European retail brand. We climb on an escalator. The students are speechless, except for one who lets out a low whistle and says: "Holy. Moly."

Hard Rock Café. KFC. TGI Fridays. The music pulses as we switch escalators, our body heat pressing into Bolivians feeling the pulse of More, many for the first time. J Lo isn't singing about the rocks that she's got, but we're rising, rising — Tommy Hilfiger, BabyCorp, Clarks — to the Dream's music, out of Bolivia and into America.

Since we're studying "sustainable development" I wanted to give the class a broad perspective, including...*this*. But I failed to scout it out first, having arranged the meeting with Ventura's director by phone through his assistant. This morning, after my usual two-hour lecture on sustainable development to lay the groundwork for our five days together in Santa Cruz and Suraqueta, I told the students about the mall excursion. A few of them simpered at this, their smirks groaning, *We* know *what a mall is, Professor*.

But now, their stumped expressions say they didn't know what a mall is. Not fully. This is the Dream on crack, Ventura's flashy architecture making the Macy's in New York look quaint, as if the investors transported a new prototype of ultra-sleek mall to Latin America's most indigenous, Pachamama-centric country.

Fifth floor. The personal assistant to Jesús Figueroa, the mall's director, ushers us to our seats in a conference room, serves us Starbucks, then close the doors. "Smells like sulfur," one student says. "The devil's been here?"

"Smells fine to me," says a University of Central Florida peer, sniffing the Seattle-spawned coffee.

Jesús makes his entry. Boyishly handsome, dark-eyed, with some of the whitest teeth I've seen in Bolivia, Jesús is fortyish, just under six feet, and clad in business shirt and jacket. What ensues is one of the slipperiest sales jobs I've seen.

He knows this isn't an MBA class. I've sent him the syllabus and briefed him. These are culturally aware undergrads who chose to take a course on race, class, and sustainability in the continent's most far-flung country. So how does he win them over?

By being himself. Jesús Figueroa embodies, unapologetically, the "growth economics" paradigm I just taught in my morning lecture.

Beaming with a pride usually reserved for one's children, he projects photos of his baby: Ventura Mall, when it was still under construction. "My dream," he says in a creamy Spanish, "of the future." He tells us about the doubters ("A mall of this scale is not feasible in Bolivia"). His faith ("'Cholitas are not just poor Indians,' I implored. 'They *will* consume, too'"). The investment flowing into his Dream, the building rising. His two years of eighteen-hour workdays, six days a week ("My kids? I never saw them"). Till finally, against all odds, he attracted the giants.

"I'll never forget the day KFC landed," he says, relating the sweat-and-tears tale of convincing them at a Las Vegas trade show. That first multinational was all he needed. "Then Starbucks landed. Pizza Hut landed…." Jesús's eyes soften, the names of chains falling from his lips like autumn leaves, each one "landing" — and that's how it feels, as if they, and this mall itself, have landed from the distant Planet of Toins, smothering vestiges of the gift economy.

The students, program staff, and I lean forward in our seats and laugh as this smooth *bachata* dancer glides us through his world, one where "destitute Bolivia" will rise, with time, to Miami's consumerist heights. "Yes, Ventura Mall is only accessible to the top twenty percent of more elite consumers now," he says, fielding a question about access, "but the rest will *aspire*. And they'll *arrive*."

I mention the decline in foot traffic I've noticed on the plaza; there are fewer people at the Victory Café. "The mall is the new plaza," Jesús seamlessly replies. "And it's actually 'Defeated Café.' Do you know why?"

Nobody speaks. He exclaims, switching to English, "No parking, no business." Jesús then passionately describes the mall's bountiful fields of parking, absent in the barren historical center, and how much safer it is inside his walls: "No crime and all-weather."

During a final tour of the food court, I think of Amaya. She's an urban preteen, and Jesús's shopping mall is primed to act as her initiation grounds. Am I doing enough for her as her father, enough to help give her both structure and freedom? Have *I* truly matured into an adult who could even hope to do so? I mean "adulthood in community," in the sense articulated by the Bolivian foreign minister, Fernando Huanacuni, who described community as "the unity and structure of life where the ant, the tree, the mountains, the ancestors...we are all here."

My musings are interrupted by the mall director. "What about franchising some of these brands in Suraqueta?" Jesús Figueroa says to me, while a hundred people around us ingest fast food. Figueroa grows distant, as if consulting a Google chip-in-the-brain. Finding the phrase, he snaps back and says: "*Es un* 'ground-floor opportunity.'"

JESÚS FIGUEROA and the Ventura Mall flummox the class.

They debate it in the bus all the way along the bumpy road to Suraqueta. Some students, won over, argue Bolivians "shouldn't be denied what we in the north have," malls included. Others fire back that this is not a *choice* "because of capitalism's unfair marketing power."

"And look at the greenhouse gas produced," one student says. "Even Jesús admitted the mall uses, for its air-conditioning, lighting, and so on, a carbon footprint equivalent to three hundred thousand Bolivian people." We calculate that Suraqueta, with about five thousand people, has one-sixtieth the energy footprint of that single mall.

Suraqueta, initially, dampens this heated discourse. The students reside in adobe eco-*casas* and tromp Amboró National Park's giant ferns for a day with Kusi as expert guide. They tour the Flor de Montaña alternative school. And one morning, we take several bush taxis up to Chorrillos, a hidden cup of humid valley above the town, to the off-grid home of friends Juan Carlos and Carolina.

Entering this Bolivian family's life feels like stepping into another world, that of ancient China's Taoist poets — society people who fled the metropolis for far-flung peace, sharing that unadvertised reclusion with whomever happens to hear about it. We've been up to their house on several occasions and are consistently astounded by the way they embody deep layers of the Sweet Life. We join Juan Carlos and Carolina in the adobe meditation hall. The air smells a tad more tropical than in Suraqueta, the silence of this hidden vale a tad thicker. In the distance, I make out the thump of a waterfall. As part of their livelihood, the family hosts ten-day retreats for seriously ill, primarily cancer patients from Bolivian cities and abroad, everybody arriving via word of mouth. They also receive folks exhausted by workaholism and stress.

Juan Carlos and Carolina talk a little bit about their philosophy — "No judgment, no evaluation, no comparison," as Carolina says at one point — and then they lead the group in a tribal dance around a bonfire. At the end of an hour and a half of dancing, chanting, and playing drums, everyone is sweating and spent. One of the students rails on the mall — its environmental impact and consumeristic values. Carolina eventually responds, as the sun begins to set, "Under *vivir bien*, we don't blame a mall. We don't judge consumerism or those people promoting it. We see, neutrally, it as part of *wetiko*, the Algonquin way of talking about a cannibalistic spirit."

The sky turns pink, the *carnavales* on the ridge seeming to indeed hold the sky aloft on their branches. Juan Carlos says: "*Wetiko* tricks its host into thinking that cannibalizing others' life force — including animals' and Pachamama's life energy — for personal advantage is a logical and upright way to live. *Wetiko* severs one's connection with Pachamama and makes the ego supreme."

Author Paul Levy, he says, rendering the *wetiko* concept comprehensible to Western people, dubs it "malignant egophrenia" — the ego acting with the malevolent logic of a serial killer, disconnected to heart, reason, and limits.

I descend the hill a little baffled. The Dream, according to this Bolivian couple, is even deeper in us than I thought. And more inextricable. The Sweet Life therefore feels even more unreachable.

On my students' last full day in Suraqueta, organic farmer Asano charms them for three hours with worms-in-the-mouth and seedlings-in-sand aplomb. But the tiny Japanese-Bolivian, at the end, drops a quiet bomb beside his guinea pig pens: An Argentinian company has just arrived, he says, and started "a huge chemical agricultural project. Industrial grapes and strawberries, hidden just above town. Pesticides into Suraqueta's watershed."

Hearing this, I offer to take, on our lunch break, any students who want to go with Melissa and me to the spot Asano describes. A dozen of us bush-taxi up to a shocking sight.

It's as if Jesús Figueroa's Dream beat us back to Suraqueta: Acres of hillside are denuded of trees. A tractor roars in the distance, toppling more forest. A small crew of men, without masks, sprays insecticides onto the grape saplings.

"Look," Melissa says, pointing out the gullies taking the contaminants right into the Chorrillos watershed that feeds our municipal water supply. Asano had explained to us that some of the previous municipal officials — who currently face numerous corruption charges in court, based on their tenure in Suraqueta

— did not apply the law requiring an environmental impact assessment. Melissa sets her jaw and says: "We must stop this."

But the near-complete warehouse and processing center makes it appear unstoppable, despite the recent municipal government shift. *Wetiko*. A cannibalizing spirit. One of the students reaches through the barbed wire and picks a strawberry so perfect it could only come from spraying away all other life. "Half a strawberry," she says. "It's got that Sam's Club generic taste. Bred for transportability and shelf life."

Fruit grown to cheaply and efficiently supply Ventura Mall's food-court smoothies.

Eighteen

A week later, the threat of agrochemicals in our town's water becomes local news and activates the "antibodies." Two years ago, blowback to the Coca-Cola blitz on Suraqueta's plaza ignited our single fruit-planting *minga*, but this more visceral threat triggers responses from all directions.

At a meeting of the town's citizen-run water and sewage cooperative, members demand something Suraqueta still does not have — potable water — and *not* a new infusion of toxins from foreign-owned industrial grape and strawberry farms. The problem, however, is that, despite the overturn of the old municipal government, corrupt elites remain entrenched in the independent water cooperative. New town-wide elections, however, will be held in four months — in July 2016 — and Melissa is considering if she'll run. Scant women and, currently, zero foreigners serve on the board. But a handful of locals have planted the idea of a campaign with Melissa.

The new mayor and town council go into overdrive; they initiate lawsuits against former officials who, an independent auditor concludes, embezzled four million bolivianos, and they spark fresh actions to benefit the town. Transition friends like Salvador and Karina, now in the government, present a wide-ranging plan for town recycling and also a historic ordinance conservation law to avoid "a Coroico" here; fifty people crowd city hall to support the heritage preservation measure, and it soon becomes law.

Moreover, several of the study-abroad undergraduates, stirred by their visit, complete coursework in Cochabamba and return to Suraqueta. "Seeing the destruction inspires me to come back and act," one of them puts it to me. "But more than anything, I need to decolonize myself." Two students conduct research on aspects of organic agriculture in Suraqueta as their final semester-abroad project, and a third stays for months on a Washington University–supported internship in the fledgling MAS municipality, assisting with Escobarian "postdevelopment" actions like implementing and funding the historic conservation law.

Meanwhile, Melissa and I receive visitors, our retiree friends Dwayne and Alison, from Brooklyn, he a former engineer, she a professor. Having popped in for four days during a Bolivia trip the year before, they decide to come back and rent a house in Suraqueta for a month. They're on vacation, but also on the trail of *vivir bien*, of the Sweet Life, looking for ways to deepen and simplify their American lives. But Alison's face goes sour when, on the plaza in front of city hall one afternoon, the interning US students tell her about the Ventura Mall and the industrial farming. She accompanies us up to Casa Guapurú, where Melissa and I are to meet with the students.

Alison hasn't seen our land for over a year, and she's overcome by the changes. The thorny *quiñes* are gone; in their place rise three-meter, flowering *tulas*. The orchard we'd planted in our community *minga* is fruiting. A student samples one of our first peaches. "Sweet!" she cries out and waxes poetic on the contrast with the nonorganic, GMO strawberries in the industrial fields above. Our soil, once the hardness of asphalt, has, over just a couple years of permaculture, come into an adolescence of fertility. All the manure we've laid down, the helpful shade of rising *tulas*, and the way we've gravity-channeled creek water through the property has not only helped us grow stronger crops but created richer habitat. The ferrets and iguanas, the *tejones* and wild guinea pigs, have started to venture back, albeit cautious of the now full-grown Boots and Adobe.

We circle up on the hillock — Alison, two students, Melissa, and I — passing around a yerba máte cup while Clea eats *guapurú* off a nearby tree. One of the students is reading Joanna Macy and Chris Johnstone's *Active Hope*, and we discuss the authors' "spiral that reconnects," where you "honor your pain for the world" — the pain of an ecocidal Dream and its underlying *wetiko* — alone, and then in tribe, finally "seeing with new eyes" and "going forth."

As we dig deeper into these ideas, I feel the rawness of my own pain surface as the students articulate theirs. One, a junior from Case Western, admits she felt comfortable in the mall. "I have a lot of happy childhood memories in malls," she says, "and I felt that nostalgia in Ventura. It's like how much cars are a part of me. You know, I can't even listen to NPR because it makes me carsick. That's because my parents had NPR on constantly as I shuttled endlessly around the suburbs from sports practices to music lessons."

La Pacha, the unified field where all of this belongs. We talk about all our good memories, about how love has been tied to and expressed within materialism, within NEVER STOP IMPROV-ING. Instead of my previous reflex to judge this — in others and most vehemently in myself — we look at it and feel its texture, without judging it.

Seen like this, we view European culture in its complexity, the "Plato to NATO" culture that gave us the Enlightenment, the In-dustrial Revolution, and eventually, the Dream. Not perfect gifts, but gifts nonetheless, and ones that Europe, as a culture, spawned and then sent around the world via exploration, imperialism, and trade, as researchers Kirk, Hickel, and Brewer point out in their 2017 paper "All Change or No Change?". Today, many in the world are adopting Global North liberal values like freedom, equality, and the rule of law, and these are part of the modern capitalist sys-tem Europeans have bestowed on the world. But isn't this system also "the host structure," as Kirk, Hickel, and Brewer write, "of the suicidal *wetiko* meme that is gradually consuming the planet? The messy truth, of course, is that it can be both." The Dream can offer great benefits to some while exploiting others and plundering the natural world to an extreme degree.

The other student eventually says that being in Suraqueta makes her realize "what a real alternative looks like, or more importantly feels like." She asks Melissa and me how we ended up here, on this land, in this community, "and with no…*car.*"

After sharing a smirk with me, Melissa talks about how she feels increasingly connected to our community and how our relationship with every square meter of soil matters. "By rooting ourselves in Suraqueta," she explains, "you see how even the soil quality of a garden bed is like money in a bank account. Each time we till in more manure, or compost from our gray-water banana circle, we're growing our capital because that soil gives bigger beets and passionfruit, producing stronger, more pest-resistant crops."

The sun suddenly slips through a weak point in the slate-gray sky. We're in a pattern: sun-warmed wildflowers, the rustle of an iguana, the boom-boom of a marching band below on the plaza. "*Mira!*" Clea says, pointing to a cocoon on the *guapurú* tree; as she grows, she's become increasingly observant of nature's subtleties. In the organic broth inside a cocoon, the organs of the new creature emerge with the pulse of a heartbeat. Growth in nature, I'm realizing more viscerally each day, happens not in a linear manner but rather through a series of pulsations. Growth is gentle; it reaches out tentatively into new terrain. I notice that is how the change is happening in myself, in my family, and in our polis. This quote from Rumi captivates me: "Your hand opens and closes, opens and closes. If it were always a fist or always stretched open, you would be paralyzed. Your deepest presence is in every small contracting and expanding, the two as beautifully balanced and coordinated as birds' wings."

Caminar preguntando. The Case Western student wonders

aloud about David Korten's idea of "Great Turning" from eco-cide to Earth culture, about the "antibodies" of human tribes and communities rising. *Walk, questioning.* "Can a new activism," she asks, "be as nonblueprinted, as…*natural,* as Pachamama?"

Our elder friend Alison, who's been silently listening, takes a *guapurú*-gorged Clea into her lap and observes, "The new Global South 'activism' seems to be tapping the sensuous, the slowness of nature." She herself is a lifelong activist, mainly on the streets of her hometown of New York City. "What is happening here can inspire us in the north with approaches beyond necessary-but-insufficient marches and advocacy campaigns." As she says this, the sky flexes gray muscle, squelching the sun. There's the tongue-feel of yerba máte, the *wawawa* of our creek, the spark of yellow on gray as birds flare south. "How little Suraqueta plays out," she says, "matters hugely to the world."

ONE DRIZZLY EARLY MAY AFTERNOON, I get a call from Androas, a German traveler I'd met on a previous visit to Santa Cruz, where he was studying Spanish. He'd asked me about Suraqueta and got excited about a potential visit when his wife arrived. I gave him my number.

"I'm here!" he enthuses, explaining that he and his wife will spend two nights at La Vispera en route to camping in Amboró.

Melissa, Clea, and I meet the buoyant and tan couple for dinner on the patio of Trent's Posada del Sol. White butterflies, having emerged from their cocoons, flutter overhead, away from the sunset as, for three or four hours, we come into intimate and enjoyable conversation with the couple. We talk about our home-stead, about this Transition Town that's morphed into an ener-gizing eco-municipality attempting to buck corporate agriculture and other aspects of the Dream.

They are also transitioning in a Suraqueta-size town just south of Stuttgart, Germany. Androas teaches physics at a technical high school. His wife, Katya, works for IBM, where she does "cloud development for high-end companies." Katya says, "I love bunching up with colleagues over laptops and coffee" to solve an interface bug. We're very different on the surface; to wit, she's a salary woman, a career IBMer using her precious few weeks of vacation in Bolivia this year. Yet we have much in common insofar as the couple has decamped from rat-race Stuttgart to live a less stressful life. They both bike daily ten-mile commutes to their jobs, along municipal bike paths, and watch the sunsets from their porch overlooking a nature reserve.

The couple percolates happiness, and it comes out that the forty-one-year-old Katya is pregnant and just told Androas today. They're overjoyed. Perhaps thinking of what's to come, they dance with Clea to the live Andean-music band, Trimate, playing at Posada. Watching my little strawberry-blonde, sure-footed dancer get down with them, I can hardly believe this girl was once the infant whose umbilical cord I cut back at an American birthing center over three years ago. She's so different from how Amaya was at this age. Whereas Amaya was always tranquil, a so-called "easy" child, Clea seems to be coming into herself as a creative extrovert, a dancer-artist with wide mood swings.

After dinner we stroll to the plaza, well-fed, well-danced, and well-conversed. We take photos with Androas and Katya, then hug good-bye.

Our dinner brought texture and enjoyment. And yet, over the coming days, a slightly unsettled aftertaste develops. It surfaces obliquely while weeding the orchard one afternoon. "Jeez," Melissa says, "*cloud development for high-end companies.*"

I hack my hoe into a stubborn wild passionfruit choking a pomegranate sapling. "*I love bunching up with colleagues over laptops.* Say what?"

Our field-banter bubbles up out of neither envy nor disparagement, but rather from a certain disequilibrium. The German

travelers did not affirm our exact version of the Sweet Life —
revillaging in the Global South — the way visitors like Alison
and the internship students do. To the contrary, they embodied
a transitional path toward "living well" in the Global North, a
sweetness *outside* our Valley of Light in which they've apparently
found happiness.

The following day, while we're at Bergwald for coffee, Clea
goes over to watch one of the guests, a midforties man, apply-
ing a wrench to his motorcycle. I sidle up behind my daughter,
then Melissa joins us, and we start chatting. It turns out he's from
Washington, DC, where he owns City Bikes.

"I know that bike shop," Melissa says. "In Adams Morgan,
right?"

He nods, pleased.

Melissa and I, having both attended grad school in DC, slip
into a spontaneous quarter hour talking Tryst and Rock Creek
Park with him. We're no longer fully in Bergwald, as a kind of DC
motion picture plays in our minds. He tells us he's on a motorcycle vacation across South America. ("Why not on a bike?" Melissa
asks. "Too slow," he responds.) He's an entrepreneur and bache-
lor living in a dynamic American city, financially and personally
free to go where he wishes. And he wishes to spend a grand total
of eighteen hours in the place we've chosen to make a life, with
Suraqueta worth a mere clause in his banter — "pretty nice place"
— before he segues into more stimulating matters.

Tourism gives the town part of its "glocal" fabric, yet I wonder how much more rooted our lives might feel without this
stream of happy-*not*-to-stay-here travelers advertising other
lives elsewhere. I've been reading E.M. Forster's *Howards End*,
set a century before, a novel I plucked from the Vagabond Library. The nature-centered country home of the title — Howards
End — symbolizes the settled and biocentric quality of the pre-
industrial world. But the estate's owner, a London businessman,

wants to sell the anachronistic home. It *un*settles him, actually, to feel rooted because he's successfully embedding into the
then-fledgling Dream, where people move as fluidly as capital.
Motion — to him, to the emerging world — is rootedness.

The following day, while I'm practicing *valluno* plaza-sitting,
a long-haired Venezuelan *jipi* approaches my bench, peddling
vegetable-ivory necklaces he's woven. Just arrived from Brazil,
he's been traveling the world for ten years ("Europe, Asia, Latin
America"), and it's his first time in Bolivia. He's allowed Suraqueta a couple of days and asks me about the area. I mention Amboró National Park, the El Fuerte Inca ruins — and ask him about
his native Venezuela. My heart clips faster as he describes various Venezuelan "Suraquetas": Mérida, surrounded by entrancing
hamlets; Margarita Island, where Lebanese, Germans, and Swiss
have settled beside Caribbean beaches, eating seafood daily. As
he croons on, I feel landlocked to the point of claustrophobia,
and I neuro-mirror his enthusiasm for those locales. Wanderlust
strikes.

Later, I sneak guiltily online to look at Santa Cruz–Caracas
flights. No, I'm not going to Margarita Island, but I hanker to.
After a while, I look up from the screen and out at the waning
crescent moon over a Suraqueta whose harmony — in moments
like this, in a world in brisk motion — disquiets, and I wonder
what it's like to be that itinerant Venezuelan, gypsying the globe.

Ariana, a thirty-five-year-old friend from La Paz, also has
itchy feet. She's been living in Suraqueta with her three kids for
the past few years, but she has decided to pack up and move
her family to the city of Valparaíso, on the Chilean coast. At her
going-away party at Republika, she tells me she's decamping from
Suraqueta in part because her German boyfriend, finding Suraqueta too small, has already escaped to Valparaíso, and she wants
to make a go of it with him. Her departure is also partly economic; like others who have come and gone, she's found the cash
flow to be more of a dribble. A massage therapist and beautician,

she had a smattering of clients here, but she expects to lure many times more to her condo home-office in Chile.

Many others in Suraqueta mirror Ariana's free-spiritedness. She and her kids are vegetarian and have long volunteered on conservation projects. She transmits optimism, and that positivity is reflected in the faces of all who come to say good-bye. I can tell that it's hard for Ariana to leave. Her kids attended the Flor de Montaña alternative school, and she's been active in Transition. The previous weekend, Ariana organized a big "*gratiferia*," or "*Really* Free Market," where everybody brought things to give away for nothing. It took place in the vegetarian café Planeta Verde, and the joint was packed. "Juan Carlos is taking over the *gratiferia*," she tells me, with a touch of pride over having started it. "It's going to be a monthly event." A stream of white butterflies passes us, flying east, though Ariana is moving southwest, representing the converse face of our community: not Transition Town, but Transience Town. Though centripetal forces do root us into "glocal" community, centrifugal forces tug at our fabric. The "fireflies," those vehicles traversing the old road to Cochabamba, shine brighter on these nights of departure, as Ivete and Mateo, and now Ariana and her family, depart Suraqueta. As I leave the party, Ariana gives me an especially strong embrace and *adios*.

A WEEK LATER, Melissa and I stop along the Camino a San Juan to chat with eighteen-year-old Beatriz, one of the violin-playing, "earmuff" kids in the Christian, orphanage-assisting German family we used to live next to at Bergwald. We've remained casually acquainted from our days as neighbors, and as we talk, Beatriz announces: "We're moving back to Germany."

Melissa asks why, and she says it's time for college, and that means Europe. "I don't really want to go," the flaxen teen says in accent-free Spanish, but she also admits that there's "no excellent music school" in a small place like Suraqueta. She and her sister have been busing, once a week, to a conservatory in Santa Cruz, a five-hour round trip. Unstated: They're done with Suraqueta. Done with reggaeton and agrochemical-fed tap water. Beatriz volunteers at the Suraqueta Refuge, feeding rescued wildcats and howler monkeys, and we talk whenever I bring Amaya and/or Clea. She always has a vibrant yet calm demeanor, as if forever hearing a symphony in her mind. But now there's uncertainty. She loves the freedom and wild nature of Suraqueta, but says: "I'm *missing out* on something here. I want to be at the heart of things, in Germany." The globe's third-richest country at the EU epicenter; territory of Beethoven and Bach, of smooth ribbons of *Autobahn*.

Transience Town. I stream the news in German on Deutsche Welle and ponder a "sabbatical" in cultural capital Berlin. I dream along smooth ribbons. Buddhists say that the first creation is in the mind, and I'm already creating a year's sabbatical in Berlin by conjuring it.

In those disturbingly xenophobic weeks before Melissa's foray to the UN in New York City, she had said to me: "Why don't we — in a year or two — move to Santa Cruz for two months. Rent out our Suraqueta house and get an apartment there. I could take French and you German at the Alliance Française and Goethe-Institut, and we could just live a kind of urban life and get our languages down." When I'd asked her why we'd do that, she replied: "Don't you remember? To prepare for the year we've always talked about…biking across Europe, working on organic farms in Germany and France."

Next, Thiago tells us he's planning to leave Suraqueta. His Colombia-*warmi* prospect gone cold, he's putting his land up for sale and says he'll move to Cochabamba where there's more permaculture activism and a larger pool of possible mates. Hilvert and Karina, too, just returned from a climate change conference in La Paz, are talking about the urban connectedness, and seem slightly down on renaturing. "I've been feeling a little isolated as a *campesina*," Karina tells me one day. "I mean we actually *ordered pizza* the other night. A motorcycle taxi carried it from Suraqueta, the whole twenty-five minutes and over two rivers to our farmstead. Ridiculous. But it tasted so good."

Are Melissa and I really rooted here? As the outer world beckons, that's the lovely and chilling question seeping in. Build a final house on our hillock? Give birth to an anchoring Bolivian baby? Melissa and I no longer discuss those questions. Humans, per Plato, are erotic, finite creatures who handle stasis poorly, all the more so in a modern Dream of multitudinous choice.

THE DARK BUSH. In part to get perspective amid turbulence, Melissa and I take a two-night retreat with Juan Carlos and Carolina.

Along with little Clea and two of the American undergraduates who have returned to work with the eco-municipality — they'll join us for the first day only — we walk the two kilometers up to their home, tucked behind a ridge of the Suraqueta valley.

When we arrive, little Clea confidently joins the clutch of Juan Carlos and Carolina's many children, nephews, and nieces, while we adults meditate, stretch, and dance. The place is empty of other visitors. Intermittently joined by the kids, we do outdoor sauna, receive head massages, and eat only raw fruit and vegetables, with the exception of one cooked vegan meal at lunchtime each day. That pattern alone — beside the distant crash of falls and wind-swoosh in the *tulas* — relaxes us deeply.

But within that relaxation is a wound. So many partings and departures. Sure, Pieter and Marga have been planted here for thirty-five years, Ludwig and Anna, too, and a hundred other native and immigrant families are intact. But there's much fission. Each person's departure — Mateo, Ivete, Ariana, Thiago, Beatriz — contains what I've come to think of as "the last interaction," during which I give the person complete attention, take in their voice, the sheen of their hair. Each person is like a puzzle piece in a different section of my heart. Unique pieces. Since nobody else fits that portion of my heart, I incline toward their distant shores.

After sauna together, Juan Carlos, Melissa, and I cover ourselves with mud and let the sun bake it in, a cleanse. "We don't know if we're committed to building a 'final' house here," I say at one point.

Juan Carlos, already mud-covered, nods but doesn't respond. That's how it is a lot of the time with him, as if he's become the bowl of sheltered forest in which his family resides — silent, receptive, free of judgment.

After a while Juan Carlos does speak, telling an Andean story that indirectly responds to what I'd said. It's about Ekeko, a real-mythical Inca man with a large belly who traveled blissfully, without goals, from village to village in precolonial times, before there was "Bolivia," simply bringing joy and laughter wherever he went. Juan Carlos talks about how Ekeko in a sense *is* Pachamama. Pachamama is not mind-externalized "nature," per the Western definition; she is rather holy and fresh and everywhere — and, most importantly, always beginning. *No house is "final"* is the oblique message I take out of this.

Later, Melissa talks about how we feel conflicted over having another child. She mentions the negative environmental impact of yet another *Homo sapiens* on a strained planet. "It's a choice we make," she says. "We can choose one less human, thereby freeing up space for spectacled bears and quetzals."

"Are you sure?" Juan Carlos says in utter serenity. "Is it possible that another child might help bring Pachamama back into congruence?"

My lingering inner New Yorker rises up in unspoken cynicism. He's got eight freakin' kids! The absolute maximum Melissa and I would have, as we've discussed, would be one more. Three kids: Amaya, Clea, and this new squeaker…spawned from three adults, or the replacement rate. It's only later, the mud washed clean, that I reflect on what I know about Juan Carlos's family. His five grown children continue on vegetarian diets, seemingly cleansed of *wetiko*, all working as natural healers or counselors — four in Bolivian cities, and one who just moved back to assist her family with massages and cooking. The three young ones are growing up off-grid and off-Dream here, exuding self-confidence and competence. The entire family radiates such obvious inner joy that it gets emitted into widening circles, and their work reaches hundreds. *Am I sure* that Juan Carlos would have helped the world by not reproducing? Would we?

BACK IN SURAQUETA, I've got Deutsche Welle streaming the latest from the epicenter-of-things when Melissa comes over and mutes my laptop.

I look up at her, and she asks: "What would it mean to really be here?"

Gingerly, she closes the laptop and says, "*Vamos al Veintisiete*" — Let's go to Twenty-seven.

May 27 is Mother's Day in Bolivia. We celebrated it at home this afternoon — and now I assume she wants to celebrate in community as well.

We step out into the moonlight, holding Clea's hands, past the thorny Moses beard and agave spines, the "live barrier" separating us from Maximo, from Rafaela, from Suraqueta. We open our gate, still padlocked daily since Grace's rape over a year ago, the trial once again delayed and the case festering.

In town, we reach Republika on the corner, all aglow with Transition-Transience cheer. Inside, I can see the Australian Jeff pulling beers, a throng of friends gathered around the bar. Melissa walks right by.

"You're passing Republika," I say, having assumed that was our destination.

Melissa leads us around a corner, and we stroll past several blocks of adobe town houses topped with *teja* roofs, the sound of dance music growing with each step. Then I spot something unusual: glowing lights from a small chapel hidden at the end of a road that abuts Asano's farm. I've never seen that sanctuary open.

"I thought that little chapel was closed."

"It is," Melissa says, "except for one day a year."

To me, that doesn't make sense. If you're going to maintain a building like this, you might as well make full use of it. Yet now, though I've never seen the door opened, a hundred or so people are gathered outside. On the chapel's patio, many dance to blaring music. Others drink hot *api*, a traditional purple corn beverage, and eat empanadas; the air smells like sweat and fermented corn. The chapel's interior, far from abandoned, is painted pure white, with pink and red touches, and impeccably clean, with an altar topped with flowers and lit candles.

I wave to folks I know as the more-gregarious Melissa makes the kissing-rounds with Clea in tow. I overhear folks congratulating her on her courage to stand up to corruption in the water cooperative by running for elected office. Melissa has Clea handing out homemade Mother's Day gifts, small crocks of the *guapurú* sauce we canned from this year's harvest on our land.

Meanwhile, a friend's mother approaches the chapel. After we *hola*, she bypasses the drinkers out front and disappears into the chapel. I follow.

In contrast with the dark, booze-soaked feel outside, it's immaculate within. I watch my friend's mom kneel, evidently praying for her mother, so I do the same. This is not a space of efficiency. Like the one-day-a-year, yellow-flowering cactus Melissa discovered at La Vispera upon our arrival, so too does this sanctuary, after 364 dark days, blossom for only one day, *Veintisiete*. Beauty, wrote Ezra Pound, prefers the forgotten places like this one, those where the "glo" in "glocal" shines less brightly than in heart-of-things Berlin and Valparaíso. Still kneeling, I close my eyes and send love to my mother, to Melissa, to Amaya's mother, to my long-departed Nana and Granny. Unearmuffed music thumps outside, a blend of reverence and celebration that feels right.

After a while, Clea and Melissa sit beside me on the bench. Melissa closes her eyes, joins her mother. Others we know gather around. I exchange warm smiles with our caretaker neighbor, Rafaela, who sits directly to my right, the one who had wanted to buy a piece of our land; she came to understand why we didn't want to subdivide Tierra Guapurú, and ended up buying another parcel she loves. I nod to Maximo, who walks in with his two daughters. "Happy Mother's Day," I silently mouth to him, and he winks back. I feel something of the spiny barrier between "them" and "us" dislodge as Melissa whispers: "It's not Sweet unless shared."

Nineteen

Hay cambio. Things change. Ludwig and Anna, in their seventies now, put their four-decade creation, Bergwald, up for sale. And Don Asano, eighty years old, tells me on the plaza one afternoon that he'll soon be unable to farm. He hopes his grandson, Hernan, a late-twenties agronomist from Santa Cruz, will take over his organic acres, but he laments that Hernan is considering a job offer to manage a lowlands industrial farm at a higher salary. Then I catch wind of something more jarring still: Pieter and Marga have put La Vispera on the market.

When I hear about it, I bike to La Vispera and find Pieter picking persimmons beside the hobbit's house Melissa and I rented when we first arrived in Suraqueta. I don't know how to broach La Vispera's sale. It's a delicate topic; as with Bergwald and Asano's farm, new owners could wholly alter it. Responding to Bolivia's strong economic growth, several corporate American hotel chains have "*aterizado*" — landed — in Santa Cruz, and perhaps one will want, like Jesús Figueroa, Ventura Mall's director, to "franchise Suraqueta." Noticing a flock of bright-yellow migrants on his white flowering Moses beard hedge, I say: "Such beautiful birds."

Pieter nods, watching the birds alight. I recall how he weaves La Vispera birdsong into his piano compositions, and I've seen entranced fowl fly over to listen to him play his grand piano. "I never learned their names."

His use of the past tense punches my gut. *Too late to learn them now.* He says that the last thirty years seem to have passed as fast as ten years did in his youth. "And I know it's thirty years because of the *molle* trees. I planted them ten meters apart three decades ago. Neighbors told me that in thirty years they'd touch. And look!"

At the edge of the orchard a fog rolls in, shrouding the bok choy stalks and red hibiscus. Rising beyond are two *molle* trees — one female, the other male, in *chacha-warmi* — their green, finger-like tips exploring each other's for the first time.

"You're selling La Vispera," I blurt.

Pieter's expression shifts. It's the first time I've seen weariness in him. Since I met Pieter ten years ago, his light-blue eyes have always flashed, his agile body roving up and down La Vispera's hill paths. Whether straightening up a cabaña room for new guests, foisting Osho's *The Mustard Seed* at me ("This is fire!" he said of the book), or playing a newly inked piano piece, he's been a man bejeweled. But today his large shoulders droop as he tells me that, for a midseventies couple, "running a farm, an herb shop, a B&B... exhausts." They're looking for a young couple with a comparable worldview to take over their life's work.

"Will you leave Suraqueta?" I ask.

Pieter nods. "Yes." He gestures up to a pair of vultures circling overhead, of the same variety that regularly patrols our acres. "I'll leave in the bellies of vultures."

He says that he and Marga, when they sell La Vispera, will keep their home and the land above. "When it's my time to go, Billy boy, I want them to lay out my body in a sky burial."

BILLY FROM NEW YORK IS DEAD.

He was a Broadway actor who'd retired to Suraqueta. Years ago, I'd occasionally see him around, and then he fell out of sight. Like poor-old-Klaus and Jesse the orange-haired Jehovah's Witness, like Ariana-off-to-Valparaíso and Beatriz-to-Germany, Billy becomes one of the stories composted into Suraqueta's soil. Jeff ties up Billy's tale for me one evening over a beer in Republika. "I was with Billy almost to the end, out in P-mo." That's what he calls

Palermo, the area twenty minutes outside Suraqueta where he and Lisa want to found their farmstead when they save enough from bartending. "Billy'd wasted down to bones. Almost no flesh." Jeff looks pained. I didn't realize how close he'd been to the émigré New Yorker. "Then I had to leave. I couldn't hold up that wasted body anymore."

Totentanz: the death dance. It's a common medieval painting. During an undergraduate year in Germany, I spotted the paintings regularly in old churches. In them, a pauper holds hands with a skeleton who holds hands with a farmer who holds hands with a skeleton who holds hands with a priest who holds hands with a skeleton... all the way up the social hierarchy to aristocrats and the pope, no one by skeletons unflanked. I'm up in the eaves, looking through the round window at white swabs of cloud cottoning the green hills. I touch our adobe wall, as hard and cool as bony hands. The other day, Melissa and I were talking about health insurance. We've let ours lapse for the past two years. "If you're terminally ill," Melissa asked me, "I assume you wouldn't go back to America. That you'd want to..." Her voice trailed off.

Die here. Perish above the tectonically subducted former continent of Nazca, atop layers of Inca and Chané, beneath the Magellan clouds and the Southern Cross? Beside Billy from New York, and Pieter with his sky burial, and probably Asano? How ephemeral, a family's quest for Sweet. Out the eaves window, a gray mist skids down from Amboró's cloud forests and over our windless *tulas*, creating the rich light of a 1930s film. I imagine such a film, but set in the future. A film without Bill and Melissa, who are already assimilated into vultures. The plaza and church below, the clay *teja* roofs, appear the same, as does the stand of pines beside the distant "sugar baron castle" — a weekend mansion owned by a Santa Cruz sugar magnate — with our vigorous *guapurús* and raspberry trees in the foreground. The once-tiny *carnavales* below the eaves are yellow summer giants holding up what remains of the seven skies. Clea is an adult, a mother, now returned to Suraqueta with big sister Amaya to sign the deed that transfers our house and land to someone else. Contemplating the fine, gray drizzle, Clea feels wistful, but she needs the money, and she doesn't come to Bolivia very often anymore; her life is in Buenos Aires, or Provence, or Brooklyn. She remembers the peace of the *guapurú* forest, the feel of *wawa*, laughing with little Adobe or Boots in the hammock with *Papá* and *Mamá*.

HAY CAMBIO. Dissolution of bodies, dissolution of marriages. It comes in an impetuous wave, stronger than the one a half-year back that split Ivete and Mateo, Anette and Thomas, and Serdar and Denise. Most are expatriate or mixed *extranjero*-Bolivian couples. There's Tina and Gonzalo, an Argentine tour operator couple together for twenty years and in Suraqueta for fifteen (one child). Severed. Jano and Anabela, who operate a bakery they started (two kids). Severed. The Suraqueteño Yuri and his Swiss wife, Karin (two kids), fifteen years together. Split. Even Christopher Columbus (the alias of the former System of a Down guitarist) and his Bolivian wife, Sol, break up, and she leaves the farm with their three kids and opens a café in Suraqueta. And so on. *Chacha-warmi*, severed. *Cuidado* — be careful — Melissa and I are repeatedly counseled.

I'm saddened by this. Melissa and I talk with our breaking-up friends, and the community in general comes together to try to listen to and mend these families where possible. But part of it is Dream-related. Transience Town. All of the former couples have at least one urbanite from another country, and the centripetal forces ripping at the *dulce vida* are robust.

Politically, too, things are fragile. The historic conservation law gets stuck in process because of a few elites who want to put up Coroico-style high-rises to garner more rental cash. And while support has built for Melissa and her water cooperative candidacy, which has further integrated us into the community fabric, the corrupt current head of the water board cancels the upcoming elections on a technicality, prompting a citizens bus to Santa Cruz to challenge the cancellation before a judge. Then, rumors surface on Grace's rape case: Evidently a judge was paid $10,000 to accept a piece of "evidence" that will release the accused rapists. Such tenuous rule of law makes us question, for our family's security, whether Melissa, now appearing on TV as a candidate, should so publicly wrangle with the establishment.

It's in a confounded state that Melissa and I once again visit Juan Carlos, Carolina, and their family in the Dark Bush of Chorrillos.

The family has eight guests here for a ten-day retreat, but Juan Carlos delegates their care to his daughter. While Clea merges with a group of Bolivian kids, Juan Carlos sits down with Melissa and me in the adobe meditation hall. As per our American habit, we dive in with a kind of pro/con wrap-up of our lives in the moment, laying out the positives — the eco-municipality, Melissa's candidacy for the water cooperative, our Mother's Day experience of *integración* — and then bemoaning the political insecurity, coupledom breakups, and that oh-so-definitive breakup, death.

Juan Carlos, after a long silence, says: "I've noticed that the Europeans and Americans who visit are, at first, almost always *here*." He indicates his head as the location of that *here*. Then he gets up and turns on loud salsa music. And we dance. The song segues to African drumming, then Andean *caporales* and Brazilian samba, as the retreatants, little Clea, and his kids, nieces, nephews, and wife, Carolina — hearing the music — join us in a meditation-hall-turned-discotheque.

How we sweat! And sing along, belting out any lyrics we know, kids dancing with elders. Juan Carlos, in his loose-fitting Tarabuco-patterned pants, positively springs around, an enormous grin on his face. After over an hour, Juan Carlos deejays the tunes downward to chill and has us circle up tight, close our eyes, and pile up our hands together in the center. Automatically, hands float up from bottom to top, the sensual touch of others, our bodies loose from the dance, nobody in their heads anymore.

In the late afternoon, Juan Carlos and Carolina take us up to the Chorrillos waterfall. It gushes less water than the falls in Carlos Peralta's section of the Dark Bush, but it is remarkable for its height, seclusion, and the variety of tropical plants growing up its finger canyon walls.

"You know about the llama salt caravans, to the south of Suraqueta?" Juan Carlos asks, launching into a story. "Well, one evening some of the shepherds leading the herds approached the *mallku* [leader] and told him that they have twenty llamas but only nineteen cords. How to tie the last one up for the night?"

The sun deepens into an amber, a hint of turquoise. Juan Carlos continues: "The *mallku* told them: 'Just *pretend* to tie him up. He's too dumb to know the difference.' So they did this, going through the motions of tying the llama to a stake. But the next morning, when all the llamas were reloaded with salt, the shepherds approached the *mallku* and told him they were all set to go, except for one llama, who refused to budge. 'You forgot to untie him,' the *mallku* said. So the shepherds went through the motions of 'untying' the llama, after which they went on their way."

As the waterfall crashes, I reflect on this allegory, knowing I'm still tied, *umbilically* even, to a need for control, to impatience, and to a nonacceptance of what is. I'm cinched to evaluation, comparison, and judgment. I tell this to others. I say that I'd thought I'd understood the enigmatic Sweet Life on that near-death precipice, in deepened community, and through relationship with our land. "But right now I feel as perplexed as ever," I say. "The cord around me feels real."

Carolina speaks. "If you change, the cord dissolves. *Chachawarmi* ruptures are not the problem. Death is not the problem.

The agribusiness above us, poisoning this very waterfall that feeds our home...is not even the problem. Acting out of 'ego' — in other words, out of evaluation, comparison, and judgment — is the nonexistent llama-cord that seems so real." She puts a hand on her heart: "The Sweet Life is here."

The sun is setting above us. I reflect on her and Juan Carlos's core philosophy of "no expectations, no evaluation, no comparison, no judgment." Over all the visits here, I've seen how this approach is actually lived. Juan Carlos cleans the toilets if they're dirty; he doesn't expect women to do anything society says they should. Carolina has no expectations of him, and she doesn't blame him.

Carolina puts a hand under the falls and says to Melissa. "Run for office, sure. But this water will be clean when you're free inside. When the cord snaps."

There's a long silence, then Juan Carlos says, the twilight warm on his face: "What I found is that beyond thoughts, beyond conditioning, is a state of peace. It's..."

Juan Carlos laces his hands together and lets them fall into his lap. His body seems to diminish, melt even, as if his will is gone and his words have been undone by the quality of the light infusing the finger canyon.

"...*amor*," he finishes very quietly.

LOVE. We leave inspired by our friends' insights, but we soon encounter perhaps the worst ax to gash into our search for the Sweet Life. It starts with a work trip to the Amazon.

I take a twenty-seater Amazonas flight from Santa Cruz to remote Cobija, on the Brazilian border in far northern Bolivia, then I catch a bus toward Riberalta. It's a scoping trip for a potential module for my NYU course. What really arrests me is the unexpected level of destruction.

I spend the night in the hamlet of Sena on the Madre de

Dios River, but I am awakened from sleep by machinery. A Chinese company, having recently arrived with hundreds of Asian workers, is building a highway between two small Bolivian cities, Cobija and Riberalta, including tremendous bridges spanning the Amazon tributaries. Until now, access has been a dirt road with ferries to carry vehicles across the rivers, and this absence of "development" has preserved not just the surrounding Amazon but the area's indigenous cultures. This new highway serves part of a development corridor linking Brazil and Peru, which will also mean heightened extraction of mahogany, gold, and previously inaccessible petroleum reserves. At sunrise, helicopter blades thwack above my cabin as another exploration team departs. The Dream has arrived.

I leave Sena for Tumichucua, a lakeside town, where I lodge in a half-abandoned Catholic retreat center. In the village's only bar-restaurant-karaoke establishment, a local resident tells me, "The *indios*" — indigenous people — "are going deeper into the bush. They still follow the schools of fish and the flocks of birds. But the petroleum and timber companies are cornering them."

Cornering them. I think of Chief Gaspar, in another part of the Bolivian Amazon. The tree that holds up the world. *"Andrew Jackson killed the Indians!"* my elementary school peers and I chanted at Nassakeag. We were really chanting: *It's our fault.*

On the flight back to Santa Cruz I don't see *la Pacha*'s unifying vision. I only see fire below. Flares from petroleum exploration test sites and slash-and-burn fields along newly cut roads. An indigenous woman sits next to me, her cheeks lightly scarred with initiatory cuts. The cuts remind me of something Juan Carlos whispered to me at his home. Quechua words. *Yachachiy* ("initiation" or "guidance") and *wañu* ("death"); together, they blend "beginning" with the cessation of life. Juan Carlos invited me, in that whisper, to do something I know I must do. He told me I must undergo initiation, on a specific day in early July that he says is portentous for me. Yet I felt, and still feel, a mix of skepticism and fear. I push the thought out of my mind.

The indigenous woman talks openly about her life. Though my elder daughter Amaya is part Amazon indigenous, through her maternal grandmother, hailing from the same area as this woman, I know little about her tribe. The woman says she's off to Santa Cruz to meet with allies because petroleum interests have approached their tribe. "They've offered us new houses, piped water, and so on, in exchange for cutting the forest. They'll give us 'good jobs,' they say. But what do we have left if the forest is gone? That's our life! But now they're telling us we don't have a choice. They're attacking our indigenous territory with lawyers, saying they'll do it whether we accept their 'gifts' or not."

I look out the window, over the Amazon forest's new ribbons of roads, over the flames defying the Law of Mother Earth. I recall Don Gaspar's words. "Be a bee," he told me. "If you go against the bee energy, you're stung." Indeed, this woman tells me her tribe is arming; these bees have stingers. "Each of us has at least one or two guns now. We'd rather die than lose that which nourishes us — Pachamama."

Twenty

In Suraqueta, I return to more fire.

"It's coming toward our land!" shouts Melissa, a few days after my return, as she runs toward the house from the orchard, a tower of smoke beyond her.

While she texts the municipality and our friends for help, I snatch a hundred-meter-long hose and a shovel and race toward the fire. Municipal staff are already there, but they.have little better fire-fighting tools than I. There's no fire department in Suraqueta. And fire insurance in the rural areas is questionable. So, to prepare, I planted fire-resistant trees on our borders, cut three-meter dry season firebreaks on vulnerable peripheries, and negotiated with a neighbor to stop burning garbage on our eastern flank. But can such preemptory measures protect our land and our home from *this*? The flames arch twenty meters, sparking on the unnaturally dry *tula* of a climate-changed ecosystem. I join the municipal staffers shoveling dirt at the fire's edges.

Melissa's text gets shared, and neighbors and friends arrive. Maximo and one of his daughters motorbike to the hilltop and connect two of the hoses to a spigot there and begin to spray. Kusi arrives with her teenage niece, Esmeralda, and they both machete underbrush beside me, all of us laboring to establish a firebreak. But a fresh round of windblown flames jumps the break, singeing my arm hair. "Get down!" someone yells, indicating I crouch and flee to avoid smoke asphyxiation.

La comunidad rallies, and the fire is eventually quelled; everybody goes home. Though I'm happy to see how effective people power can be in a crisis, I'm nevertheless alarmed. The charred trees outside our north firebreak are far too close to the three hundred fruit and forest trees we've planted and tended, not to mention Casa Guapurú. And recurring fire-causing droughts will only increase in what Bill McKibben calls the new, human-warmed planet "Eaarth."

That night, noise.

I awake, dreaming it's the Chinese company's bulldozers and helicopters. But it's an electronic music festival at a private home below ours, mostly urbanites from Santa Cruz. The low-frequency bass sound of their speaker towers penetrates everything in Suraqueta, even our forty-centimeter adobe walls, pulsing into our sleep. The party continues through the next day and into a second night. Though neighbors complain, the new government is overwhelmed with too many other priorities to enforce a just-passed noise ordinance.

At 2 AM on the second techno-night, I'm weak and insomniac. Weakened by Suraqueta's broken marriages, by noise and Amazon destruction, by fire. It's a moonless night, as I step out onto our pulsating porch. Without a flashlight, I walk through the almost tactile din, through our orchard, to the hillock where our vision of a final house weakens each day. Sure, we've talked about how the hillock naturally buffers the town noise, like this festival, and how we could soundproof the bedrooms with double windows and foam in the roof. But we can't soundproof the Dream because its pulse is everywhere, including inside of me even now.

A cold wind, a *sur*, blows through the noise, knocking eucalyptus and *soto* leaves down, to get composted into our land, just as all our stories — Pieter and Marga's La Vispera, Asano's organic farm, Bill and Melissa in vulture bellies — are composted, and there's no plot in compost. No Athenian statue. No One Thing. The Sweet Life weakens and resistance to Dream appears to collapse. Like the impractical arming of that tiny Amazon tribe, a romantic last frontier in Conquest, Transition Suraqueta's "glocal" tree burns on an Eaarth unfit for another baby.

I fall to my knees and pound the hillock with my fist, pound what I love. *Wawawa* and *no-hay-guapurú* and our family hum. Exhausted, I finally fall into a half sleep under the *soto* tree. When I awake, the noise has stopped, and I manage to hear Juan Carlos's whisper: *You must die/begin/initiate.*

JUAN CARLOS'S WHISPER IN MY EAR, I'm ready to walk, alone, up the mountain to the Chorrillos Dark Bush.

But it's also election day, which is always a Sunday in Bolivia, and Melissa is up for election to the water cooperative board. The fate of safe drinking water for thousands is at stake, and I spend the first anxious morning hours of that July morning with Melissa at the town's sole polling place, a splendid old building on the plaza. Melissa and the fourteen other candidates are required to spend the whole day seated in front of the ballot boxes, both as live visual cues of who's running and as observers to electoral transparency.

The corrupt old-guard officials have been running strong campaigns, but the municipal landscape has changed. Previously, the inner circle squelched information about the elections and sent in their own handpicked "voters" to ensure their own victory, but these elections have been featured on community TV and radio stations, on the internet, and postered throughout town. By noon, voter participation is a remarkable twenty times what it has been in the past.

Media packs the voting hall, along with the mayor, a national congressman for our province, and the deputy governor, and it's strange to see Melissa on the stage with these dignitaries and fellow candidates. I take care of Clea, along with other *mamas y papas* providing spontaneous child care, and it gives me joy for Clea to see Mommy up there, one of only two women running. Not to mention that the males who have dominated this position have used it to bolster their feudal interests and very rarely to exercise their power for the common good. Melissa has long supported "women's political participation" projects with her work at the UN, and she is finally a woman politically participating. She's also the only foreigner running. The statutes say that anyone with Bolivian residency who is a water cooperative member is eligible.

I'm apprehensive that Melissa will be disappointed. As I watch the voters stream in, many of them clad in *pollera* skirts and rubber-tire sandals, indigenous *valluno* and Quechua folks, I think of how different Melissa is from 97 percent of the voters. Not long ago, Melissa, Clea, and I were *jipis* held in that cold immigrant detention cell. Will she receive any votes at all? Sure, her open spirit, intelligence, and constant efforts to integrate us into the community have earned her many friends, several of whom wink at her after voting. But she only knows a relative handful of folks among the thousand voting, and it remains to be seen whether they can look past her skin color — and gender — and see her as a future official.

The waiting and suspense is excruciating. But it's time to go.

Melissa knows what I must do today and understands. It's the day Juan Carlos assigned for my initiation; for reasons I don't fully understand, it's an important date, our Dark Bush *amigo* says, that aligns with the lunar cycle. Melissa nods to me from her place behind a ballot box, and leaving Clea in collective child care with our friends, I walk at a fast clip out of town, across the river, up toward the sugar baron's castle, and then beyond it into the forests of the Dark Bush.

I'm heaving with exhaustion when I reach my destination: the hidden waterfall far behind Juan Carlos and Carolina's home.

I strip off my shirt and sandals, down to my shorts. Above, swallows thread through the ribbon of falls, and *patuju* flowers — the national flower, its red, yellow, and green the colors of the Bolivian flag — drop from a patch of giant ferns.

Time passes. I stare into a river pool freckled with leaves and seeds. I let my gaze glaze its surface. For a while, I'm thinking of Melissa and the voting below, feeling anxious about the results. A wasp makes perfect circles, two feet in circumference, and then begins lazily carving figure eights.

After a long time, I'm no longer looking at a pool; it has seeped inside of me and merged with the two-thirds of my body that is water. Closing my eyes, I feel its dimpled surface, its cool foreign depths. The figure eights prickle, and I'm smiling, eyes closed, with little conception of time. Sitting there hearing and feeling the constant thrubbing of the falls, I enter into a kind of trance.

The forest and falls and I snap into place together. I feel a shiver, then take out what I've brought along. A long sharp thorn, from one of the last *quiñe* trees I felled on our land.

This aberration — so much larger than a typical thorn: knife-size, knife-sharp — surprised me, and I kept the spike for this initiation.

Juan Carlos's whisper. *You must…die. Begin. Initiate.*

I watch the drizzle of droplets separating from the falls behind it, and then my eyes lock into other eyes. Mammalian eyes. Dark ones.

Juan Carlos has tracked me, but he does not approach. He stands silently, fifty meters away in a patch of fern trees. Only his shimmering eyes are visible.

I look at the *quiñe* barb in my hand, tickle its razor tip along my wrist. A Greek root of the word "character" is *kharakter*, or "marked with sharp lines." With initiation cuts.

I glance up, but Juan Carlos has vanished. As he told me before, I'm the only one who can cut the cord.

I walk into the river and along a tributary, up and up, to a smaller falls. There: a small evaporating pool, with several hundred black tadpoles on the verge of death. Their mini-sea of rainwater has evaporated so much that it is now just a shallow puddle. The tadpoles don't know anything is amiss. They swim lazily, eating from the pool bottom, and siphoning off what lands on top, oblivious to the fact that their pool is about to dry up.

No replenishing rain clouds in sight. They're doomed, but frogs are not doomed. Likewise, 99 percent of the little stunted *sotos*, *tulas*, and *carnavales*, the tiny saplings shaded from the sun under the tree canopy, are doomed. But trees aren't doomed. Nature spreads out a thousand seeds of amphibians and trees, and some survive.

I sit by the puddle and look at the black-and-gray creatures, glossy as the sinking surface, feeling a déjà vu. I had a bizarrely similar experience with tadpoles, a decade back, while living in the twelve-by-twelve cabin in North Carolina. I wonder at the synchronicity of it as they nibble at the wet clay bottom, swerve and slice, one past the next, and some of the larger ones rim the water's surface with parted lips, sucking off what they can and leaving a thin wake.

I take out the *quiñe* barb, running it over the water's surface, getting my courage up to do what I'm to do.

I remember Carolina: *The Sweet Life is here*, she said, indicating her heart. It isn't in Transition Suraqueta. The Sweet Life I've been searching for has always been millimeters away, the luminous everyplace where spirit meets clay. The Sweet Life is not a place but rather a state of change, of shifting perspective, learning patience, relearning culture, sharing your world, leaving your world, growing another world.

I smile, thinking of Thiago, who now lives in Cochabamba — from there roving out to give permaculture workshops throughout the continent — but he's back for a visit. "Eco-*nomadism!*" he said to me a few days ago. "It's now one of the pillars of the Global Ecovillage Network. Settled community is one path. Another is taking the same ecological consciousness into one of *Homo sapiens* bipedaling or busing or biking together."

How joyful to see my old friend. We launched Transition Suraqueta together, went through the dry season of my *chikungunya* and his addictions and breakups together. And there he was, throwing my favorite Rumi back at me, quoting the mystic poet with a smile: "Your hand opens and closes, opens and closes. If it were always a fist or always stretched open, you would be paralyzed. Your deepest presence is in every small contraction and expansion." He let that sink in, then added: "The same is true for Suraqueta. It's contracting and expanding — people leaving, new ones coming in — that's the town's 'deepest presence.'"

Growth in nature, and in Suraqueta, it would seem, happens through a series of pulsations. Transition town, Transience town: a single place.

The sky magnificent, a waterfall crashing, I feel my cherished mental concepts withering as I begin. The godhead here is Yahweh: Inhale, *Yaaah*; exhale, *Weh!* — the divine is presence, our breath — *now* — absorbing the Sweet. Tadpoles perishing beside me, I wonder what it would mean for another Billy-from-New-York to die. To die to the false idea that I am separate from the rainforest destruction I saw in the Amazon, and instead embody Carolina's mysterious observation that the forests will heal when I do. Die to impatience and nonacceptance. How many times in Bolivia have I been wounded or hurt, depressed or insomniac… over what *is*? These tadpoles aren't worrying; they're living. What would it mean, at long last, to begin?

I am ready. I plunge the *quiñe* spike into my palm, hard.

Screeeaam! My yell echoes through the canyon.

Blood drips onto my forearm, into the mud. Pain. *Ahhh!* I scream again. But then I laugh, as more than blood drains out.

I thrust my bloody palm into the clay pool bottom, squeeze

silky mud through both hands. I pull out my hands, shellacked in deep brown, the sun gleaming off the rippling water. I walk into the forest with gleaming brown hands.

This is not an Amazonian scarification ritual. It's my ritual. Juan Carlos had whispered: *Draw blood*. Drain into your larger body, Pachamama. Initiate into a space beyond Mind.

Later, I discover that, at the very moment I screamed, and as the breeze was peeling away all that wasn't me, the final votes were being tallied below, revealing that a woman, and a foreigner, had received the highest vote count in the fifteen-candidate field. "You change, and it ripples outward," Carolina had said. Melissa swore in amid the dignitaries as copresident, along with a man of highlands indigenous descent. Together, a foreigner and a *colla*, both outside the water cooperative's corrupted networks, pledged their commitment to protecting the headwaters in which I stood bleeding.

Back at the falls, I place my sore hand in the water to rinse clean the clay. Then I step into the spray. It pounds down on me and I'm someplace else entirely: nowhere, with a waterfall in there. The present where the camel-cord vanishes, the Dream dissolves, and I begin.

Twenty - One

The months pass. Another Suraqueta rainy season arrives to our once-ravished-by-ants jasmine plant spreading lush along the portico, encouraging us to spend more time in hammocks enveloped in blossoms and fragrance. Clea and I pick the first orchard crops of flavorsome passionfruit, figs, and apples; peaches, pomegranates, and limes. *Wawa* gushes in the creek bed, merengue pulses below in the square, and both sounds belong. Later, the feel of skin, breath, and bone of other mammals — ones named Esperanza, Amparo, and Natalia — cycles around in a couples-switching *rueda*, as I dance with the salsa group I helped start called La Candela de los Valles (The Valley Flame) in a show at the Suraqueta cultural center. Immediately following our group, Melissa and three-and-a-half-year-old Clea perform on the trapeze, the fruit of their classes with Maria, a revillaging Buenos Aires acrobatics teacher.

In December 2016, Amaya, now nearly twelve, arrives for vacation. As we stroll through town, people call out "Amaya!" and run over to kiss her. Though she hasn't been to Suraqueta for months, she belongs. We visit the new municipal library, a renovated historic adobe building financed by a donation from the Korean government; we read for hours before heading to La Chakana café on the plaza to play blackjack. Amaya doesn't know poker or betting or bluffing, so a world opens up to her as I demonstrate the subtleties of poker faces, passing, and folding. We spend two leisureology-approved hours on that porch playing cards, while friends stop by to greet her.

So goes Amaya's vacation. Sleepovers at Soami's and Lukka's, biking around town on her own now, staying up until midnight with a friend to catch frogs in our moonlit pond. "We caught eleven!" she announces, eyes dancing, and mud to her waist. I feel a torrent of pride, and not because of anything she's achieved. It's how I've felt throughout her visit. Maybe it's a less-conditioned parenthood that I've shifted into, one before manuals. It's a sense of happiness that any species must feel when healthy, as it feels good to breathe deeply or exercise, a natural feeling of love and wellness that arises through being with your children. I realize, too, how much my children have taught me about the joy of always beginning.

"You're happier than when you first arrived in Suraqueta," Rulas Maradona tells me, one afternoon, at his new house. Amaya, Clea, and I have come up to see the beautiful wattle-and-daub eco-*casa* that Rulas constructed himself, partly with the money he earned building ours. As I ponder his observation, Clea is outside singing the landscape: "I love Adobe, love Boots, love Pacha-mama, love Suraqueta, love trees…" She's up in a peach tree with two of Rulas's children, and they all start singing, too, as the three of them shake the tree, the fruits raining to the feet of Amaya, who gathers them up. I don't think of the happiness I feel now, as a base state, as mine. It's natural as trees dropping peaches. Just as sight happens on its own when the obstacles to vision are removed, happiness happens when its obstacles — evaluation, judgment, comparison, and so forth — are removed.

Rulas seems to be waiting for a response. I don't know what to say. Eventually, we start talking about schools. Flor de Montaña school, already four years old, just received official government certification, and new teachers and programs are flourishing. Rulas is considering sending his kids there. A nursery school and kindergarten linked to Flor de Montaña has opened in town, several blocks from our land, and Clea spends three hours there each morning, playing, gardening, painting, and singing mantras. Her Andean-Amazonian eco-educational school anchors and deepens our connection to others, intergenerationally, and also includes both Bolivians and expatriates.

Eco-building feels more inclusive now, too. I think of Rulas's father's home, in town — a simple adobe similar to the home of Kusi's grandfather — and then his son's home, with materials similar to his dad's, but also with gray-water recycling and water catchment. Transition. Rulas hands me a yerba máte cup, and we pour hot water and pass the cup and its metal straw back and forth in silence, watching our kids eat peaches beneath the tree. I remember Kusi's grandfather's definition of Living Well, so poignant in its simplicity: "Eat well, sleep well, love well."

After one fun evening dancing salsa at home with Amaya and Clea, Melissa and I cuddle on the sofa, the girls crashed out on their beds in the mezzanine above us, and I suddenly feel that life is at once so much richer and so much simpler than I'd once imagined: STOP IMPROVING and seize as much leisure as you can. Cut the cord to anxiety. Resist the chip in the brain and become animal. Work at something you love, if you can, and wherever you live, lend bikes and dance and catch frogs. Eat well, sleep well, love well.

MY SISTER AMY AND HER FAMILY come to Suraqueta for several months, swapping Vermont and Big Rock Candy Mountain for a rental house in Bolivia. "Where even *are* we?" asks their culture-shocked youngest when they first arrive. Amy and Andrew work remotely and send the boys off to Flor de Montaña each morning. By the time they leave, my nephews seem part Bolivian, with their *valluno* accents, love of Bolivian professional soccer, and a taste for *guapurú*. Later, in emails, Amy tells me that they have absorbed a bit of the Sweet Life. Sweet *Lives* —

plural — actually, since the way each individual and family lives it is unique, and ultimately it's not a model, but rather a way of always beginning that can be practiced anywhere.

You change, and it ripples outward.

La luna wanes and waxes, and wanes again. At times, I recall Carolina's words; I feel balance and equanimity, the love so softly spoken of by Juan Carlos, up in the Dark Bush. Melissa feels it, too, and we share this common sensation in glance and touch.

At times, I take a break from the laptop and step outside to lean against the now-towering *soto* tree below our hillock. I gaze into branches that support the world, my feet the *soto*'s roots, my legs its trunk, my chest its branches and leaves, my mind the sky. I know that Carolina is not being overly simplistic by focusing on personal transformation. She isn't denigrating the need for structural change, for speaking truth to power and joining popular movements. She means: When we surrender into the joyful state of *la Pacha*, the unified field of life, such surrender delicately ripples out and affects outer reality. It also gives us the equanimity to notice external change.

Hay cambio. Suraqueta changes. On the water cooperative board, Melissa helps usher in victories. The municipality declares the swath of acres above the Chorrillos Dark Bush waterfalls a protected area, thereby curtailing the agro-industrial grape-and-strawberry operation. A potable water–processing plant, the first in Suraqueta's history, goes live.

Melissa and I receive a foundation grant through the World Policy Institute to deepen local Suraqueta actions and capacities, while linking global allies and local Bolivian efforts. The "Suma Qamaña project," as we dub it, fosters the practical application of the indigenous Andean concept of the Sweet Life. We establish the Living Well Collaborative to offer a physical and virtual home from which — through actions, research, and writing — the "tree" of regenerative economy can support real-life connection among happiness levels, community building, and people's care for Pachamama.

Partly through our work with the Living Well Collaborative, the newly passed historic conservation law for Suraqueta is grounded, and several proposed Coroico-style buildings are redesigned. A dormant noise ordinance is updated, setting decibel limits for the kind of parties that undermine community well-being. And we accompany our Transition friend Salvador, now the city manager, as he secures funding for organic agriculture and clean energy. He and the mayor go to La Paz to liaise with government officials in an attempt "to make Suraqueta not a minor footnote but a massively ecological municipality." This postdevelopment process is one Melissa and I live, within our community, from the bones out, not from the head down.

You change, and it ripples outward. Nor does Carolina mean that the luggage arranges itself — all too perfectly — in the journey. After the Dream, disarray and pain remain. Amazon deforestation continues in Bolivia. A proposed gigantic dam could flood half of Madidi National Park. The government passes a decree to allow petroleum drilling in national parks. Climate change continues to hurt our local farmers, as one "driest year in recorded history" follows the next. Two new malls poise to open their doors in Santa Cruz.

Xenophobia remains. Though much more integrated into local life than when we arrived, Melissa and I still feel it, and we remain unsure whether we will build a "final" house on Tierra Guapurú. Business-as-usual remains. I'm enlivened to work part-time — as I've come to do — directly with Salvador and others in city hall, and I'm sometimes discouraged on those dark and stormy days when local elites push back against eco-municipal activities.

But now I have more balance and equanimity. The thundery days don't shake me like they used to. I notice the ways the world can, and does, come into balance. It's encouraging to see two former Suraqueta officials from the previous government convicted and jailed in Santa Cruz on corruption charges, with another major lawsuit still pending. In Grace's case, in a groundswell of support, citizens show up to monitor each step of her complicated trial. The verdict is finally delivered: guilty. The two adults (age twenty-five and eighteen) get the maximum twenty-five-year sentence, while the youngest, a sixteen-year-old minor, receives a four-year sentence. An editorial in *El Deber*, the most important newspaper in the region, praises Grace's perseverance to get a conviction in a context where violence against women normally goes unpunished.

Melissa and I discover, too, a deepening community. Farmer Asano's grandson returns to manage, and eventually own, the Suraqueta farm, ensuring that its organic abundance surges into the next generation. Pieter and Marga find an eager young Bolivian couple to take over La Vispera, and they maintain its spirit. Republika's Jeff and Lisa save enough to start building their adobe dream house on their P-mo permaculture acres, where they hope to settle in the next few years. And back in New York, "Al" retakes his name. "I'm Ahmet again," he writes, adding: "My trip to Suraqueta and meeting Carlos Peralta…it started me on the path to some big changes. I quit my job. I've got some savings, for now, and we'll see what I do next for work. My imagination is larger than any investment bank."

AFTER MY DARK BUSH INITIATION, after the Dream, I feel more reflective than before. "Those who contemplate the beauty of the earth," naturalist Rachel Carson wrote, "find reserves of strength that will endure as long as life lasts." I feel this strength, one afternoon, walking past a Campeche field now free of the erstwhile Pilfrut bag litter — after a seven-hundred-person-strong municipal cleanup *minga* and improved garbage collection. I stop and gaze out, noticing, maybe a kilometer away on the other side of the valley, Casa Guapurú.

A minuscule hammock swings. Probably Clea. The tiny red shirt is Marisela's. Adobe and Boots are too minute to see. Gazing at this miniature of my family, the now-healthy forest we steward, I feel my "urgency" moorings are flung loose. I'm in a *soto* tree's Deep Time, and this both liberates and disquiets. Impatience is a lifelong habit that once felt inextricable. Now time passes and then circles back again, a renewable resource within *la Pacha*. Melancholy, too, blows through my branches.

"When I die, Papi," Clea said to me on our hillock the other day, "I want Pachamama to turn me into a flower. And you will be a petal in my flower. So will *mi hermanita* (my sister)." She added that Mommy will be another flower growing next to her, "a friend." The wind was soft static in the *soto* leaves above, the air fragrant with eucalyptus scent, as Clea added more softly: "But we don't decide what we are after we die. Pachamama decides."

Even here in Deep Time *hay cambio*. How is it my sister and her family have come and gone, already composted into Suraqueta's collective memory? Our *casera* Serafina still asks for them, as the kids still ask: "*Y los primos?*" — And the cousins?

During that time, my parents came for a two-week visit — my mother's leg now fully mended — and everyone celebrated my father's birthday at Trent's Posada del Sol.

My father beamed: his wife, two children, all five grandchildren dancing to a friend's band, a fusion of Andean music and jazz. One of them, the *charango* player, wore a scarf with the colors of the Bolivian flag. Green, for the trees that hold up the world; gold, for the minerals of Pachamama; red, for the bloodshed in freeing a plurinational country. The colors, so meaningful to me now, blended together as the musicians bobbed and I twirled my glowing mother.

The distant hammock in front of Casa Guapurú stops swinging. I turn toward home.

AFTER A BOLIVIAN ACTIVIST collective translates part of my book *New Slow City* into Spanish, I speak to a packed auditorium in La Paz. Then I speak at a similar powwow in Santa Cruz, that growing metropolis, with a hundred folks turning out to explore "glocal" alternatives to Speed. Joining us are urban "antibodies" — a transparency collaborative called Revolución Jigote; a city bicycling group; an urban forestry group called Colectivo Árbol — all challenging a "the-mall-is-the-new-plaza" advertising offensive. Melissa, Clea, and Amaya accompany me to the Santa Cruz event, along with twenty friends from Suraqueta. My two daughters usher folks in and distribute copies of *New Slow City*.

After the gathering, we step outside, and the first thing I see is a Coke billboard. Bright red, on the side of a building. Where is the inner turmoil I once felt seeing that red pillar on the Suraqueta plaza some years back? Instead of gazing upward — which really means gazing *away* — I accept Coca-Cola as part of *la Pacha*, the unified field.

I walk toward the Santa Cruz plaza, Melissa ahead talking with a friend and a little hand in each of mine, Clea on one side, Amaya on the other. We merge with an unusually large crowd streaming in the same direction. It all feels so…city. The smell of exhaust, the traffic, the tall buildings. I think about the birthday party Amaya's been invited to at Ventura Mall. She'll get more such invitations, and she'll continue to be an urban child, since this is her home, and Suraqueta will continue to be for vacations. I accept all of this, my feet rooted into something beneath the concrete.

Then I feel a touch of the old trepidation, and Amaya seems to intuit my feeling. She squeezes my hand and points to a bit of graffiti. It's by Mujeres Creando — Women Creating — a Bolivian feminist street collective. Amaya reads it aloud: "*No soy originario, soy original.*"

This hard-to-translate gem tickles me in the gut, especially when read by my elder daughter, who's a mix of Bolivian indigenous, Portuguese, and Irish heritage. Roughly, the graffiti says: "I'm not an 'original inhabitant,' I'm an original." "*Originario*" or "original inhabitant" is a cultural/political term for "pure" indigenous, so the wordplay captures a tricky political concept. It isn't celebrating an individual's separation from the group. It means: I'm textured. I'm neither a political concept of who's indigenous and who isn't, nor a cog in McWorld. It means: I've cut the cord.

Arriving at the plaza, we suddenly realize why the crowd is so large tonight. All surrounding blocks are closed to cars, and masses of celebrants stream in filling an undefeated Victory Café, swelling a plaza adorned.

"Gorgeous," exclaims Melissa. The square is festooned with pastel Chiquitano indigenous ribbons, an artistic revival of the culture of my be-a-bee friend, Chief Gaspar, and others who have marched across the country. They — the people — have stopped, for now, some of the burning I witnessed in the Amazon. The moratorium on a highway through an Amazonian indigenous protected area holds firm.

This isn't to say that forest destruction is stopped. Bolivia is not unblemished ecological harmony. Her agricultural frontier is pressured, her petroleum is pressured, and she often stumbles, questioning. Bolivia is in transition. What's Sweet about the country is its rebelliousness — stopping water privatization, ousting exploitative presidents, pioneering constitutional Earth rights — and its underlying ethos of Sweet, from which we all can learn. That ethos is an antibody that will continue to rise up to help heal ecocide.

A BOOK MIGHT APTLY END on such up notes: colorful banners unfurled, Santa Cruz's plaza renewed, long-oppressed women creating, and the so-called neoliberal consensus challenged on a fertile Global South fringe. An up note with Amaya as a textured *original*, and her dad with a "transitioned" northern psyche. An up note confirming the Great Turning and the power of neo-ancestral *vivir bien*. But the story wouldn't be complete if left here. I'm walking one more, irresistible question, one that exists beneath words. I walk it — a week after Santa Cruz — up to the Chorrillos Dark Bush, to Juan Carlos and Carolina's home, for a community seed exchange.

Word of mouth fills the family's acres with Suraqueteños, most having hiked an uphill hour to come here. We share a pot-luck meal and then out pour the seeds. Hundreds of bags and envelopes and jam jars of them. This diversity is something that the marketplace does not provide. I've been buying my seeds at the little agro-shops down by Suraqueta's market, and they each carry the exact same fifteen varieties. But this "glocal" gift economy yields *valluno* seeds and also the offspring of seeds brought from afar, from Germany and Thailand, from La Paz and Sucre.

After the exchange, when we are all wealthy with seed (Melissa and I gather sixty varieties), Juan Carlos lights a bonfire, and we create a mandala together with yellow *carnaval* flowers and plump purple *guapurú*, spices and coca leaves. Then a couple — the *chacha-warmi* — steps forward to place the mandala over the flames, sending our community intentions into the sky.

The twosome gently lifts up the mandala and walks toward the fire. He's darker-skinned and wears an olive-green cowboy hat. She's thin, with military khakis and a red bandana. Maximo and Kusi are a couple.

They started dating six months ago and recently moved in together. They've expanded their now-joint honey business, and they are talking of marriage, and kids, should the customary one-year *chacha-warmi* cohabitation work out.

Maximo and Kusi, looking stunning together, place our mandala on the fire. Then each of the fifty of us gathered, in turn, takes a bottle of local wine and pours it onto the four sacred directions around the fire. The burning and *k'oa* goes on for an hour, Melissa at my side, Amaya playing guitar with a clutch of kids, Clea gazing admiringly at her sister. Though half of us here are from other nations, most of us have lived in Bolivia long enough to have participated in this outdoor ceremony of seeds, fire, air, and chanting, this *k'oa* ritual, so many times that it feels routine, yet not rote.

I think of Amaya's forthcoming initiation, one that Melissa dreamed up for her, a Pachamama-centered coming-of-age ritual — *die, begin, initiate* — for her entry into the teen years. The prototype for it came out of a two-day, intergenerational women's retreat at Karina and Hilvert's flourishing experimental permaculture farm in Paredones. Melissa attended the retreat, along with Alison, who returned from Brooklyn, and two dozen other women from our friends circle and from Santa Cruz, and it includes a sweat lodge and dancing.

Does humanity need to invent entirely novel rituals, or might it help, sometimes, to go 180-degrees-forward? This does not mean backward. Turn smack around and take a powerful step *forward*. Whether you live in the North or South or West, whether you're in a village or a suburb or a city, you can turn around and see the abundance of Earth-based rituals, like this *k'oa*, that already exist, and stride into the flesh of the world with them, all the while using technologies that serve.

Like the internet, where, earlier that day, with Amaya and Clea, I pulled up the satellite photo of Suraqueta's Old Town to help demarcate the historic preservation area. Our own five acres caught my eye and I zoomed in. You can see, from space, Casa

Guapurú and the orchard; see the fishpond in the hole hollowed out when we dug clay for our adobes. You can see that our once asphalt-soil now appears soft and green with the hundreds of planted trees and the hundreds more we liberated from the thorny *quiñe* shrubs. And I think you can see from space the changes in me, the changes in a family and a community.

Kusi picks up a guitar. "I wrote this," she says, tuning the instrument. "It's called 'Sweet Life Everywhere.'" Other musician friends gather around with *sampoña* reed flutes and drums and a trumpet, and they follow Kusi as she riffs on "Sweet Life Everywhere," a tune with no lyrics. As I listen to the hybrid composition, I find myself looking up into the sky where the smoke dances. It heals, this transition to a story of union with Pachamama, to a story in which we are consumers and givers equally. It's a story into which my heart says that Casa Guapurú could be home to another child, knowing that Melissa and my happiness does not hinge on whether or not it comes to pass.

As "Sweet Life Everywhere" segues into another song, I notice a mosquito biting my forearm. I share a house with her, watching her swell with my blood. It's nourishing to be edible. The seeds we've exchanged today are deeper than mind, the plants sweet enough to make us wish to propagate them; jasmine and pomegranates and passionfruit eating sunlight before we eat them. Something clarifies in my heart. I know, in a place firmer than my analytical mind, that the divide between what we call "spirituality" and "ecology" does not exist. A Buddhist's present-moment awareness *is* reunion with the tree that holds up the world.

I stop walking and root, treelike, beneath questions. The philosophy we require is nothing less than our animal bodies sensing a honeyed world. Life. Is. Sweet. The Dark Bush bright with sun, I take Melissa's hand, in tribe. Home.

It's Bolivian Independence Day, August 6, 2017. Clea's up in a *pacay* tree with the red, yellow, and green Bolivian flag she waved on the plaza earlier today, as her mom, the water cooperative co-president, marched with the new municipal officials. Clea's now singing her love for the trees and the land, and she asks for one of the coca leaves I'm popping into my mouth. She takes it, kisses it, and cries out "Pachamama!" before letting it flutter to ground.

Melissa appears, down the south path, past our gate, which now remains unlocked to the pueblo, her long hair cascading over her tank-topped shoulders. "Just got a call," she says. "You passed!"

The final naturalization test. It's been a grueling process, but via parentage of Amaya, I'm now a dual citizen. Melissa tells me we'll have to go to the capital, La Paz, to pick up my Bolivian birth certificate.

"*Birth* certificate," I say. "That's odd. It's not like I was born in Bolivia."

Melissa smiles. "Are you sure?" she asks.

The design for our new adobe house on the hillock is on our kitchen table, with its open-plan main space to host groups who walk questioning along with us. Melissa and I are silent as Clea climbs down from the *pacay* and nestles between us on the ground. "What should we do today?" I ask.

Melissa says, "Let's begin."

Acknowledgments

To my wife, Melissa, for your literary critiques, for your love and sustenance.

To my mother and father for a lifetime of care and encouragement; and to Amaya and Clea for hugs and fun during the years it took to write this book.

To Jason Gardner for so deftly editing this and the other two books in the trilogy; special kudos to Jeff Campbell for sensitive copyediting.

To Monique Muhlenkamp, Munro Magruder, Ami Parkerson, and Tracy Cunningham for bringing *Twelve by Twelve*, *New Slow City*, and *Dispatches from the Sweet Life* to the world.

To Michael Bourret, my agent, for your thoughtful support of these books.

To Louisa Putnam and Rowan Finnegan for upholding these words and a shared vision.

To World Policy Institute's Kate Maloff and David Stevens, I am grateful.

Thank you to Stephanie Mady and Shalomit Draper for outreach; to Martin Kirk, Jason Hickel, and Joe Brewer for ideas in chapters 17 and 18; to Nancy Romer for inspiration and encouragement; and to John and Lucy Draper for generous use of your Mattakeese homestead.

Abundant gratitude to our friends and community in Bolivia; our shared lives and challenges are this story.

Finally, I am in debt to the extraordinary early readers who took the time to comment on and improve initial versions of this book: Taylor Reed, Nataka Crayton, Joy Holdread, Duncan Sill,

Zeynep Cilingiroglu, Mary Jane Di Piero, Nancy Clarke, Priscilla Orsi, Chelsea Gilmore, Charles Thoman, Klaus Villanueva, Jennifer Shriver, Jean Riquelme, Marilyn Batts, Vanessa Voller, Amanda Martin, Cathy Markatos, Michele Wucker, Brenda Gillen, Faith Krinsky, Eve Wright, Sam Wurzelmann, Betsy Amin-Arsala, James Spartz, Sandrine Szlasa, Justine Szlasa, Judy Moores, Mary Stucky, Cameron Haight, Susan Forman, Elena Cristiana Jove-Edens, Nick Buxton, Lois Wauson, Karleen Reeve, Angela Gaye-Horn, Evan Meyer, Andrew Faust, Linda Raven, Annie Aviles, and Anna Madrona. Thank you.

Glossary

adobe: Building material that uses sun-dried bricks made of clay and straw.

aguayo: A rectangular piece of patterned cloth, used in traditional South American communities to carry children, goods, and so on.

arquitecta: Female architect.

bachata: A style of romantic music originating in the Dominican Republic.

biocentrism: A view that extends inherent value to all living things, in contrast to *anthropocentrism*, which places the rights and needs of humans above all else.

camba: Refers to people from eastern Bolivia, especially in and around Santa Cruz; generally, a regional identity of Amazonian and lowland Bolivian culture, in contrast to highland *colla* culture (see below).

caminar preguntando: To walk questioning.

campesino: A small landholder/farmer.

casera: A go-to seller that a customer frequents.

chacha-warmi: Literally, "man-woman"; the unified male-female energy field.

ch'alla: A traditional blessing ceremony, celebrating reciprocity with Pachamama (see below), and including various elements in different contexts, such as burying llama fetuses, burning an offering (see *"k'oa"* below), or pouring alcohol onto the ground.

charango: A small Andean guitar, traditionally made from an armadillo shell.

chicha: A fermented corn-based drink.

chikungunya: A mosquito-borne viral disease common in Africa and India; a major outbreak occurred in the Americas in 2015.

ciudadano: Citizen.

co-housing: An intentional community of private homes clustered around shared space and often including conserved green space for common use.

colla: Refers generally to ethnically indigenous Andean highlanders from western Bolivia, in contrast to the eastern lowland *camba* identity (see above).

comparsa: A group of people celebrating carnival together, wearing the same costume.

comunidad: Community.

cuñapé: A cheese-based bread pastry typical of eastern Bolivia.

cupola: Dome.

extranjero: Foreigner.

finca: A small farm or property.

gray-water system: A domestic, natural-waste-processing system that integrates wastewater produced from baths, showers, and clothes washers into productive use, such as for irrigation or other needs in line with permaculture principles. Wastewater generated by toilets, kitchen sinks, and dishwashers is called *black water*.

guapurú: A native Bolivian grape-size fruit that grows on the tree's trunk.

guayabilla: Wild *guayaba* fruit.

Hay cambio: Literally, "There's change."

jipi: From the English "hippie" (pronounced HEE-pee); common parlance for musicians, artisans, etc. who travel through South America.

k'oa: Andean ritual that pays respect to Pachamama by burning an offering in her honor (one particular type of *ch'alla*; see above).

luna: Moon.

macha: Female version of "macho."

MAS (Movimiento Al Socialismo): Translated as Movement Toward Socialism; the current ruling party in Bolivia, headed by Evo Morales.

micro: A half-size bus used in Bolivian cities.

minga: A communal labor-sharing work day.

oferta final: Literally, "final offer."

osiologo: Literally, "leisureologist," or a lover of free time.

la Pacha: A unified vision of life: beneath, above, and within, an essential wholeness in all of existence; one of the four facets of the Bolivian "sweet life" (see "*la vida dulce*" below).

Pachamama: Mother Earth, or the planet itself as a living body, known in the West as "Gaia."

Paceño or Paceña: A person from the city of La Paz.

permaculture: A holistic system of agriculture and community that centers on observing an ecosystem's natural patterns and then designing landscapes and human settlements in harmony with those patterns. The term *permaculture* was coined in 1978 by two Australians, environmentalist David Holmgren and biologist Bill Mollison.

plurinational state: The coexistence of multiple ethnic "nations" within one contemporary political state; in 2009, Bolivia changed its official name to the "Plurinational State of Bolivia," in recognition of the country's multiethnic nature and the enhanced position of Bolivia's indigenous peoples under a new constitution.

pollera: A layer-cake skirt common in the Andes.

postdevelopment: A theory that criticizes the Western ideas of "progress" and "development" as ethnocentric, since they seek to make poor countries like rich countries and often dismiss many ancient philosophies and traditions despite their long histories of success. Postdevelopment thinkers like Arturo Escobar call for diverse, bottom-up (rather than top-down) approaches to "development."

quiñe: A very thorny, shrub-like tree.

revillaging: A trend where people move from cities to towns or rural communities to enjoy their small-is-beautiful benefits; the opposite of "urbanization."

singani: Bolivia's national liquor, distilled from white Muscat of Alexandria grapes.

suma qamaña: The Aymara term for *vivir bien* (see below).

sur: A cold front coming in from the south.

tajibo: A hardwood tree typical of eastern Bolivia.

teja: Ceramic roof tile.

tejon: A type of badger.

tipa: A fast-growing Bolivian tree species.

tula: A fast-growing "pioneer" tree species in Bolivia that takes over a landscape quickly but lives a short life of roughly five years.

valluno: Literally, "valley dweller"; refers to folks native to the valley region west of Santa Cruz, which includes Suraqueta. *Vallunos* have a unique identity, which comes from a blend of cultures, including indigenous lowland Chané and Guaraní and upland Quechua of Inca pedigree, plus Spaniards, Sephardic Jews, Turks, Greeks, and Croats.

Vice Ministry of Decolonization: The branch of Bolivia's national government responsible for uncovering and rooting out the ways in which society and culture are influenced by foreign control, including examining "development" as a neocolonial endeavor (see "post-development" above).

la vida dulce: Literally, "the sweet life"; another way of saying *vivir bien* (see below).

vivir bien: Literally, "living well"; known as *suma qamaña* in Aymara. The phrases refer to happiness achieved through deep human community in balance with nature; a holistic embrace of harmony with self and others, including nonhuman life, the physical world, and metaphysical energies.

Washington Consensus: A broad set of free-market economic ideas, generally supported by the International Monetary Fund, the World Bank, and the United States; these ideas include, among other measures, free trade, floating exchange rates, and the privatization of state enterprises.

wiphala: Bolivia's second official national flag; its checkered rainbow colors represent the colors of a "plurinational state" (see above).

yerba máte: Warm tea drink, common in South America.

About the Author

William Powers is a senior fellow at the New York City–based think tank World Policy Institute, where he focuses on international development, environmental policy, and sustainable consumption and currently leads the Living Well Collaborative project based in Bolivia. He also teaches on the adjunct faculty at New York University. His award-winning book *Twelve by Twelve* (2010) was a national green-living bestseller. He also is the author of *Blue Clay People: Seasons on Africa's Fragile Edge* (2005) and *Whispering in the Giant's Ear: A Frontline Chronicle from Bolivia's War on Globalization* (2006).

For two decades, Powers has led development aid and conservation initiatives in Latin America, Africa, and Washington, DC. His essays on global issues have appeared in the *Atlantic, New York Times, Washington Post*, and *International Herald Tribune* and have been syndicated to three hundred newspapers around the world and translated into a dozen languages.

He has been a keynote speaker, lecturer, or panelist at over one hundred events in the United States and abroad. Powers has worked as a fellow at the World Bank in Washington, DC; head of programs for Catholic Relief Services in Liberia; and chief of party of the USAID/Conservation International rainforest conservation program in Bolivia. He holds international affairs degrees from Brown University and Georgetown University's School of Foreign Service.

www.williampowersbooks.com

Read the other titles in William Powers's Beyond the American Dream trilogy

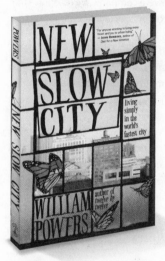
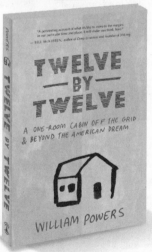